S0-AIP-576

IMMORTALS BY MY SIDE

IMMORTALS BY MY SIDE

Rosemary Brown

HENRY REGNERY COMPANY · CHICAGO

© Rosemary Brown 1974. All rights reserved.
First published in England in 1974 by Bachman & Turner, London,
under the title *Immortals at my Elbow*. Reprinted 1975.
First published in the United States in 1975 by
Henry Regnery Company
180 North Michigan Avenue
Chicago, Illinois 60601
Manufactured in the United States of America
Library of Congress Catalog Card Number: 75-13248
International Standard Book Number: 0-8092-8173-2

Contents

*The key to immortality lies within us: we turn
the key in the lock when we identify ourselves
with the Infinite Spirit*

*9th April, 1974
(From Tovey in spirit)*

CHAPTER 1

The Awakening

We slip into this life out of our mother's womb. We enter an independent existence instead of being part of our mother's body. We become a separate life which can be sustained by external means.

In the beginning of time, were we part of a Cosmic Consciousness in much the same way as we were once part of our mother's body? Did we slide out of the womb of Eternity to experience a separated consciousness? Is there a great Source of Life from which we sprang and to which we shall one day return?

These are questions which seem virtually unanswerable. They are questions which reflect the whole mystery of Life and Death and the Hereafter.

If we believe we are creatures with souls, and not merely a mass of physical components serving a transitory function, we must believe in our own essential immortality. The flesh perishes, but Spirit cannot perish because its very nature is imperishable. Whatever we believe or do not believe, the origin of Life, its purposes, and our future are subjects that will stir some interest in most of us.

Out of the vast halls of Space and Silence came forth Life. Yet nothing can come from nothing, therefore Life must always have been existent. Life in this sense is what some people call God, but the word God has been used to mean so many different things that it is probably less confusing if we substitute for it the phrase "the Creative Force". It is difficult to prove that God exists as a Person, but the evidence of our own senses can show us that a Creative Force certainly does exist.

For many of us in this world, it is more than enough to cope with its pressing problems and urgencies, and to bear with its pleasures and pains. Therefore thousands of people may give little more than

7

a passing thought to anything other than their own immediate concerns. Those of us who reach out in thought towards wider horizons may find ourselves on uncharted seas if we venture beyond the stereotyped conceptions of Man's being and his Creator. Yet the next logical step in our evolution would seem to be the expansion of our intelligence beyond the limitations of our physical senses.

Throughout the ages, in order to survive, we have had to concentrate on conquering our environment and utilising its resources for the preservation of life. In the midst of the maelstrom of nations in conflict, in the midst of the rat-race for material gain, for personal acquisitions, prestige and power, we can overlook the fact that within us may lie the seeds of inner powers which could give us a deeper understanding of ourselves and a greater mastery of Life. Most of us neglect or ignore these inner potentialities or dismiss them as non-existent without so much as making any attempt to discover whether they do exist.

My own experiences in Extra-Sensory Perception, and especially my communications with those we mistakenly label "dead", have made me realise there are worlds within worlds and worlds outside our world. To me, this realisation has given Life a fuller meaning, enriched my outlook, and deepened my awareness of God or the Creative Force.

Many of those who communicate from the Next World do so because they want to help people who are seeking for greater understanding; they want to help us to evolve and become spiritually quickened. It is difficult for many in this world to become fully enlightened because they are so hemmed in by tradition, superstition and various dogmas. In the next world, it seems that a more comprehensive outlook is attainable which enables one to see that there are many paths to Truth and to God.

In my first book, *Unfinished Symphonies*, I described how a number of great composers of the past have communicated with me and transmitted many new musical works of theirs. The object of this exercise is not simply to give the world further compositions, but to show by an outpouring of music unmistakably characteristic of themselves that they continue to live beyond the Vale of Death.

Why should these composers want to prove that Death is not the end? Is it to reassure us, to comfort us, to help to allay our fears and give us hope? They tell me there is far more to it than that, which is one of the reasons for my writing this book.

8

A growing number of people are becoming aware of deeper levels of consciousness within themselves which may give them rare flashes of insight into things and events: flashes that supply information which could not be obtained by them through any of the normal, recognised means. Down the centuries, any investigation into such matters has been discouraged by various establishments. Were the establishments afraid that the populace might get to know too much? Or were they afraid for themselves, afraid that the results of any investigation might challenge some of their doctrines?

Of one thing we can be sure: that is, that those who value truth above all other considerations will not be amongst those who oppose the search for greater knowledge, whether that knowledge be related to the material and physical aspects of the Universe, or to the spiritual and psychical ones.

For many people, Faith is their only solace in the face of death. There are a number of well-authenticated instances of communication from beyond the grave, some excellent examples of which have been quoted in a book written by a well-known member of the Roman Catholic Church. If instances such as this were made more widely known, a great wave of reassurance could be given to those who strive faithfully to believe whilst perhaps wondering whether there is any real foundation for their tenacious but tenuous faith.

The Anglican Church in this country made a long and careful inquiry into Spiritualism, but suppressed its report which was favourable. One good clergyman whom I know expressed his opinion that is was wise to suppress the report in case it sent people flocking willy-nilly to mediums as a result. There are many good mediums, but also many poor ones, and the inevitable frauds, so one has to guard against gullibility and remember that no medium is infallible – though I myself have encountered more than one who claims that his or her mediumship is NEVER wrong! This assertion that their mediumship is never wrong has invariably been contradicted by some of their outpourings.

The vital question is whether we are going to be content to go on functioning on one cylinder, mataphorically speaking, using only part of our brain, and turning a deaf ear to the voice of intuition and a blind eye to our Extra- Sensory faculties. Must religion be stationary or can it march forward like a noble vanguard, leading us to great, new revelations?

Religions are invariably founded on a belief in the continuance of Life after Death, otherwise there would be little meaning in them.

9

The Christian religion is no exception to this, its entire structure hingeing upon the after-death communications of Jesus. In spite of this, there are people who proclaim that it is wrong to communicate with the so-called dead, or, to put it another way, wrong for the dead to communicate with us. Quotations from the Old Testament are often the favourite ammunition used to fire this misplaced broadside, a warning that was uttered against communication of an undesirable nature being taken to include communications of all kinds.

It is good to have faith, and even better to add knowledge to faith. Blessed are those who believe in God and leave all that is not immediately understandable in His hands; more blessed still, perhaps, are the dedicated pioneers who brave the winds of criticism and the tides of bigotry in their endeavours to increase our knowledge through painstaking research into the intangible realms of spirit.

Do these words strike a spark of response on the tinder of your heart and mind? If so, perhaps you are one of the vast company of souls in the world today who believe that it is our duty to gather wisdom and devote it to the betterment of Mankind, who believe with all our hearts in the rightness of the quest for Truth.

Can we give credence to any belief that God wishes us to bury our heads, ostrich-like, in the sands of ignorance? Or can we accept that the Will of the Almighty would be for us to expand our intelligence to its utmost limits in the effort to become greater in the highest sense? The choice is ours if we have the courage to make it.

In this book, I will describe the views of some of the composers and others who dwell in the World of Spirit. It is interesting to see how some of their ideas about God and Life have changed since their departure from the material world. As Chopin once remarked to me, "Matter is like a blindfold that prevents people from seeing the light. It is not until we reach the after-death state that we are able to see just how blind many of us have been."

One wonders what sort of eye-openers we may experience when we move on from the dense world of matter into the finer realms of spirit. We are, of course, spirit here and now in this world; but, enveloped in the flesh as we are, we may be deluded into thinking that our physical bodies are the sum-total of our being. Indeed, unless we have experienced "out-of-the-body" consciousness, we may find it difficult to imagine how we could continue to function without the physical body. There are cases on record where people have found themselves able to observe what is happening while their bodies are unconscious under a general anaesthetic; and cases where people have

10

died temporarily, and, before being resuscitated, have found themselves experiencing an awareness totally detached from their momentarily dead body.

I know that these out-of-the-body experiences can and do happen, because I have had many such experiences, usually during the sleeping state. As an experiment, whilst separated from my body I have chosen places to observe which I know with certainty I have never seen or heard described; carefully noting details which could easily escape the eye of anyone but the keenest observer, I have been able to satisfy myself when actually visiting these places at a later date that my out-of-the-body observations were correct. This proved that there is some way of being able to see without depending on one's physical senses: that one's Astral Body – or Soul – has eyes of its own or some other substitute for sight. The Astral Body, perhaps I should explain for those not familiar with the term, is the spirit equivalent of the physical body into which it merges during one's earthly lifetime. It is attached to the physical body by what is described in the Bible as "the silver cord" which acts rather like the umbilical cord between mother and child. At death, the silver cord is severed or dissolves away, leaving the spirit free to move in the Astral Body; until then, it keeps the Astral Body linked with the physical one.

It might be possible to prove conclusively through systematic investigation that we can function independently of the physical body and brain. This would lend strong support to the surmise that death is not the end, but merely a transference into another body and dimension. We have a very long way to go yet in such research, for we have to do battle against a great deal of scepticism, prejudice, and obstruction by some religious factions. But it is doubtful whether anyone can halt the march of Science which will surely turn its attention more fully to such matters. We are only just emerging from the repressive influences of the Middle Ages; we have to shake off the miasma of black magic; we have to avoid the multitude of misleading offshoots of an alleged psychic or occult nature. We need serious research into the entire matter, which is of serious import for us all.

Sir Donald Tovey, who communicates frequently from the Next World, remarked one day to me – rather pithily, "Too many cults spoil the cloth!"

He had been discussing with me the numerous cults springing up all over the world nowadays. I gathered that he was expressing his opinion that many people in their eagerness to blaze new spiritual

11

trails were getting drawn into blind alleys and side-tracks. We have quite a glut of self-styled messiahs in the world today, most of whom, he said, are harmless, self-deluded individuals; but some of them are power or position hungry, and not true worshippers of God at all.

"People will often clutch at any new movement without analysing its use and merits because they are bored or suffering from a spiritual vacuum. Instead of truth, they want glamour; instead of facts, they want fantasy; they do not realise that reality can be the most exciting and stimulating discovery of all."

So said Sir Donald. He was talking about spiritual reality, and not of the everyday humdrum or harsh reality of present-day life. But I remember how often he has insisted that spiritual reality is intrinsically part of everyday life, and that the neglect of this aspect is the very cause of much of the harshness and dullness of our existence.

"Human beings are in essence spiritual beings, although their behaviour sometimes might lead one to doubt it; therefore it is not being unrealistic to seek spiritual values and apply them to the material issues facing humanity."

When I asked Sir Donald what he meant by spiritual values, and how he would advise people to find them, he replied that each person must seek them individually because that is the best way to acquire a true sense of values. Also he specified that the scale of spiritual values varies inevitably from person to person, although a basic common thread runs through them. To word his meaning another way, he said that each one of us must cultivate his or her own soul, and that no one else could fulfil this rôle for us.

Since my first book was published, I have had a tremendous number of letters, and some writers have inquired about the spiritual implications of my work with the composers. I hope this book will answer some of their questions. The vast majority of letters has consisted of inquiries and requests of a personal kind which would keep me occupied for decades if I answered them all. Occasionally, I have received a screed from one of the 'know-it-alls' whom most of us know only too well. Some of these well-meaning souls have told me how I should live, what I should believe, and how their particular creed is (so they say) the one-and-only right one. It is amazing how many one-and-only right ones there are according to the adherents of the respective beliefs.

I should like to express my thanks to all who have written to me with goodwill. I am sorry it is quite impossible to reply to all the letters that reach me, but I appreciate deeply all the kind thoughts and encouragement sent by well-wishers.

A large proportion of the letters are from people appealing for help with their personal problems and difficulties. Alas! I have not the time nor the energy nor the knowledge to supply solutions, but I always pray for such people to have the strength to cope with their troubles and for help to come to them. It seems we need a vast army of Samaritans to deal with the misfortunes of countless people.

Surprising – most surprising of all, I think – was the large number of correspondents claiming to be in touch with one or other of the composers with whom I work. I know the composers help as many as they can, but it is obvious that some people let their imaginations run away with them, often through wishful thinking. I have had more than a few write asking me to confirm that Liszt or Chopin or Beethoven or one of the others is in touch with them; if they are definitely in touch with them, of course, they do not need any confirmation; if the contact is so uncertain that they feel the need to have it verified, it is useless, anyway.

People – women in particular – seem to think that working with the composers is a romantic thing. In reality, it is a very hard task requiring terrific concentration which certainly leaves no room for indulging in romantic thoughts. Not that the work is without its compensations. It is wonderful to get to know these great souls as individuals, and to share with them the occasional moment of humour or sense of triumph when some particularly complicated phrase of music has been successfully transmitted by them to me. To get anything as elaborate as a piece of music across clearly, without any mistakes in transmission, is an almost impossible feat. Imagine the joy of the composers when one of them has managed to convey a new composition accurately. Still greater is their joy when these compositions are acknowledged by eminent musical experts to be not only true to type, but bearing the unmistakable hall-mark of authenticity.

It must be difficult for many people to imagine that anything like this breakthrough in communication with the Other World can take place, especially if their minds are preconditioned by a disbelief in or bias against such a happening. But I believe that we are on the threshold of a widespread breakthrough in communication which will be established eventually by Science. Religious bigotry and persecution will be dispelled slowly but surely by the light of true knowledge, and the only thing likely to remain intolerable will be intolerance.

We witness in our time one mighty nation trying to free her people from the discord and disruption of opposed religious views by inducing them to adopt Atheism. Perhaps this does offer an escape from the endless distraction of arguments about the validity of various religious beliefs. The pages of history bear sickening accounts of religious persecution with an attendant stream of vile torture and dreadful toll of human life. These fiendish acts of persecution, far from adding prestige to the religions concerned, may well have helped to undermine the influence of the relative churches, and led to the present day lack of regard for them.

One still hears the rumblings of attempted religious intimidation in some quarters, often from unorthodox cults. The threat of misfortune of some kind is held over one's head with the admonition to join some particular group or believe what they say you should believe if you do not want this misfortune to overtake you. The threats vary from the old-fashioned one that everlasting hell-fire awaits you, or that you will be denied Eternal Life, right down to a more original hand-out of twenty more incarnations in this world if you do not obey the injunctions of their order. Yes, I was told in all seriousness that if I did not join in the activities of a certain small sect in this country, I would find myself forced to return to this world over and over again. "So what?" I retorted. This seemed to flummox the person uttering the threat who believed, apparently, that this was calculated to strike terror into my heart!

It rarely seems to occur to people that anybody converted to a belief through fear is not likely to be fully sincere. To conform through fear probably means one is conforming outwardly whilst still lacking an inner conviction. Fear must produce many hypocrites and make people swear allegiance to certain causes in the hope of saving their own skins or souls.

Do we want a rational society? A society where we can reason things out together quietly? Or do we want a society where we are bludgeoned into submission, where people either as individuals or as groups get what they want by the use of violence? True, all down the ages, people have employed violent means to obtain their ends, good or bad, but do we have to continue indefinitely in this manner? Does not violence always bring repercussions, either through protest at such methods or in actual revenge? Will we find violence is becoming an effete and ultimately ineffectual means of obtaining its multifarious goals? Will it become apparent that only through willing co-operation can satisfactory and durable settlements be

14

reached? Can we bring ourselves to negotiate peacefully, or must humanity go on plaguing itself with strife and pillage?

These are questions that must arise in the minds of many thinking people. They are also questions with which many souls in the Next World concern themselves. They are, we say, at a crucial cross-roads in human development. We can drift into chaos, unrest, and pollution not only of our atmosphere but also of the human spirit. If we cannot or do not balance out the world's resources, and some groups monopolise or hoard whilst other groups remain deplorably deprived, they predict more frequent and disastrous upheavals than we have ever experienced so far. It is becoming obvious to more and more people that the economy of each nation reacts more and more swiftly and more and more drastically on other nations. This is partly due to the faster exchange of goods through speedier and farther-ranging transport, and partly due to increased absorption of goods owing to the growth of world population. To keep up with the increased demand for goods, there is a need to plan and organise on a wider and more far-sighted scale. And this, they say, calls for mutual co-operation between nations and peoples, without which famine, disease, and disorder could spread across our globe accompanied by inevitable and prolonged riots.

Why should those in the Next World be concerned about us? Do they have a profound degree of compassion for us as we suffer the onslaughts of this world whilst they dwell in peace, untroubled by earthly burdens? Their concern does spring partly from compassion, but they also seem anxious to preserve our planet and try to prevent the human race from destroying itself. This leads to another question, which I put to them myself. Why should they be so enormously concerned to preserve our world when there is another life after this, and other spheres where we can continue to exist free from the tribulations of the material world? This brought forth an answer which could provide a clue to the *raison d'être* for our world: that we need to incarnate on earth or a similar planet in order to become conscious of ourselves and develop into self-motivating beings so that we can take an active part in the Universe. Before our entry into matter, we lay unconscious in the cradle of Infinity, mute, passive, and unaware. The great Principle of Life then stirred us into movement, and launched us on our journey of self-discovery. To put it very simply, being born on earth is like a child being sent to school to learn. Whether we learn and what we learn depends on our opportunities and our response.

15

This gives us a thought-provoking picture of the view of our world as it can be seen from the Next World. The detached point of view of those who dwell in that world might help us to attain a keener sense of the Eternal values which are destined to concern us all sooner or later even if we take no interest in them here and now. If we came to know these values in full, and applied them to the business of living in a practical sense, we might find a solution to many of our problems.

This is not preaching from Beyond, nor moralizing, nor an attempt to impose a point of view or creed. Their efforts are directed at trying to give us greater understanding so that we can make the best of life on earth, and be the better prepared for our transition to their world.

As we proceed in this book, I will outline some of the present viewpoints of several of our great thinkers such as Einstein and Bertrand Russell. There will also be quite a lot of comment from Sir Donald Francis Tovey, who has plenty to say for himself from the Next World. Sir Donald, a great musicologist, brilliant lecturer and gifted musician, has turned out to be one of the prime movers in communication; as he passed on in 1940, there are still living a number of people who knew him well and can testify to the authentic ring of his conversations with me.

Some of our fellow creatures would try to deceive us into believing that communication with spirit is wrong, worthless, pointless, and goodness knows what else. In reality and in truth, communication can be enlightening, uplifting, and a beautiful, holy experience. When conducted with good motives in a sensible, God-guided way, and communication is entered into only with "good" spirits, it is like a breath of pure, wholesome air blowing away the stale atmosphere of religious stagnation. In shutting out the Next World, we may be shutting out the way to this world's salvation. For who knows what revelations might not come from Beyond?

16

CHAPTER 2

Testing the spirits

Quite a few people I have met seem to think I must be a credulous kind of person. This is far from being the case, and I have stood on one side and weighed up the pros and cons of my own work with great care. I regard my work as being partly experimental, and it is, naturally, unpredicatable. It is very difficult to test work of the psychic class, because one cannot command results. A great many members of the public jump to the wrong conclusion that mediums "call up" spirits. I doubt whether they do call spirits in that sense at all. Spirits seem inclined to come and go when *they* choose, and not when we desire. The nearest one can get to 'calling them up' is to send out a mental message requesting contact – rather like ringing someone up on the telephone: the number may be engaged or there may be no reply, or it may even be out of order.

We are exhorted to test the spirits in the New Testament, and this is certainly wise advice. We have to remember that when people pass over into the Next World, this does not change their nature. If they have been irresponsible or wicked in our world, they will be the same in the next – unless and until they learn to mend their ways. It is strongly recommended, therefore, to be sure to keep the door closed against such types, unless one is deliberately running what is known in Spiritualist circles as a rescue group which takes on the task of trying to help spirits who are in need of guidance.

From childhood, I have led a prayerful life, always beginning and closing each day with spontaneous rather than formal prayer. I am a great believer in the efficiency of sincere prayer as a protection against undesirable spirits. It is interesting to note that music came to me from the composers at first only after I had been deep in prayer. Now, after several years of working with them, a brief period of

17

inner prayer or silent meditation seems to suffice to attune me with them.

I have carried out extensive and constant tests on my own mediumistic abilities, and also checked very carefully each composer or other spirit wishing to communicate. I still do this checking to this very day – much to Chopin's amusement, apparently. He came a few days ago to begin dictating a new piece of music to me – a Ballade, so he said. Suddenly he looked at me with a very solemn face, and said, in his broken English, "Ah! I have forgotten to bring my identity-card. What shall I do?"

That was so typical of his bantering manner that it was proof enough in itself. Liszt, usually more serious than Chopin, reacts in a different way. One day, I was eyeing him up and down to make sure it really was he and not an imposter, and he asked in a rather quizzical way, "What is the matter? Do you not trust me?"

I assured him hastily that I trusted him completely but that I was merely satisfying myself that it was he.

"But by now you recognise my presence without having to see me," he went on. "So please do not let us waste time with unnecessary preliminaries."

It was true. I have become so accustomed to the presence of Liszt and some of the other composers that I am able to sense when they are with me before I see them or hear them speak. Many readers may have experienced a similar sensing of a presence – an unseen presence – although they may not have been able to identify the manifestation.

We recognise people we know through the use of our physical senses, either by sight from their appearance or by hearing if we are sufficiently familiar with their voices – or possibly we can guess who they are through our sense of smell should they be in the habit of using a distinctive pefume. In sensing the identity of a spirit without using the faculties of sight, hearing or smell, a further sense is evidently called into service. Is this kind of sensing, in fact, an example of telepathic rapport? Or should it more aptly be named intuition? Does such recognition occur as the result of an impingement on us of certain vibrations or waves of some kind being set up by the spirit concerned? I turned to Liszt for an answer to this involved question, and he stated that each person has his or her own dynamic field which can be sensed or "picked up". This so-called dynamic field is muffled to some extent, he added, while we are living on earth because matter has a deadening effect. He also asserted that each person's dynamic

18

field is peculiar to that person only in the same way that fingerprints are individual. Could our advancing technology one day design a machine that could scan or register these dynamic fields, and perhaps even record the impact of a burglar's or intruder's field to aid detection and arrest? Technology has already outstripped the limits to which the average imagination might have stretched a century ago, and its future achievements could reach beyond our wildest dreams.

Speaking of technology has reminded me of some mechanical tests which were applied to the music I receive from spirits. I was invited to take part during May 1971 in a television programme in Birmingham, to be interviewed by Wendy Cooper about my work and my first book. A musicologist and mathematician, Stan Kelly, appeared with us on the screen, armed with a computer which he had been using to analyse and assess the music. The computer was a multi-variate analyser which supplied correlation factors. Stan Kelly, who has a special experience of computers, punched up paper tapes representing random samples of music written by Liszt, Chopin and Beethoven during their life-times, and also random samples from the music I have taken down from the same composers. The evidence evinced by the use of this technique indicated strong correlation, especially with Chopin. This did not surprise me as Chopin seems the most capable of communicating music clearly and quickly – or else he is able to attune himself to me more easily than some of the other composers. Mr. Kelly said that scores of over sixty are sufficient to show correlation, and that the scores obtained were in the eighties and nineties.

The method of employing a computer to analyse and assess the music could prove sometimes to be more reliable than obtaining human opinion. You see, opinions always vary about everything. One critic will laud the music, extolling not only its beauty, but also maintaining that it is true to the composers named. Another will not be so enthusiastic, and may allege that the music is an unconscious imitation on my part. I have found, sad to say, that jealousy often colours opinions, and this will sometimes prevent a person from giving a really impartial criticism. I am a musical nobody, and it irks some musicians (especially if they aspire to be composers themselves) to think that so much publicity has been given to my work. I wish they could look beyond personalities to the music itself and the elevated goals of the composers working with me. I do not matter, and I wish they would devote their attentions to the actual work instead of carping at me and conspiring to dismiss the music with

19

false explanations. But the majority of musicians who have examined my work have conceded points generously even if not fully convinced of the origin of the compositions.

With the help of friends, we have sometimes acted upon a plan to obtain as unbiased an opinion as possible regarding the source of the music. We once slipped an item of music given me by Schubert in with a programme of Schubert piano works. Then we challenged the audience to 'spot" the piece which was not written by Schubert in his life-time. No-one was able to distinguish the piece, and several were quite emphatic that the piece transmitted to me was without any doubt whatsoever one of Schubert's own works! When my first record was being issued by Philips (now Phonogram) Record Company, Jack Boyce, then manager of their Classical Records Division, played a tape-recording at a sales conference of an excerpt from a String Quartet I had "received" from Brahms. He then announced that it was part of a String Quartet written by Brahms in 1969 (the date when I received it).

"You mean 1869," interjected one of the audience attending the conference.

This audience consisted of sales representatives and agents and the like, including people very familiar with Brahms' work. They were all cajoled into accepting the excerpt as genuine Brahms – which it is, of course! This may have seemed like "pulling a fast one," but it is often the only way of getting people to be really open-minded in their verdict.

Even if people do believe my work is authentic, it takes courage for them to say so. They may find themselves jeered at by sceptics or frowned upon by establishments who are too set in their ways to accept a new conception. It is, perhaps, exceptionally difficult for anyone to take a stand for my work if they have a big reputation at stake. But I am grateful for ever to more than one celebrity and musical expert for sponsoring the work with enthusiasm and undisguised belief.

An instance of unexpected and quite dramatic support occurred in May 1973. I was invited to take part in a Festival which included the Arts and Music. The organiser, Leonard Pearcey, a very gifted and able young man, arranged for me to be interviewed by none other than Sheridan Morley, the son of Robert Morley, the distinguished actor. Sheridan asked me a number of questions about my work, then I followed this up with a performance at the piano of various compositions that have been passed to me by the composers who

20

communicate from the Beyond. The audience was then invited to ask questions, and several people did so. A young man arose in the audience and said that he had no question to ask, but that he would like to say something if permitted. He said that he thought he should announce himself first so that people would know that he knew what he was talking about with regard to my work.

"I am John Lill," he said quietly.

A gasp of surprise and delight came from the audience. I had never, until that moment, had the honour of meeting John, but had naturally heard of his reputation as a great concert pianist. I wondered what he was going to say, and my joy knew no bounds when he stated without hesitation his conviction that my work is completely authentic. This conviction, he told the audience, was upheld by the fact that he had been informed by no less a person than Beethoven that my work is absolutely genuine. At this, there was a stir of even greater excitement. John explained that he has a very close rapport with Beethoven and is able to converse with him.

Beethoven had told me that something very exciting would take place at the Festival, and that a man in the audience would say something of great moment. Since this first meeting, Beethoven has given John Lill and myself a number of amazing and detailed cross-references. He would tell me something, and say he would also inform John. Later I would check with John, and find that he had indeed been given exactly the same message. Telepathy, the sceptics might comment. Unlikely, I would retort, since the messages were sometimes very complex and did not, in any case, come to us at the same instant time.

British composer Richard Rodney Bennett, whose fame is growing fast, said that he couldn't have "faked" the Beethoven music himself when referring to my Beethoven-dictated compositions. That is indeed a wonderful tribute from one of the most brilliantly gifted composers of our time. Professor Ian Parrott, of the Department of Music at the University College of Wales in Aberystwyth, wrote that he is quite happy to accept the utter genuineness of the phenomenon of my spirit-dictated compositions. Humphrey Searle, one of Britain's leading composers and a Liszt expert, after examining "Grübelei", a piano composition I have received from Liszt, said, "It is the sort of piece Liszt could well have written, particularly during the last fifteen years of his life."

I could quote many more testimonies from musical experts, many of them well known, but this might be mistaken for trumpet-blowing

21

on my part when I simply wish to demonstrate that the music is considered by many musicians to be clearly the creations of the composers in question.

Besides the music, there are often highly evidential messages for various people. I have chosen to quote from reports made by Dr. H. van der Haas on my mediumship. He is a qualified chemical engineer and the author of *The Enterprise in Transition*, an analysis of European and American Practice. I first met him in 1971, after he had written to me from Holland at the suggestion of Professor Tenhaeff, the distinguished parapsychologist, who had already met and examined me.

Dr. van der Haas kept a record on a tape-recorder of our conversations, and gave me permission to quote what follows. The first meeting was on the 23rd of June 1971, when the doctor's late wife appeared to me, and I was able to describe her in detail. She spoke, recounting many details of her life, then referred to someone he knew who was about to go to Ostend. To quote word for word from Dr. van der Haas's report:

"My daughter, just married, crossed to England by way of Ostend for her honeymoon. I did not know where she would cross. This was on the 27th."

The 27th meant a time-lapse of four days between our meeting and his daughter's crossing, which ruled out any suspicion of mind-reading.

Spirits often reminisce when communicating, probably because it is one way to help prove their identity and show that they do remember. Here is my account of some of Mrs. van der Haas's conversation with me, and her husband's comments and confirmation in brackets.

"She had a little pink cushion, battered, but still in use. It has compartments."

(*Correct, an inflatable little cushion used on picnics.*)

"She worked very deftly in raffia."

(*Correct. My wife had to learn this when training to teach children.*)

"She is talking about boxes for seeds, rather shallow, which were put one on top of the other, and stored in a slightly damp place with an earthy smell."

(*My wife always worked in the garden where there is a hothouse. Seeds were planted in boxes, and around June they would be empty, and stored on the floor of the hothouse, near the rainwater overflow, where the ground is always moist.*)

22

"She was fond of poplar trees, there is a whole row with slight gaps in between."

(*Correct. There is a long row on one side of the garden*).

"She liked to grow creepers, things that climb."

(*Correct. There were a number of creepers in the house and along the garden walls.*)

"Now she speaks of a haystack quite near a farmhouse, and then a little farther there is a very beautiful old willow tree."

(*This is exactly the situation at the back of the garden.*)

"She liked to make a sort of pancake which you had to eat right away. She would cook it in a pan, turn it, and bake it quite thick, with cheese inside."

(*Correct. Made from two thick slices of bread with a slice of cheese in between very frequently prepared.*)

"She was very fond of birds, and at one time there was a pet bird that would sit on her hand."

(*Love of birds – correct. Nothing known about pet bird, until my mother-in-law informed me that some 25 years ago there was one in their house.*)

"She says you have been to a place recently where there was a small, short waterfall. You were looking at it for a few minutes; it was tucked away, so that you came upon it unexpectedly."

(*Correct. In Paris in the Bois de Boulogne.*)

"You went to a scent factory with her. There were pictures of the flowers the scents are made from."

(*Correct. At Grasse, to the south of Grenoble.*)

"There was a lot of mimosa, which she liked very much, add plants with leaves like palm-trees, sharp thick leaves."

(*Correct. A good description of the agave plant.*)

"You have a goblet, a tankard, in the house, which is a cherished possession. There is just one; it is the sort of thing that could have been an award, a prize. It has only one handle; it is made of dull silvery metal."

(*Correct. A prize made of pewter, awarded in Indonesia, where my wife and I spent some ten years.*)

"I smell the odour of sweet-pea; it is her perfume."

(*Correct, although never identified as the scent of sweet-pea. Visiting friends at Assen in Holland whom I did not know, but who were very old friends of my wife, I found they had lots of sweet-pea in the garden, which had exactly the smell of the perfume.*)

Psychic imvesigators look for all kinds of explanations, often

23

attributing results to mind-reading which, if true, would indicate a remarkable telepathic ability! But, as Dr. van der Haas remarked, there were items which could not be explained away by the mind-reading theory, such as his wife's foreknowledge that her daughter would cross via Ostend to England, and her reference to the pet bird of whom her husband did not know.

Sometimes evidence comes in a foreign language of which I am completely ignorant, providing even better proof. I will illustrate this point with an example that can be corroborated. It concerns Elizabeth Parrott, the talented artist wife of Professor Parrott, M.A., D.Mus. (Oxon) of Aberystwyth University College. One day, they visited me in my home, when the spirit of Mrs. Parrott's mother manifested beside her. This spirit claimed to be very close to Mrs. Parrott, then began speaking in her own tongue which was Russian. Having no knowledge whatsoever of the Russian language, other than having read in the newspapers that the word, "Niet", meaning "No", often seemed to be on the lips of the politicians, I knew that the words could not be emanating from my own subconscious mind. It is obvious that nothing can emerge from the subconscious mind unless it has first been absorbed into it, which dismisses the second theory sometimes put forward by investigators that all messages from the so-called dead are merely the products of this ubiquitous faculty. I repeated the words being spoken by Mrs. Parrott's mother to the best of my ability, struggling to pronounce them in the same way. It was very difficult, but Mrs. Parrott was able to understand in spite of my stumbling attempts to copy the sounds.

Dr. van der Haas made further tests of my psychic abilities, and his wife communicated several times. Once she mentioned how she had a slight lisp, pronouncing some words with a sibilance. Dr. van der Haas said this was correct, and that his wife often made a sibilant sound where words commence with a letter Z which is *non*-sibilant in Dutch. She said she wished to give him "a great many marigold flowers", and the doctor replied that it was her favourite flower and that their garden was at that very time full of them. She spoke of another incident which the doctor did not remember. This was about a box of chocolates with a pale-blue ribbon around it. Dr. van der Haas wrote to me to report that about one month after she had said this, he was checking the contents of a drawer for some other purpose, and found the pale-blue ribbon which then revived the memory of the chocolates.

At yet another session of communication, the following conversa-

24

tion emerged. Again, my remarks are in inverted commas, with Dr. van der Haas's responses in brackets in italics.

"Recently you were engaged in a controversy with someone about psychic communications. This was a man, one of a group of two or three. A stocky-built man; rather blustering type of person. He tended to be an antagonistic influence in experiments."

(*A few months before, I received a telephone call from the man mentioned in Mrs. Brown's statement, whose mental and physical properties tally exactly with the description given. He invited me and somebody else to discuss setting up experiments in the parapsychological field. A first attempt was made with photography, but it soon turned out that this person was basically in disagreement with the experimental line chosen. It is interesting to note that Mrs. Brown has more than once mentioned photographic experiments in her sittings.*)

"Your wife says that something has happened to one of the poplar trees. It is in the middle."

(*There is a row of poplar trees on one side of the garden. A year ago, one of the trees, in the middle of the row, died, leaving an open space.*)

"There is something which needs planing off – a large whitewood table. The surface is rough."

(*A table answering the description, which was used in the garden for making tea, etc., had been varnished during windy weather, so that the surface is now very rough because of inclusion of sand-grains in the varnish. This table was once used in my wife's room in Indonesia.*)

"Recently you were working with a big screen, not cloth, but looking like it, and there was something went wrong with it."

(*This screen, of the type used for film projection, recently fell off the hook when slides were to be shown.*)

"Recently, you almost got the to Bank, and then you changed your mind and decided not to go there. It was a Tuesday."

(*Completely correct.*)

"Your wife had a model of a windmill, this size (indicating about 25 cms height). The sails could turn. Some way they jammed, and would not turn."

(*Correct, also the height. The sails jammed at a certain moment. It is interesting to note that this little windmill was used last Christmas for the first time since years, and that I spent quite some time trying to make the sails turn adequately, without succeeding altogether.*)

"You were in a church in the Netherlands, recently, a rather big one, where you called as a sightseer. There was no service, and it is a beautiful church, but you felt it was rather empty spiritually."

(*This is completely correct; the church is the old cathedral church of 's-Hertogenbosch.*)

At my next meeting with Dr. van der Haas, he handed me a little gold chain belonging to a lady who is a friend of his. Here is the doctor's report of this occasion, taken verbatim from his own typed account:-

"She" – the lady in question – "sufferers from mental depressions, and the idea was that in a sitting perhaps details might be revealed which might help in the cure. Mrs. Brown mentioned a great many details about the lady's past, about her response to treatment, and about the way the treatment should be adapted. Those about the past were discussed with the lady who agreed they were correct. Those about the response to treatment were appreciated as correct. The advice given about improvements in treatment was followed, and first indications are that the response has become better in a number of aspects."

The doctor's wife had joined us at this meeting, and gave further messages, including one about a recess near the fireplace in the doctor's house (which I have, of course, never seen) where she said she hid a present for him once. She said she liked to buy him presents, and teased him, not telling him where they were, or else giving false clues. The doctor confirmed this as completely correct. He said that on the 5th December, a traditional feast with the Dutch, surprise presents are given, and that he and his wife had continued the old custom of hiding presents. She hid them, he informed me, very craftily, and provided all sorts of clues, also false ones.

Among the numberless instances of evidential communication I have received from the Next World, there is one which rates as particularly interesting as it concerns Professor Einstein. The interest of Professor Hermanns of Standford University, U.S.A., was aroused when he read in my first book the account of my contact with Einstein. He knew Einstein very well, and was naturally all the more intrigued to think that I might be in touch with him. Professor Hermanns came to London, where we met on the 19th June 1972. He began to question me closely about the contact with Einstein, and I was very glad to see we were joined by the great man himself in spirit. Einstein began to talk quite volubly about his life and his work, mentioning a number of details which Professor Hermanns verified as being correct. It was certainly a most exciting meeting – it is always a great sensation to find that great souls have not just become extinct at death, but retain a mind which functions as keenly

26

as ever. What stood out in my mind most as a highlight of the meeting with Professor Hermanns – and Professor Einstein – was the humorous reply made by Einstein to a question posed by Professor Hermanns. He asked me to inquire of Einstein whether he could remember anything in particular about him, and Einstein's answer was definitely unexpected but totally accurate.

"Yes," came the rejoinder from Einstein, "I remember he always ate his food far too fast."

This observation from Einstein, which I repeated for Professor Hermanns to hear, drew a chortle from Hermanns' secretary, Ken Naughton, who was with us at this momentous meeting.

"He still does", volunteered Ken, whilst Professor Hermanns was still looking a trifle amazed that Einstein should recall his eating habits!

How good to think that our friends who have gone on into the Next Life should be able to remember us so well! Although there may be some things about us that we would want them to forget!

We have seen from the accounts of the meetings with Dr. van der Haas that those in spirit can be conscious of us and what we are doing and where we are. It would seem that spirits can watch us fairly freely, but Liszt says this depends on the amount of interest felt, and that usually it is those who love us in spirit who watch over us most and try to help us. The details related by spirit, also demonstrate that they retain many memories of their earth life. As Liszt declared a moment ago, whilst I was actually typing this chapter, "The thread of life does not end with death; it is simply transferred to another spool."

27

CHAPTER 3

Intelligence after death

If Life does continue after Death, to what degree do we remain the same, and does this sameness continue indefinitely? These are two questions I find are frequently asked by the serious inquirer. Two questions that I have asked more than one of my "spirit" contacts to see what they would have to say about them.

I will quote first of all from Bertrand Russell, since his after-death statements should interest many people.

"After breathing my last breath in my mortal body, I found myself in some sort of extension of existence that held no parallel, as far as I could estimate, in the material dimensions I had recently experienced. I observed that I was occupying a body predominantly bearing similarities to the physical one which I had vacated for ever; but this new body in which I now resided seemed virtually weightless and very volatile, and able to move in any direction with the minimum amount of effort. I began to think I was dreaming and would awaken all too soon to that old world, of which I had become somewhat weary, to find myself imprisoned once more in that ageing form which encased a brain that had waxed weary also and did not always want to think when *I* wanted to think.

"Several times in my life, I had thought I was about to die; several times I had resigned myself with the best will that I could muster to ceasing to be. The idea of B.R. no longer inhabiting the world did not trouble me unduly. I felt the world had had enough of me, and certainly I had had enough of the world. Befitting, I thought, to give the chap (myself) a decent burial and let him be. Now here I was, still the same I, with the capacities to think and observe sharpened to an incredible degree. I felt earth-life suddenly seemed very unreal almost as though it had never happened. It took me quite a long time to

28

understand this feeling until I realised at last that matter is certainly illusory although it does exist in actuality; the material world seemed now nothing more than a seething, changing, restless sea of indeterminable density and volume. How could I have thought that that was reality, and the last word of Creation to Mankind? Yet it is completely understandable that the state in which a man exists, however temporary, constitutes the passing reality which is no longer reality when it is passed."

My first contact with Bertrand Russell came as a complete surprise to me. Why should a man of such lofty intellect want to communicate with me? Well, of course, he probably did not particularly want to communicate with me at all, but saw me as a possible channel of communication with the world. I pointed out to him (unnecessarily, no doubt) that if I did pass on what he said, there was no guarantee that it would be accepted as bona fide messages from him. He replied:

"My influence on the thinking of the masses was negligible, but a strange quirk in human nature leads some people to pay more attention to messages from supposedly discarnate beings than to any from the mouths and pens of mortals. Therefore I am hopeful of my disembodied utterances being at least a source of diversion amongst those who foster an attitude of greater respect for the dead than the living."

When he said this, I suspected he was having a sly dig at the type of person who hangs open-mouthed on every word emanating from the Next World as if it is a tremendous revelation from on high. Not that I exclude the possibility of great revelations from the Beyond, but I know well – and serious investigators know – that a great quantity of banalities emerge from contact with the average after-death communicant. At the same time, we have to remember that these very banalities are the meat-and-drink of our everyday social talk, and I do not see why we should be surprised when those who have passed on continue to indulge in this habitual practice.

Suppose you knew a man who lived in the next road, and his main interests in life were a football match and a glass of beer: if he "died", and had a shot at communicating with you after his death, would you expect him to pour out a stream of pious eloquence? Would not you be tempted to doubt his identity if he did? People can only prove their identity by being themselves, and acting and speaking in their usual, recognisable way.

"A superficial examination of the facts rarely reveals the truth. There are those whose summary consideration of a controversial matter dismisses their opinion as shallow and immature."

What did Bertrand Russell mean by that, I wondered. He explained in more simple terms that he could appreciate now, from his position of increased perception into people's minds, that the majority of us do not give a really considered opinion on many issues.

"I did not realise, 'he added,' just how many people there are who are unwilling to consider all possibilities with regard to the hypothetical aspects of religion. There are so many possibilities which they want to exclude without giving them any thought or allowing others to give them any thought. We are no longer in the Middle Ages when a man could not question the existence of God or anything about him except on pain of death. We must let it dawn on us that if God exists and is a reasonable being he would prefer an honest doubter any time to a credulous cretin."

I thought the expression "credulous cretin" was a little too sweeping, and said so. For the first time in his talks with me, he showed some irritation.

"If you are going to take it on yourself to edit my speech," he remonstrated, 'I shall say even more outrageous things and insist you do not expurgate them."

I was a little amused, since I felt I held the whip-hand, and could choose to omit any portion of his remarks whenever I liked. On the other hand, I am endeavouring to be a truthful reporter, and would not be fulfilling my mission if I began to delete any passage I decided to leave out. I will proceed, therefore, to quote him verbatim as in his following view of human character:

"The assessment of any man's value rests not only upon the sound judgement of those who sit in judgement, but also upon a profound penetration into the hidden attributes and tortuous labyrinths of his mental processes. No human being is as simple in psychological function as might have been construed a century or two ago. There is rarely a straightforward assumption which can rightfully be relied upon to state a man's composite attitude; motive is almost invariably mixed with sundry and subtle undercurrents in the individual's own interests which would build a cynical view if one did not regard the main motive as the true indication of character.

"The human mind works very much upon the principle of computerisation if it is endowed with healthy intelligence and primed with adequate knowledge; it will weigh up all aspects programmed for its prognostication therefore taking in its stride both the altruistic and the self-seeking venues. The final decision in any matter may be one

30

that is not a clear-cut issue and is often arrived at prematurely before the inbuilt computer of the mind has been allowed to assimilate all the known facts and complete its assessment. Complete and effective programming is the secret of efficient mental activity; and how often can we be certain that our programming is absolute and accurate, unbiased by false propaganda from the outer world and distorting influences from within ourselves? Can we ever be one-hundred-per-cent dogmatic in any of our opinions without risking a fiasco at some future date when greater awareness of ourselves and the world we live in comes upon us by accident or design? We live in a world of shifting values which most people twist to suit their own purposes, seldom seeking truth for its own sake. How, then, can we find a sure and certain hope or any logical foundation on which to stand firm and look at the world about us without the threat of being undermined by an unexpected cause for reversal of outlook?"

He speaks in this passage as if still in our world, perhaps still taking such a close interest in the evolution of the human mind that it is as if he remains among us. In another conversation with me, it seemed apparent that he had altered some of his conclusions since his transition into spirit. Here it is:

"The scientist cannot be reproached if his study and research have sometimes drawn him to wrong conclusions which later discoveries have caused him to recant. Those scientists and philosophers who have the courage and honesty to admit the errors of their concepts merit our respect, and demonstrate that they are discerning disciples of the truth which they are willing to pursue no matter whether its growing accumulation contradicts some of their own patterns of belief or previous deductions.

"The habit of practising more latitude in one's attitudes even when they seem to be supported by incontrovertible principles and laws, will contribute much towards a speedier retrieval of a position which has become untenable following the production of fresh data outdating that which has already been collected.

"An examination of the process of evolutionary thought will reveal that it has a directional impetus very like a watch-spring which has been released from its tension and widens its concentric rings, becoming free from being geared to time. The primitive brain can deal only with the present moment of time; a brain more sophisticated can review the past and preview the future. Even in the world of matter it is possible to transcend time in thought and in actual fact to a distinctive degree by fast travel removing one from parochial

31

time. Time and location are inextricably interwoven to such an extent that one begins to conceive that time is a place rather than a process."

On another occasion, he delivered the following speech to me:

"Shedding light on humanity's path is not going to be an easy task, whoever attempts it. Ideas and ideologies can only be introduced slowly into the thinking of the populations of the world, and the means of doing this is still limited to personal conveyance amongst millions who remain to this day semi-illiterate or totally so. The facilities of radio, television, and newsprint may be available in abundance to the Western Hemisphere, but less accessible to the populations of the Eastern Hemisphere which are far more dense in comparison, and far more heterogeneous; to reach these peoples is going to be a long and difficult task, especially where they have already been indoctrinated with insular policies and dictatorial measures.

"Throughout the world, many the person who convinces himself if not others that his line of thinking is superior and best for the populace in general. The acid test of priming the populace is in the test-tube of the experience which follows for those subjected to the priming process. Is their experience the richer materially or mentally and are they healthier or happier through having had certain ideas moulded into their minds? Are they living more constructive and co-operative lives as a result of having submitted what intelligence they may possess to the manipulations of others?

"History has demonstrated that many a dictator sets out with benign motives fully intending to occupy the position of self-appointed saviour of his people, only to fall victim to an over-developed sense of power and self-importance which leads him to presume greater authority than he is capable of wielding wisely and beneficially. Sooner or later this leads to discontent and rebellion, and the dictator finds himself overthrown and replaced by another individual or corporate body of deposing contenders who may prove to be even less salutary. If a ruler or government wishes to be lasting, it would seem wise to be malleable but unwise to be too malleable.

"It seems difficult for nations to adopt a system of government which is satisfactory to the whole populace, and there must always be the dissenters who cannot agree with the policies practised by the current leader or leaders. By some strange freak of outlook, almost all dissenters are regarded as seditious influences – as indeed they may prove to be in many instances; but the remnant who cannot be

32

so classed may consist of genuine well-doers whose aims are solely to introduce reforms that will rectify various evils both social and economic."

When Bertrand Russell was talking to me, I listened carefully, trying to record faithfully each word he uttered. There are, of course, difficulties in communicating between the world of matter and the world of spirit, and messages may not always come over clearly. I had a message once from Sir Donald Tovey which I sent to Dr George Firth, O.B.E., of Edinburgh to read. Dr. Firth queried one word –"flagrant" – which he thought must be incorrect. I duly checked with Sir Donald at the first opportunity, and found that it was, indeed, incorrect; the word should have been "blatant", but it was so similar in sound that Sir Donald had to spell it to me letter by letter before I grasped it. The text from which this query arose is included in a later section of this book. Sir Donald remarked when this query occurred that in my attempts to transcribe his speeches I was "faithful in effort if not in effect" – typical of his phrasing, so the Firths assured me.

Bertrand Russell said one day that he had concluded when in this world that there were many questions about the Cosmos and Creation for which, perhaps, there were no answers, or if answers existed, it would be well-nigh impossible for us to obtain them.

"I was positive I knew the answers to many questions including the vexing one concerning the probability of taking up a new life after this one has ceased. I use the word probability rather than possibility because I believed in the possibility of many improbable things, and preferred to consider problems in the light of probability rather than in the half-light of possibility."

Science has moved from the realms of basic matter into more ethereal realms during the past few generations. We know now that the atmosphere about us vibrates with countless sounds, images, and waves of which we are oblivious, some of which we are now able to detect as demonstrated by radio and television, to name but two examples. Shall we be able to build apparatus one day which will enable us all to perceive and hear spirits? Anyone who answers that question with an emphatic "no" is probably being too cocksure, and in danger of having to eat that word at some future date.

What if we do eventually design apparatus which enables us to communicate with those in the Next World? If there is a Next World, it seems not too absurd to assume there must be some means of contacting it: after all, those who have passed on have reached it –

33

without any special apparatus. So far, we have had to depend largely on mediumship, seership, "divine" visions, and so on, for glimpses into that world. But this means many people have to rely on others for any contact with the World of Hereafter since we cannot all be mediums. This also means relying on the integrity and efficiency of the mediums who can give this service, although the involvement of the human factor is for ever fallible.

What sort of repercussions would such apparatus cause? Would it, for instance, enhance the status of religion or detract from it? Take the official religion of Britain, Christianity: how would it be affected? Proving that Life after Death is a reality will verify its most important issue, and could lead to a great revival in Christian belief, perhaps with some modifications on certain points. It might seem to the modern thinking worshipper that we must be prepared to move forward with the times, hallowing our faith but accepting an expansion in outlook where it is consistent with the principles of Christianity. And this willingness to be prepared to progress in outlook would apply to peoples of all religions if they are open to new ideas, new developments, and new light on their pathway.

Liszt has often conversed with me about Man's endless search for truth and his varying beliefs.

"Belief is often based on fragmented knowledge which has been passed on through various means including reports made by people who are, it goes without saying, not infallible. These people have often had their words mistranslated, misinterpreted, and misapplied. People cannot be blamed if they do not comprehend the obscurities and discrepancies in sacred books. But they can be blamed if they possess normal intelligence and yet behave deliberately in a manner likely to be detrimental in any way to their fellow-beings."

That seems to be their attitude in a nut-shell in the Next World, that it is not so much what we believe that matters as the way we behave. Whatsoever a man soweth, that shall he also reap, we were told long ago. That, they say, applies to each one of us, and we are building our future life here and now. They assure us that from their own experience they know that maxim to be true.

We are in this world possibly to learn; no doubt we shall find we still have much to learn in the Next World . . . and perhaps the world after that, then after that. . . . In this world we seem doomed to learn through suffering; in the next, we can learn in greater happiness and through glad service to others. All this, I am told, is no wishy-washy piety but practical reality; a joyous reality which we can bring

34

into effect in this world when we gain greater understanding of ourselves and others and Life itself.

Speaking of learning, and the theory that this world is a sort of school, if we have only one life here, it would hardly seem to give every soul a reasonable chance to acquire an adequate amount of wisdom. This raises the question of reincarnation, a highly controversial issue, which might throw us into even deeper waters if we allow ourselves to get carried away by some of the claims advanced in support of the idea. In order to give everyone a fair range of opportunities in earth-life, it might appear that the only way would be through allotting more than one incarnation. For instance, it would seem grossly unfair for one soul to experience an extremely limited life in primitive conditions, denied education and any other means of developing his mind, whilst another has access to schools, libraries, museums, universities, and all that modern culture can offer.

Somewhere, sometime, if justice rules supreme, there must be the same opportunities and privileges for every single soul; if there is not, then the idea of God is a mockery and a myth. We may, of course, find that all we have missed out on in this life is awaiting us in the next; but can a world of spirit provide a successful substitute for all of the experiences available on earth? Can we, for example, really grasp both the feminine and the masculine rôles without incarnating alternately as female and male? Would it be absolutely just for us to have a life only as a woman or only as a man? Are we always one or the other, throughout all time to come? Are we male or female by virtue of the fact that we occupy a male or female body? Or are we either masculine or feminine within ourselves?

Experiments are now being conducted by reputable hypnotists in "regression", that is, retracing the history of a hypnotised subject by moving him or her back in time by hypnotic suggestion. This technique might eventually throw a great deal of light on the vexed question of reincarnation, since it appears that some subjects have been regressed to a period prior to birth, and given accounts of previous lives in which they have been of the opposite sex to their present one. Some of these accounts of apparent earlier incarnations might, however, be the inventions of an imaginative sub-conscious mind, and need to be tested in some way for their accuracy.

The people who claim to remember a previous life often maintain that they were some great figure in history – which causes one to suspect that they are compensating themselves for a feeling of

35

inferiority by providing themselves with an alternative as a grand personage. I was once at a small gathering where a number of the guests laid claim to having been kings, queens, great warriors, eminent statesmen, noblemen, heroes, all. One lady turned to me with a somewhat patronising air, and asked me whether I could recall who I had been.

"Oh, I expect I was a scullery maid or something," I replied, having no reason to believe I was previously some exalted person.

The lady in question glared at me in a rather malevolent fashion, and there were a few seconds of uncomfortable silence in the room, during which I realised that I was suspected of irony.

On another occasion, I witnessed two ladies almost coming to blows because both claimed to have been the wife of a great pharoah. I had already met two other ladies who firmly believed they were the wife of the pharaoh at stake, and wondered whether there might not have been a real free-for-all had they been present as well.

Strange that people should so much want to have been certain well-known figures. After all, the prominent people in our world are often far from good, pleasant, or likeable! The ones no-one ever hears about are just as likely, or perhaps more so, to be the ones really worth knowing.

One often wonders, too, what good can be achieved by dwelling on past lives. If the memory of them will in any way help us to lead better lives now, or assist in solving some of our current problems, well and good. If not, it would seem just so much waste of time and energy to try to delve too much into the past which is over and cannot be altered.

It is easy enough to produce arguments both for and against the case for reincarnation; it is easy enough to produce arguments for and against most things. To help settle such arguments, we need to get at the facts. Possibly the experiments in regression will supply some of these facts. Possibly those who communicate truthfully and lucidly from the Next World can help to clear up some of the confusion regarding this matter. At least they may know more than we do about reincarnation, but if they cannot give definite proof one way or the other, the case will still be not proven.

In my first book, "Unfinished Symphonies", I outlined Liszt's views on reincarnation: he maintains that the same person never incarnates more than once, but that each life is a unique expression of the soul which can infuse part of itself into what he calls, "an earthly vehicle" – that is, a physical body. In other words, he is

36

saying that the whole self does not return, but that one can project part of one's self into an earthly existence. Logic tells us that the identical self could not be born more than once on earth since this would require the same parents who would also have to be exactly the same as they were previously. This would involve an endless chain of identical ancestors and identical conditions in a world where conditions are continually changing and people continually evolving. The Liszt assertion regarding reincarnation seems far more plausible than any idea of total return.

Or perhaps an analogy given by Einstein expresses the process in a majestic manner:

"The sun itself does not visit the earth, but its beams reach, touch, and merge with the world. So also does the soul beam down into earthly existence, like a ray from its own centre becoming clothed in matter."

CHAPTER 4

Standards of mediumship

No one who has ventured into the fields of mediumship, culling messages and information in search of a goodly harvest, needs telling about the wheat and the tares that spring up side by side. I have had highly evidential and very helpful messages from other mediums from time to time; I have also had a bellyful of nonsense from some. Not only do standards of mediumship vary sharply, but there are plenty of phoneys and featherbrains scattered around to mislead the unwary.

This emphasises the advisability not only of testing the spirits, but also of sounding out the sincerity of mediums. Some of the experiences I have had with other mediums have shown me how cautious one needs to be, as illustrated by the following story.

In February, 1971, the publishers arranged for me to go to Paris for promotion of my first book. This turned out to be a whirlwind weekend. To begin with, there was a period of delay in air-travel due to a strike which obliged passengers to fly by a different air-line. Eventually, I landed at Orly Airport where I was met by representatives from the Paris publishers. Hardly had I set foot on French soil before I was snatched away for a hectic series of recording for Television and Radio. Finally, a big press conference had been arranged, at which I was required to answer the usual flood of questions, and to play a few examples of the music from the composers working with me. At last this event drew to a close, but people were still milling round me asking further details, when a woman thrust herself in front of me and said dramatically, "Look me in the eye! I am a medium, too."

I felt a nudge from the faithful Liszt who hurriedly whispered "Do not take any notice of this woman." He need not have whispered, anyway, for no-one else could have heard – and the self-styled medium did not hear, either, that was obvious. She went on to say that I must not fly back to London, that I must cancel my flight and go by ferry instead.

"I see something terrible for you if you fly," she stated.

What was she up to, I wondered? Did she hope to panic me into heeding her? I managed to muster enough French to reply that I was not afraid because I knew I would be safe. She looked a little crestfallen at this – was this because she was genuinely afraid for me, or because she was disappointed at being unable to perturb me? Anyway, I flew home as arranged, and have flown several times since without any mishap. I wondered whether she had some plan in mind to claim that she had averted a disaster for me by her dire warning. Or did she really think she foresaw disaster for me? Worse still, did she wish disaster for me out of jealousy? Liszt said she was just trying to "ruffle" my calm. Perhaps, though I doubt it, her utterance was a strange way of trying to test my own mediumship.

I have had many prophecies made to me by several mediums. Out of all these, only one – the least likely – turned out to be correct. This was a prophecy made some years ago. It took place in 1963 when I joined a small group of people in a South London house who met weekly to pray for the sick. There was a man in this group who sometimes went into a trance during which a spirit spoke through him. One week, this spirit, who claimed to have lived in China many centuries ago, turned his attention to me.

"In less than ten years, you will be world-famous, lady," he announced in a very positive tone of voice.

I was too astonished to answer. What on earth could ever make me world-famous, I asked myself silently. I seemed a most unlikely candidate for fame, and it was a distinctly terrifying prospect as far as I was concerned. I love quietness and peaceful surroundings; I prefer to live un-noticed, a modest, simple life. I decided the spirit was either kidding or mistaken. Perhaps, I thought rather facetiously, the name of this Chinese "guide" should be "Foo-ling-you." Now I have to eat those unspoken words for his prophecy has been well and truly fulfilled within the span of time named by him.

At the time when that prophecy was made, I was a very impoverished widow struggling to bring up my two children alone. I was slaving away in school kitchens, scrubbing floors and scouring pots to make ends meet. At the end of the day's slogging in the kitchens, I had all my own household chores to do as well as the

39

children to look after, trying to be both mother and father to them. All these labours left no time or energy for any other activities; in fact, the weekly prayer meeting was almost my only diversion whenever I could manage to get a friend to look after my children while I attended it. My chances of fame – which I certainly did not want, anyway – appeared to be nil.

There was one prophecy which was made repeatedly to me by more than one medium: that was that I would marry a second time. But I think that was a false prophecy made, possibly in all good faith, by people who thought that it would comfort me. More than twelve years have elapsed now since my husband passed away, and the passage of time has diminished any chance of remarriage even if I wanted it.

There is no need to list the numerous other prophecies which depressingly, or sometimes mercifully, failed to come true. There have been amusing moments, too, such as the time when another medium informed me in all seriousness that Liszt had told her that he wanted me to grow my hair long and wear it in plaits, to wear dirndl dresses, and goodness knows what else! She was a fairly well-known medium, and in spite of the absurdity of the suggestions, I was inclined to take her seriously at first. But afterwards I asked Liszt myself about her statements. "Do you really want me to grow my hair and wear it in plaits, and do all those other things that she said?" I asked – rather indignantly, I must admit, because I thought it was making a fool of me.

Liszt was gazing at me earnestly.

"Why," he asked me, very much on his dignity, "Why should I go to another medium to give you a message when I can talk to you direct?"

That seemed to answer that. I did not like to think that the lady had been deliberately making it all up, but if she was not a phoney at least I wondered if she were not just a little scatter-brained! I don't think for one moment that Liszt would be the least bit interested in my hair style or anybody else's – he has more serious business to attend to with his mission to help humanity.

Then there was the medium who swore that I was George Sand in my last life.

"Ah, but George Sand is in the Spirit World," I said, "And what is more, she has talked to me."

That scotched that little idea! George Sand apparently wanted to tell me that she and Chopin had "made up their differences," and

40

this is what she came to say one day.

All this must sound as if I have little faith in mediums in general, but, in fact, I have met many fine mediums who more than compensate for the frauds and fakers.

What, then, can we do to weed out those who practice deliberate deception? Or restrain those whose intentions are good, but who are deluded by their own imaginations? This would be no easy task, since there are so many people aspiring to be mediums these days, and the tricksters will naturally work furtively in the background.

The Spiritualist Movement itself endeavours to keep some kind of check on those mediums who come to its notice, and the Editor of the Psychic News, Maurice Barbanell, is always on the alert for fraudulent mediums. Mr. Barbanell, an able and unflagging exponent of Spiritualism, would be the first to expose any false medium of doubtful repute. The fraudulent mediums and the incompetent ones give a bad name to Spiritualism, and detract from its chances of taking part in a great spiritual awakening.

For mediums to improve their standard of mediumship, it is essential for them to be completely honest with themselves and with others, and to learn to distinguish between imaginary and real communication. It may be very difficult for some to distinguish between imagination and the real thing; the dividing line between the two can be very thin, and only by constant watch can one prevent one's own mind infiltrating into the processes of psychic perception. When psychic manifestations become more palpable as with direct voice, or even more tangible with materialisation, the interference from imagination will not pose so much of a problem.

If Spiritualism can prevail upon people to strive to ennoble their souls, and not merely seek messages from the so-called dead, its image in the eyes of the Churches might be brighter. It is, after all, registered in this country as a recognised religion, although many people are probably unaware of this fact. Although religious tolerance is called for nowadays, especially in view of the different religious beliefs of immigrants now settling in countries other than their own, there is a deplorable lack of tolerance amongst certain sects. Spiritualists are often in the firing line to this day on account of their beliefs, and can be the victims of scurrilous attacks which in some cases might entitle them to sue for slander or libel.

It is as long ago as 1937 when Dr. Cosmo Gordon Lang, then Archbishop of Canterbury, set up a commission on Spiritualism, which drew a highly favourable report. When a journalist asked Dr.

41

Mervyn Stockwood, Bishop of Southwark, why the report of the commission was not published, he replied, "They did not have the guts to publish it."

The official reason for non-publication was that "the war made it inopportune". Dr. Stockwood said he thought the reverse would have been the case.

"In times of national emergency – and especially at that time, with the destructive forces of Adolf Hitler massed against us – men are readier to consider the prospect of death, and what, if anything, may lie beyond," commented the Bishop.

Had this report been made available to all, it could have eased the anguish of many a bereaved person, and perhaps helped many to be braver in the face of death, knowing from the report that it is not the end. Does anyone have the right to withhold the truth from the people? Who dares to deprive people of the sure and certain knowledge that life continues after death? How long will the quibbling continue and the truth not be made known to the whole world? It is surely high time the public was told the facts together with a caution against dabbling with psychic powers in an irresponsible way. Psychic powers, like any other powers, can be misused: hence, no doubt, the warning in the Old Testament so often flung in the face of mediums by people who take a specific meaning to be a general one.

Scientists, as well as parapsychologists, are beginning to turn their attention to the mysterious extrasensory faculties which some people possess. When these faculties are fully understood, they will not, of course, be mysterious any longer. This may disappoint those people who like to create mystery and mumbo-jumbo around things which must be subject, like all things, to natural laws. As long as we regard communication with the Next World and anything to do with psychic abilities as unnatural, these matters will continue to inspire a certain amount of apprehension which may hinder the breaking down of the barriers between us and other planes of consciousness.

There are so many apparently strange things occurring in the world nowadays; blunt razor blades left overnight inside a cardboard model of a pyramid are found to be sharp again by morning; A Leningrad housewife can make a compass revolve by staring at it; another Leningrad housewife can separate the white of a broken egg from the yolk by staring at it; a lady from a village in the Urals can read with her elbow – yes, her elbow. How much is there, in fact, that we do not know about ourselves and the unseen forces surrounding

42

us? It is no use turning our backs on these matters and saying we don't want to know. Someone sometime is going to investigate them, and we had better be prepared for startling news about the latent powers of our own beings and the untapped range of energy waves.

One thing seems certain: that we can become, or already are, transmitters of energies which we do not yet fully understand. In view of this, it is not so unrealistic as the unbeliever thinks to pray for peace, to pray for healing, to pray for anything constructive, because concentrated, fervent prayer may be releasing great waves of energy. We may be veritable generators who merely need to learn how to release and direct our potential powers.

We need to go forward with open minds if we are not to remain ignorant of our true selves, our full relationship to the world, and our interaction on all about us. We need to know ourselves in order to manage and direct ourselves for the best possible results; if we do not accomplish this, we will remain puppets in the hands of our own unplumbed natures, thrown hither and thither with no real say in the process.

Those who are discerning will begin to see more and more clearly the importance of acquainting ourselves as fully as possible with all our faculties of extrasensory perception, not simply in an effort to build a network of communications with the Next World and other spheres, but also to delve deeper into our entire being to discover and make good use of every potential. We do not hesitate to make use of all the material resources in the world; to strike a true balance, and perhaps restore Mankind to its rightful spiritual stature, we should also make wise use of all our inner resources of mind and psyche.

Those who would keep closed the avenues to psychic enlightenment may indeed be hindering the spiritual advance of humanity. I have used the expression 'psychic enlightenment' advisedly for the search must be for enlightenment and not for personal ends if the aim is to be for the higher development of Mankind.

As Bertrand Russell put it, when communicating recently. "If revelations come which present a challenge to some of our present ideas, we must accept them and designate their position in the scheme of things. All the formulations in the world will not arrest the tide of advanced thinking from sweeping away false conceptions and false gods.

"The intellect in Man has been used for observing and recording facts of Nature, that is, the material world. Only in recent times has

43

it been turned towards an interpretation of Man himself, his mental habits and aptitudes. The next step in self-mastery lies in the advance of mental science and paranormal psychology."

The mention of intellect brings me to another point in relation to extrasensory perception. From the observations of researchers and my own experience it would seem that intellect has little connection with the function of extrasensory perception, and it has been remarked that mediums are often people of limited intellectual pretensions. There are, however, a number of mediums who are not only highly intelligent but highly cultured. One suspects that the intellectual types may have an equal amount of extra-sensory perceptive faculties, either dormant or active, but that with intellectuality there may in some cases come an intellectual pride which leads them to disdain any non-intellectual aspects of themselves or others. Most mediums and psychics who come to notice are female; again, this may not be due simply to a greater feminine aptitude but to the fact that there may be a tendency in men to regard extra-sensory faculties as being at variance with male dignity.

In any truly civilised society, male and female dignity would be equally valued. Which brings back to mind the strange exhortations of one medium – a woman herself – who tried to lay down the law to me. She alleged she was in touch with Liszt, and proceeded to tell me that I must obey him in all things because he was a man I a woman(!), always obtain his permission before accepting any invitations for lunch, dinner etc., and generally kotow to him. She was obviously one of the all-too-numerous people who adopt a servile attitude towards those who communicate from the Spirit World. It has to be borne in mind that people are still only human beings even when they have made the transition into spirit. To set them up on pedestals is inviting trouble just the same as it invites trouble to set up anybody in this world on a pedestal.

Liszt, having worked with me for a considerable time, must have known my outlook which is one that recognises us as all being equal in the sight of God, though we may be at different stages of development. He would also know that I am one who elects to make my own decisions, and that I would not ask him or any other composer what I should do, but would turn to God for guidance. I thought the lady who was giving me these alleged messages from Liszt might have an ulterior motive. If she could persuade me that she was really in touch with Liszt, and prevail upon me to bow in servitude, she could then issue her own orders pretending they originated from

44

him. A cunning plan to manipulate me for her own ends? It would not be the first time someone had tried to do just that.

Chopin remarked to me one day that "they found it easy to work with me because I did not regard them as some kind of zombie or saints with budding haloes". This remark portrays the two extreme attitudes adopted by certain people, either classifying all spirits as demons or as angelic beings!

Chopin and Liszt know well that I would be the first to pay homage to those who possess great genius or nobility of character. They also know that all talents come from God; therefore, as Beethoven frequently says, "To God alone be the glory".

I share this sentiment, believing that we cannot claim credit for our intelligence or gifts, but only for the use to which we put them. The gifts are bestowed on us; it is up to us whether we develop them industriously as far as circumstances allow.

The vast majority of mediums whom I know do recognise very well the fact that spirits retain their human traits, and these very traits can manifest and help to establish the identity of the communicators. There is every opportunity in the life hereafter to improve one's character if one makes the effort. Liszt himself said to me one day with touching humility, "I have purged myself of many of my less worthy characteristics and hope to grow into perfection through continued effort."

He spoke of the way that his soul aspired while he was on earth to reach God, but how his earthly nature enslaved him. He pointed out that a similar battle takes place in all human beings, the higher nature seeking to triumph over the earthly nature, one's better self "waxing stronger" through its struggles with the lower self.

"You speak," I said to him, "As if we are two selves, but surely this is not possible?"

"You have but the one self," he answered, "Your spiritual self. This is your real self. But when you incarnate you take on a body of flesh which is like another entity in itself. This body is not you, but you identify with it while it is living, rather like an actor identifying with a rôle. The body has a life of its own, a will of its own if you like, and its will may clash with the will of the real self. Then you can be torn with inner conflict as so many are on earth. The whole purpose of earthly incarnation is to learn to identify with the real, immortal self, and to become spiritually orientated. This does not mean you have to be impractical; you live in a material world and have to deal with material things, but the ultimate purpose should always be kept in

45

mind."

As you can see, in his conversations with me, Liszt is something of a spiritual teacher. I expect a lot of people have drawn the conclusion that his visits to me have consisted only of sessions of musical dictation and instruction. But once I came to know him well enough to feel I could venture to ply him with questions – on subjects other than music – I began to ask about his views on God, and soon found that he is a deeply devout soul whose earnest desire is to open the frontiers of spiritual consciousness for as many as possible.

Chopin held a long conversation with me one day in one of his rare moods of serious metaphysical contemplation. At least, he rarely reveals this side of his nature. He spoke with quiet reverence of the Holy Spirit and left me in no doubt that this is for him the great reality which he worships and serves with steadfast devotion.

Mediums often get what is sometimes referred to as "higher teaching" from certain spirits. Sometimes these teachings are very beautiful although perhaps nothing out of the ordinary. Sometimes the so-called "higher teaching" is no more than a mouthful of trite repetitions of theological anachronisms. It all depends, one must conclude, on the spirit giving mouth to the utterances and his or her command of language. Such teachings may help to improve standards of mediumship when they are sincere, enlightening, and from "higher" intelligences. The fact that they rarely provide evidence of a personal category does not matter if the aim is to build a bridge of communion rather than communication. The highest form of communication might indeed lead to communion with the Highermost.

CHAPTER 5

My own search

As a child, I was always having visions, prophetic dreams, and hearing voices. Madness? So some people might say. But if they wish to dismiss the instances of my psychical and mystical experiences as delusions, they must also dismiss every single vision of every saint and mystic and prophet in the same abrupt manner. Such a dismissal would certainly not be acceptable to the Churches, Synagogues, and Temples, and would make nonsense of religion.

We can, if we wish, choose the path of cold science, believing nothing that cannot be seen, heard or felt with the physical senses. But we cannot be sure that our physical senses register all that there is. We do know that there are sounds which are inaudible to the human ear. We do know that the naked eye is incapable of seeing things which are beyond its range or focus, or too infinitesimal to be observed. As we move towards the end of the Twentieth Century, life is becoming more complicated but all the richer through our increasing use of invisible waves which carry sights and sounds across the world to our television sets and radios. To presume we have now reached the utmost limits of discovery would be totally irrational. How many other things revolve around us unheard and unseen we cannot even guess. He who rejects the idea of other dimensions, other planes of consciousness, other spheres of existence, is rash indeed, and in for some big surprises!

Since I had visions and heard voices from the beginning of my life here, they seem to me to be completely natural phenomena. The fact that few people have the ability to see and hear in this way does not imply that such phenomena are *not* natural. Rare, perhaps – but a thing is not made unnatural by its "rarity". It is possible that we have made such things seem unnatural by burying our heads, figuratively speaking, in that which is tangible, and pretending the intangible does not exist.

As a small child, I did not realise that not everyone could see and hear as I did. In time, it dawned on me that I seemed to be the odd one out, and I began to feel an abysmal loneliness because of it. As I grew up, my mother related from time to time stories of her "second sight", as she called it. But her experiences were few and far between, and usually took the form of an intuitive insight into things and people rather than actual clairvoyance or clairaudience. It was some comfort to me to find that at least she had this gift, which had been inherited from her own mother who was Scottish.

One of the first 'spirits'" whom I saw was none other than my mother's mother. I was saddened by the fact that she seemed unhappy about my mother's lot in life, and promised her that I would do all I could to make things easier and brighter for her daughter. At first a little apprehensive because I had such access to my grandmother, eventually my mother grew glad of the link because she and her own mother had been very devoted to one another. Messages flowed from my grandmother in great detail which left my mother in no doubt whatsoever of their reality. Soon I grew to love my grandmother who had died before I was born, and as I came to know her I realised what a good woman she was – which my mother confirmed enthusiastically. She was – or I should say, is – a very unselfish person and very devout, and her influence, though she was in another dimension, was like a guiding star in those early years.

Later in my life, my mother's father made contact with me from spirit. It did not take me long to realise that he was a brilliantly clever man, and that he bore a great affection for my mother. Messages poured from him, and I found him so kindly and so interesting that I felt sorry I had not met him before his death. Clearly, my mother was relieved to have word of him, and delighted with the wealth of evidence he gave her.

An interesting side-light on my grandfather which helped to link me up with mediumistic work was revealed by my mother. She told me that my grandfather had worked for many years with Sir William Crookes, and assisted him in his psychical research. My mother said she could not remember Sir William herself – she must have been little more than a child at the time – but that her father spoke of him with great admiration. A perfect gentleman, so my grandfather averred, and a scientist of unwavering integrity and fine principles. My mother told me she remembered vividly a prophetic remark made by Sir

48

William to her father, who quoted it more than once to her.

"Mark my words," cautioned Sir William when discussing with my grandfather the extraordinary success of some of his psychical research, "There are sure to be some attempts by posterity to discredit me in order to throw doubt on the conclusive nature of the research."

I am glad my mother had passed on before the scandalous effort made in a publication released in 1962 to defame Sir William's character – she would have exploded with indignation! It is a wonder that Sir William does not return to haunt the author of the book in question. Perhaps he will meet the author when he joins him in the Life Hereafter, and take him to task for his deed. Uttering defamatory remarks about someone no longer present to defend himself is very much like hitting below the belt, anyway.

Life had been catastrophic for my grandparents. Grandmother came from a wealthy family and had married well into the family of Sugg, the Gas Engineers. During my mother's childhood and early girlhood, all was well. She was brought up in the lap of luxury, adored by both parents. and enjoyed a social life in cultured circles. But this was not to last. There was no sudden reversal in fortunes, but a gradual sliding from riches to abject poverty, and all, if reports are true, because my grandfather was an honest man.

There was a syndicate of three men consisting of my grandfather and two others. One of the other men devised some kind of gas-mantle which he wished to put on the market, but first it had to be approved by the two other members of the syndicate. The second man agreed to the proposal to market the mantle, but my grandfather was not satisfied with its quality. The inventor of the mantle pointed out that they could all make a great deal of money out of the sales, but my grandfather was adamant. He stated bluntly that in his opinion selling such a mantle would be a swindle since it was definitely faulty This infuriated the man who had designed the mantle, and he swore he would ruin my grandfather for his refusal to consent to its sale.

My mother never told me all the squalid details of the family's slow financial disintegration. The man who had threatened my grandfather with ruin brought it about methodically and insidiously, making sure, not by fair means, but by foul ones, that Grandfather never got any contracts, was turned down for any position for which he applied, and was left with no means of livelihood to support his wife and children. Such a thing could not, one hopes, happen nowadays, though doubtless there are still such villains in existence.

Grandfather, a brilliant scientist, inventor, and artist, and a great

49

linguist, became a broken man. He had to move his family into successively smaller and humbler homes, selling everything that was saleable. Snobbery was rampant in those days, and none of their old friends wanted to know them after the change in their fortunes. Not only were they now desperately poor, living in the shabbiest surroundings, but they had no-one to turn to for commiseration. All this left a terrible mark on my mother who was in her early teens, and she remained embittered to the end of her days.

So I was brought up by a mother whose life had gone through devastating changes, who had witnessed the shattering of her father's spirit, and watched her own mother die an early death as a result, probably, of the terrible strains and straits. Was it all these tragedies which made by mother deeply religious? Or had she always been so? The family were brought up in the Church of England tradition, but had found the Church unable to offer them any consolation in their troubles. My mother however remained steadfast to her faith in God to her dying day.

She taught me to pray regularly, but did not insist that I attended Sunday School or Church.

"Half the people who go to Church are hypocrites," she often said. One day, when she was a young girl, disgusted at the bad behaviour and downright unkindness of some of the congregation at the church she attended with her family, she protested to her mother. Grandmother replied, so my mother told me, that one must not expect people to be good just because they go to Church, but she added a caution, "They are not bad *because* they go to Church. In fact, they might be a lot worse if they didn't."

It seems that Grandmother was something of a philosopher. Whenever she was suffering great pain while she was dying, or before then whenever there was hardship or trouble, she would tell her daughter that perhaps she had herself been bad in a previous life and was now "paying off the debt". Stories such as this one, which my mother recounted to me, introduced me early to the idea of reincarnation and its attendant theme of "karma." In those days I did not know the appointed word "karma", but my mother certainly set me thinking about the possibilities of reincarnation and its train of chain-reactions.

As I grew up, I wanted to know more about all these possibilities and began to explore various avenues. I wanted to know about other religions as well as Christianity. It did not seem fair to give a hearing only to one Faith – and how could one know whether the other

50

religions were true or not without studying them? So I set out on my long and continuing search for God – or what I named rather naïvely as "The final truth."

I went to as many different churches as possible, covering as many denominations as I could find. With the down-to-earth logic of adolescence, I tried to reason out why there were so many different forms of Christianity. If they all believed one thing, why were they not united? Why did they seem to vie with one another instead of working together? Why did they argue so much about certain points? I began to feel there was too much splitting of hairs, too much petty squabbling, and not enough Christian spirit.

I attended our own Parish Church for some time. Alas! it has recently been demolished since it had become a dangerous structure through the onslaught of woodworm and death-watch beetles. It was called Saint Stephen's, and was a very picturesque church in what was then a quiet road. I was told by a member that it was a rather "low" Church. I must say I did not think any Church worthy of the name should be called "low", but eventually I found out what was meant by the term.

When I first attended services in this Church, the congregation all rose when the Choir entered. Then a division in opinion took place amongst the worshippers as to whether the congregation should or should not stand when the choir appeared. It all seemed so silly to me. If we stood, well, it was like being polite to guests when they arrive. Like a greeting. If we remained seated, well surely the Choir was not going to get huffy over that! But the split widened, sharp words were exchanged, and the whole issue became a major one.

One morning, as the Choir entered, I was not sure what to do. I didn't think it really mattered either way. But most of the congregation stayed firmly glued to their pews, and I wondered whether the Vicar had asked them to do so. One or two defiant figures stood up, and I shall never forget the lady in front of me who sprang to her feet as if a sergeant-major had barked an order at her. She was very soberly dressed in black, wearing long black gloves which were carefully buttoned. I often watched her at services as she turned the pages of her Prayer Book or Hymn Book with her hands still encased in those gloves, and wondered how she managed to do it. There she stood on this occasion, with a black hat perched high on her head. The hat had a long ostrich feather sprouting up from the brim, and I will never forget how that feather absolutely bristled and quivered with righteous indignation as she maintained her stiff, unyielding

51

posture.

The whole business was quite ludicrous, and the atmosphere in that Church was charged with hostility. At one moment I thought how comical the situation had become; at the next moment, I felt rather sick at heart that the human species could indulge in such pettiness.

It all ended in disaster for the Vicar. He was a very conscientious, sensitive man, and all the endless back-biting and disturbance which erupted from the rift in his flock undermined his health. As a result, he had a stroke which almost cost him his life, and left him partially paralysed down one side.

A new vicar had to be appointed, and when I attended the Induction, I was very stirred to hear the Bishop having to reprove the congregation for its un-Christian behaviour.

I was about twelve years old at the time, and, as you can imagine, this unfortunate series of events in the Parish Church did not make a good impression on my young mind. I tried to understand why the members of this particular Church had fallen out over such a minor issue, and saw plainly that a religion can be made or marred by its adherents. The same disillusionment was to overtake me again and again throughout life as I studied comparative religion and a number of esoteric movements. It took me a long time to resign myself to the truth that a belief does not necessarily alter a person's character or behaviour.

Over the past two thousand years or so, several very fine major religions have arisen. The Sufi Movement recognises the value of each one of these religions, and combines the teachings in their ceremonies. There are other movements which amalgamate the main religions and philosophies of the world, and the Theosophical Society is an example of this effort to study and respect all beliefs.

By the time I had reached the age of sixteen, I had visited many different religious centres, and read a multitude of books about people's ideas of God. At first it was rather bewildering to find how much opinions could vary concerning the nature of God and the way we should worship Him. So many clashing beliefs, so many conflicting systems, so many contrasting doctrines . . . where would all of them end? Would humanity always be torn by warring creeds? The only solution seemed to lie in a universal religion acceptable to all. I wrote a long and involved thesis on the whole predicament, urging the embodiment of universal religion into every separate Faith, comparing it to a United Nations Organisation, in which each nation retained

52

its own nationality and boundaries, whilst co-operating with all other nations. Second thoughts told me that many people were so encrusted in their own personal belief that they would never entertain the idea of real tolerance towards other types of belief, let alone the idea of creating a unified belief. I abandoned by youthful ideal of becoming some kind of evangelist for a world religion. A crackpot ideal, most people would decide! I did not think I would be very popular with the sects who did battle to assert their particular belief as the only right one, anyway. But there was a ray of hope, I hazarded, for some degree of reconciliation in the Hereafter – surely there would dawn greater understanding in that realm of many mansions where it would become obvious that Life continues for all of us and not exclusively for those of one selected persuasion.

For many years I was an active member of the Theosophical Society in London. They seemed to study everything under the sun, including teachings from the Far East – all the well-known systems as well as lesser known ones. The teachings of Krishnamurti attracted my attention, and have become a life-long interest.

In every single belief which I studied, I found some light thrown on my pathway. But although God was expressed in those beliefs, He was not the beliefs themselves. They were pointers which might help to show the way, but I still had to tread the path for myself. I had to seek through meditation, prayer, observation, and through the encounters and experiences of everyday life. This search, pursued both as an inner and outer process, is the underlying thread of my very existence, and I solemnly believe has been the key that has opened the doors of greater awareness. Awareness not only of people who dwell in spiritual realms, awareness not only of exalted and angelic beings who toil for our salvation, but awareness of the very presence of that which we call God. I do not claim for one moment that increased awareness makes me in any way superior to others. I am still very much a human being subject to limitations; I am still a learner, a speck in the vast scheme of things as indeed we all are.

Human beings are sometimes prone to become full of their own self-importance. Thinkers may surmise that we are important only for our contribution to the whole. Gazing out into space at the myriad stars and heavenly bodies journeying onward, we may feel awed and overwhelmed at our sense of minuteness. Yet the very immensity of the firmament can give us a feeling of room in which to stretch our souls, of scope for infinite development, of expanse for uncramped expression. The spaciousness of Creation contradicts the narrow-mindedness which asserts that Eternal Life is only for the chosen few.

In my childhood I was taught to regard God as a personal being. I believe many people need the idea of a personal God because they are unable to grasp the idea of a being who is not an individual in our sense. We have to define things within our own range of experience before we can understand them. So we have to try to visualise God, to give Him a form, to condense that which is Infinite into the confines of our limited perception. We need an embodiment of the idea of God, we need a representative for God on which to concentrate our thoughts and worship. We have to fix a point of consciousness for ourselves in our approach to the Deity. This is where the great religions of the world display their spiritual value: they enable us through their figure-heads to take that step in consciousness which brings us into God-consciousness through our own minds. For each of us can only come to God within ourselves; we cannot do so through anybody else because we cannot get into anybody else's consciousness.

Each major religion has its central figure, its teacher, its leader. Each is often claimed to be the sole agent of God. The decision regarding this can only be a matter for the individual conscience, and each person must choose that path which he or she believes is the right one for him or her. As long as we are truly seeking God, Truth, whatever name you like to use, the form of our belief is surely of secondary importance.

Not long ago, I was discussing religion with a Roman Catholic priest. I was pleasantly surprised when he told me that he did not believe God would condemn any soul for an honest disbelief. Then he added, that should we acquire a deep religious conviction but fail to observe it, this would certainly be wrong. It was, I suppose, his way of saying that we must be guided by our own consciences – which is exactly what Liszt always maintains.

Whenever I have questioned Liszt or some of my other spiritual contacts about religion, they have emphasised that there are many paths to God. As I was born and brought up in England, a supposedly Christian country, where Scripture was taught in the schools, it was natural that I should wish to ask Liszt specifically about Christianity. In reply to my questions, he stated that Jesus was an actual historical figure whose nature was so holy that Christ manifested through him. He averred that Christ can also manifest through each one of us when we are sufficiently at one with Him. However, he maintained stoutly that the Bible was not always accurate, and that a great deal of it was allegorical, which makes it very difficult for us to get at the truth.

Many years before I had heard from earthly sources of the Holy Shroud, Liszt told me about it, declaring that it was the genuine Shroud from the body of Jesus. He pointed out that even conclusive proof that the Shroud once enwrapped the corpse of Jesus would not indicate whether he was the Messiah or not. So people will still be free to draw their own conclusions – or to conclude that no firm conclusion can be drawn.

When I was a child I used to wonder why God did not manifest definitely so that we could not doubt whether He existed. I was thinking, of course, in the terms of a personal being. In my teens I came to reason that an Infinite Spirit, an Immeasurable Being, could not condense its entire Self into one location at one moment of time. I thought this would cause the collapse of the whole of the Universe since its moving spirit would have emptied itself into a single, small section, leaving a vacuum! But I also reasoned that a single drop of water comprises the same constituents as a whole ocean, and, similarly, the Spirit of God could occupy one tiny atom or countless universes. The macrocosm in the microcosm, as it is more aptly expressed.

Reasoning powers do little to convince the majority of people one way or the other of the existence of a God, and many sophisms can be raised to confuse the issue. Perhaps we shall never know for sure in this world, although millions of us may *feel* sure through an unquenchable intuition. There is every indication from those with whom I have spoken in the World of Spirit that there is no room for any doubt about God in the Life Hereafter. The Law speaks for itself, they report. One reaps there what one has sown here; one lives in exactly the environment one has built for oneself by one's thoughts, aspirations, motives, and behaviour. Reward for one's deeds – or misdeeds – is automatic. Compensation for suffering is a natural sequence. The Motivating Power behind Life, the Moving Spirit, which is the Law, is impartial but exact. They can change their environment in that World by changing their attitude, and progress into better conditions by "making good". Even if they have sunk to the lowest depths in this Life, they can still rise to the greatest heights in that Life through a reformation of character. Such improvement in oneself is speeded up if one turns towards the Godhead, who is both the Law and its Administrator. Entrance into the highest plane follows only when the soul becomes one with God, when the Christ Spirit has been allowed to flood into the heart and mind.

In this fashion, so Liszt advises us, is the Spirit of God our Redeemer, transforming us from imperfection into perfection. Other religions than Christianity may employ names other than that of Christ; they may worship God from a different aspect, with different rites; but the one Great Spirit encompasses all, the Divine Cause which is also the Divine Purpose and the Divine Consummation.

So have my metaphysical studies been augmented by teaching from that World to which we are all, without exception, destined to travel. Thus do the dwellers in the Hereafter confirm our belief in an Almighty Being. Heaven or Hell is of our own making: the choice is ours and ours alone.

CHAPTER 6

Preparation for destiny

Is there a destiny that shapes our ends? That is anybody's guess, but looking back on my own life, I seem to detect some influence working to achieve a purpose, acting to restore order when my life had become chaotic, and weaving in the loose ends that straggled aimlessly in the pattern of my existence.

From the beginning I seemed destined to oppose my parents' wishes. I was even born against my mother's wishes. When I arrived on the scene, she already had two sons, and yet another mouth to feed was something she wanted to avoid. As I grew up, she told me quite frankly that she had not wanted me, and had tried hard to get rid of me – short of having an abortion which in those days would have been hard to come by even if she had gone to such desperate lengths. There were times when life was so disagreeable that I wished she had succeeded in her efforts.

She was always busy. With three children to care for and a business to help to run, she had no time to fuss over us, and we were brought up the hard way. The rich may delegate their offspring to nannies and governesses; the poor often have their offspring delegated to the background by the pressures of domestic drudgery and hardship – at least, that is how it must have been with countless poverty-stricken families such as ours at that time. There were no labour-saving devices to free women from some of the slavery of housework, and there was my mother – who had never held a broom in her hand in her sheltered life as a young girl – having to labour all day and half the night to keep our big house clean.

There was the assembly hall which was incorporated into our residence as part and parcel of my parent's inheritance. This was a doubtful asset, because although they let it for parties, meetings, and

57

dancing classes, the profits were very small by the time they had paid for the heating, lighting, rates, and upkeep. The bookings also varied in number, and a reasonably good season was likely to be followed by several disastrous ones.

It was not long before I was called upon to assist in the household chores. I was glad to help my mother to try to make life a little easier for her, but sometimes I felt I was the Cinderella of the family. One evening, when I happened to be very tired, my father set me some task to carry out in preparation for one of the bookings. I had school homework to do, and for once in my life I dared to demur since I was afraid it would mean my homework would not get done. I had noticed that my brothers did not seem to get saddled with any housework, and ventured to ask my father why it was always I who had to do the work. Needless to say, he made me very sorry I had even asked such a question, for he believed in harsh measures. Incidents like this were calculated to turn me into a women's liberationist! Meanwhile, I could only oppose my parents' attitude silently.

Mine was not a happy childhood. There were the ever-recurring bouts of hardship, the drudgery, and the parental bullying. This latter was so noticeable that an aunt of mine once protested to my mother about it. One of my cousins told me how she overheard my aunt – my father's sister – saying to my mother what a shame it was the way they cowed me. It seems to me now, however, that their treatment conditioned me into becoming more and more of a rebel, possibly part of the plan for my destiny. For I have certainly had to be something of a rebel to think for myself and brave the wrath of the conventional thinkers.

I believe I was an ordinary child inspite of my psychic gifts. A child who longed for affection the same as other children, and who could be naughty from time to time, although the naughtiness was often prompted by good motives or childish logic.

The assembly hall had a beautiful maple floor which shone like a looking-glass when polished, and was the delight of small children at the dancing-classes. The little girls used to slide up and down with shrieks of pleasure on the slippery surface until the exasperated teacher called them to order. One day, I thought I would be helpful and polish the ballroom-floor ready for the class. I had seen my father scattering a white powder from a tin with a perforated lid all over the floor-boards; then he would take a mop and rub away until there was a beautiful shine. I found what looked to me like the appropriate tin of powder, and tipped it lavishly on the floor, thinking

58

that the more powder I used, the better it would shine. But when I applied the mop vigorously, no magic shine appeared. I had, in my childish ignorance, covered the floor with scouring powder, a mistake for which I paid severely when my father discovered it. A mistake which also made me think how unjust grown-ups were to punish one for something that was intended to be a good deed!

As my reasoning powers developed, I began to see that both my parents and outsiders rarely took motives into consideration when dealing with people. They saw the end result, good or bad, and never stopped to find out what aim had been behind it. There was a need, I decided, to look into people's motives before judging them. My parents had led me to take the first faltering steps towards the psychological study of human nature.

One of the few bright spots in my life was the weekly dancing-class. Somehow my mother, who was clever with her needle, managed to scrape up the means to buy the materials for the little costumes we wore at the annual dancing display. The first part I had to play was that of a frog – which I did not like very much as it involved squatting on the haunches and hopping about in an uncomfortable simulation of a frog's movements. At four years of age, I was a rabbit which was much more fun. I still possess a snapshot of myself in the rabbit costume, complete with fluffy powder-puff for the tail: the original bunny-girl, so my husband teased me, when he saw the photograph. Later, I was promoted to Fairy Queen which I enjoyed still more.

My training in dancing, which covered all branches from Ballet to Ballroom, proved to be a great asset later in life when I was called on to face cameras or mount platforms to face sceptical as well as kindly-disposed audiences. Through many years of practice, I had learned to walk on to a stage without feeling too awkward or self-conscious. I had also learned how to deal with embarrassing moments such as the following one.

When I was about ten years old, I was performing a solo dance at a big theatre, when my dress suddenly fell off. I had been draped with a length of diaphanous material over a glittering body-suit, and I was right in the centre of the stage with all eyes upon me when the length of filmy cloth slid off without any warning. My mother, who was watching in the wings, said she thought I would either become rooted to the spot in panic or make a desperate dash off stage. She let out an audible sigh of relief when I stepped as daintily as I could to one side of the offending garment and continued to dance as if nothing untoward had taken place. I got away with the manoeuvre

59

so well that some of the audience thought it was meant to happen.

Besides the annual display, our dancing school was in demand to perform for a number of functions. These were often in aid of various charities, the Waifs and Strays Society, St. Dunstan's, the Sunshine Homes for Blind Children, and so on. We were also invited to more illustrious places such as the Scala Theatre. I recall that I danced once at the Connaught Rooms, and it was somewhat nostalgic to find myself again in that building in 1970 when the Philips Record Company organised a distinguished gathering of the Press for the launching of my first record.

My travels as a child-dancer enabled me to see many facets of society. My heart ached for the poor children in the Waifs and Strays Homes, some of whom were cripples; it ached for the old and impoverished folk in the Workhouses which were still in existence then. At the Sunshine Homes, I marvelled at the cheerfulness of the sightless children and the way they actually ran about without colliding with the rocking-horse and other toys in their play-room. I danced sometimes for the wealthy section of society, and now and then before royalty. I used to wonder why some people were so rich while others were near starvation. I was beginning to observe the social and economic disparities which march side by side in this world, and to become aware of the sufferings of the less fortunate members of the community.

I could see that there was a lot wrong, and wanted to help put it right, like many more before me. What could I do about it all? I prayed to be guided to find ways to help to relieve suffering.

The first time I danced before royalty, one of my childish illusions was shattered. My mother was amused when I told her that the royal personage, a princess of rather advanced years, was "only a little old lady in black who never smiled once". I had apparently expected a glamorous fairy-tale figure, since the only princesses I knew about were the ones in fairy tales.

By the time I was in my teens, I knew what I wanted to do with my life. I wanted to be a ballet dancer. Having attended classes from the time I could walk, won many medals, and passed many examinations, it seemed the natural sequence. I was shocked and heartbroken when my parents refused to countenance the idea. I begged and pleaded, but they would not relent. I even thought of running away from home to fulfil my ambition, but I could not bring myself to do that in case it upset my parents. It was quite ironical, really: they did not care how upset *I* was! I realise now that they probably

60

had my welfare at heart, and thought a stage career would be precarious and hard going. Little could they have guessed that my life would turn out to be extremely hard going, anyway.

In my despair, I withdrew into my small attic room. There I poured out all my trouble to God, and entreated Him, if it were His will, to let me take up Ballet. It was more than just dancing to me; it was a sacred art to be used to uplift people. I believed it was my mission in Life. Surely my parents would not be allowed to defeat that mission? Well, all my entreaties were in vain. I ended up in the Civil Service, about the last thing I wanted to do.

Had I been permitted to have a career in Ballet, probably I would not be writing this book now. And perhaps I would never have had the privilege of working with Liszt and other composers. Was it the hand of Destiny which held me back from Ballet? I had offered my Life in great earnestness to God at the rather precocious age of twelve. Did He take me at my word, and allot me the work which I now do to break down the barriers of ignorance and fear? Whatever the sceptics may say, I believe this work to be my chief mission in Life: a contribution, I hope, to Humanity's happiness.

I am glad to think that the many years of training in Ballet were not altogether wasted. How I could have faced the hostile critics without the stage experience I had had, I do not know. But the hostility is something to be endured for God, from my point of view, which makes it less unbearable.

My parents' attitude towards my ambition to go into Ballet as a career was identical. They both wished me to go in for something that would give the maximum amount of security. That was understandable, since they themselves had experienced so many vicissitudes and probably wanted me to avoid any more. But in most things their attitudes were at cross purposes, which caused a great deal of discord in the home.

One of the major differences in their outlooks lay in the direction of religion. My mother, as I have said, although not a regular churchgoer, was a deep believer in God, and tried to live her life in accordance with the true Christian principles. But my father was a total atheist. I endeavoured to understand both points of view. My father's atheism arose, as far as I could make out, from his uncomprising disbelief in any Life after Death. This was rather strange, because he was evidently psychic to some extent, and I remember clearly one particular apparition he told us he had seen: an apparition subsequently seen by others.

One night my father awoke, and saw in the dim light shining into the room from the lamp-post outside the house a figure dressed in white. At first he took this figure to be my mother in the long white nightdress which she wore. Then he turned over and saw that she was in bed beside him. He looked again, wide awake and startled by now, to see the figure still standing there. Hurriedly he roused my mother who awoke in time to see the white figure as well before it disappeared.

There was a strange sequel to this event. My father told his brother, John, who lived next door to us, about his experience. The very next night John awoke in the middle of the night, and saw, to his consternation, the white figure of a ghostly lady standing in the bedroom. He told my father about it next day, and they agreed that it was probably the same apparition since it was the same height and build. They named it the "White Lady."

In the house next to John's lived another member of our family, a sister of my father's. The following night after her brother John had seen the White Lady, she also woke at dead of night to see the apparition standing nearby. When she told her two brothers about her alarming experience, they remarked that the apparition seemed to be going along the road from house to house. Sure enough, the following night it paid a visit to the next house in line where my father's mother lived. It began to cause quite a bit of excitement in the road, and the lady who lived in the next house along became very apprehensive that it might call on her next.

My mother told me that the following day she met the lady – a Mrs. MacDonald – who said to her, "I woke up in the night, and thought of the White Lady. Och, my dear, I had such a panic in my breastie, and I didna dare open my eyes in case she was there."

Whether Mrs. MacDonald would have seen the apparition had she not kept her eyes shut tight, no-one liked to say. All the others who had seen the White Lady were members of the family, but she was not, although she was a close friend and her son, Eddie MacDonald, ran ballroom classes in our assembly hall at that time. Later on, he was to become one of the leading lights in the Ballroom World.

All this happened before I was born. My mother had a curious idea that the White Lady might have been none other than me, taking a look at the family I was going to join shortly. But whoever she was, I never saw her myself.

My father loved to hold forth on his views, but any attempt at discussion usually ended in violent arguments. I used to listen and not say much. He had some fascinating ideas. One was that we were all a dream in some Being's mind, and that this Being would wake up one day and end the dream. This idea was not very consistent with his disbelief in any God, but I knew if I pointed that out that it would be sparking off yet another argument.

Perhaps he would have remained an atheist to the end of his days had he not become absolutely convinced through my mediumship that there is another Life. After becoming convinced, he was a changed man. He began to make great efforts to control his violent temper which used to terrify me as a small child. The day before he died, he told me how sorry he was that I had not had much of a life.

"Goodbye," he said, "Goodbye. I shall die. I'm sorry . . . I'm terribly sorry. . . ."

I was almost in tears. I knew what an effort it cost him to speak those words, but I smiled at him and patted his hand. I was very moved that he had managed to say he was sorry. I sat with him most of that day, but when he eventually passed away the next day, I was not in the house, He died in 1944 during the War, and I had to be on duty on the day of his death. My mother and I took it in turns to sit with him, and the way it turned out provided my father with the opportunity to give an evidential message to me after he had arrived in spirit.

My mother was alone with him when the actual moment of death took place. We had no telephone ourselves, but the ground floor of our house had been turned into an Air Raid Wardens' Post, and there was a telephone in their office. My mother went downstairs and asked the Warden on duty to telephone the office where I was working to inform me of my father's passing. The time by then was about four o'clock in the afternoon. Although my father and I had not been on the best of terms, I felt a great sadness that he had gone – gone in the physical sense, that is. I left the office at once to return home.

While I was waiting for a bus, and hoping there would be no air-raid to delay me, I became aware of my father right beside me. There were a few other people waiting at the bus stop, and I sneaked a look at them to see whether they could see the ghostly form of my father. No, they looked quite oblivious of the ghostly presence. He began to speak quietly – was he afraid of being overheard by the queue, I wondered?

"Hallo," he said in a very matter-of-fact way, "I'm all right now, although I haven't quite got my bearings yet. Tell Mother I was out of my body before it actually died. I watched her sitting there and gathering up her courage. After a while, she touched my forehead. Then she moved my slippers and took away the jar."

I should explain that the jar was one provided to act as a spittoon. He died of lung cancer, having been a very heavy cigarette smoker, and the jar was a grim necessity.

When I arrived home, I found my mother very calm. She was an extremely philosophical soul, as a result of her hard life. My father was still at my side, urging me to pass on his message to her. I decided she was in a calm enough frame of mind for me to tell her, and did so. The three things my father had mentioned were exactly what she had done – touching his forehead, moving his slippers, and taking the jar away, in that order. She was obviously comforted by the knowledge that he had been there right beside her in his new body, the spirit body.

After my father had passed over, he and I became much better friends. I think he understood me better; anyway, I found his attitude towards me had undergone a complete change. And perhaps he could see that I had quite an affection for him although he had been the blight of my life in many ways. He had many fine qualities which compensated for his disagreeable temper – which perhaps he could not really help. He was a person of complete integrity and high principles, like my mother, in fact, these common qualities may have drawn them together. I had much to be grateful to him for, since he had encouraged me to think for myself, and been instrumental in introducing me to the Spiritualist Movement. After getting the evidence through my mediumship which had convinced him of an After-Life, he decided to investigate the subject more fully. So he obtained books about it which he let me read as well, and began attending public Spiritualist meetings and my mother and I went with him.

The first medium I ever saw was Estelle Roberts, famous for her wonderful clairvoyance and clairaudience. My parents and I took our seats in the large London hall – I believe it was the Aeolian – and as we waited for the meeting to begin, I felt a tremendous power gathering about us. I recognised this to be a very powerful and holy spirit presence. When Mrs. Roberts appeared on the platform, the concentration of power intensified still more. She went quietly into trance whilst the announcements were being made about future meetings. Then she rose, her eyes closed, and began to address the audience. Only it was not Mrs. Roberts speaking. It was the deep, slightly guttural voice of a man: it was Red Cloud, her chief guide.

Newcomers to spirit communication – or even old hands – are

64

sometimes rather nonplussed by the fact that quite a few "guides" are drawn from other nationalities including North American Indian, Chinese, Egyptian, and so forth. But if we expect guides always to be people from the white population, we must suspect ourselves of racial discrimination. There is no doubt that some of the people of ancient civilisations were highly cultured and highly intelligent, and we might be able to learn a great deal from them. As for the North American Indians, of which Red Cloud was one, we must realise that they were not all a bunch of primitive savages, and that some of the more advanced tribes had a culture of their own and great intelligence. Added to this is the salient point that a "guide" in spirit is often just that: one who acts as a guide to a higher being who cannot communicate direct owing to lack of skill or lack of knowledge of the complexities involved in such communication. Red Cloud, so he informed us himself, came into this category, acting as a messenger for one higher than himself.

Whatever or whoever Red Cloud was, his address impressed me very much. It was the address of an obviously enlightened soul, urging the audience to awaken to the fact that Life continues after Death and that we must all face up to our deeds when we pass over into the Next Life. But it was not just his words which impressed me so much; there was an undeniable feeling of being in the presence of goodness, a hallowed atmosphere which may not have been apparent to everyone present. Imagination on my part? Why should I imagine anything like that? I had not gone to the meeting expecting any such manifestation. I remain convinced to this day that behind Red Cloud was a holy spirit striving to uplift human consciousness.

My father took me also to public demonstrations of clairvoyance. Mrs. Roberts poured forth the most amazing messages full of evidence, but what was more significant to me was the eye-opener it brought when I realised I could see and hear the spirits *she* could see and hear. Sometimes I would even see them before she became aware of them, and I was quite relieved when one spirit lady who had been trying to attract Mrs. Roberts's attention for some time succeeded in doing so at last. What a good thing it was to find there were others in the world beside myself who could see and hear spirit! I had felt so much the odd one out, the one who was looked at as being odd if I mentioned any of my psychic experiences; now I knew I was not alone in this respect, and it was an enormous relief.

Two important features had been introduced into my life in preparation, if we believe in that hand of Destiny, for my work with the composers. One was the stage training which helped me in later years to face audiences without being overwhelmed with nervousness. The other was the introduction to Spiritualism and mediumship in general which inspired me with courage to follow my own natural mediumship. There are many eccentric people in Spiritualism, true, but so there are many in other movements. Disregarding the cranks, there are a great many fine, sincere people in Spiritualism, and the dedicated work of genuine mediums proved to be an excellent example which prompted me to take heart in my own task.

In connection with my father, I had an interesting message passed on to me from Mrs. Ena Twigg, one of the most gifted mediums of our time. I called to visit her in her home, and she began to relay a number of messages about various contacts with spirit. She stated that she was in touch with my father. Always the sceptic, in spite of my own psychic abilities, I waited to see whether she would add anything to indicate she was really in touch with my father. Suddenly she looked at me very directly and said, "Your father could have broken you."

This left no doubt in my mind that she was actually contacting my father. He was an old tyrant, but very few people outside the family knew this, and nearly the whole family were deceased. There was no-one who could have passed this information on to Mrs. Twigg.

She gave me quite a lot of evidential messages, but there were some inaccuracies. This troubled me, knowing the high standard of her mediumship. Later, however, I read the book about her, entitled *Medium Rare*, and was put more at ease to learn that a few such inaccuracies crept into her usually impeccable mediumship. This, one must realise, can happen with all mediums for they are not infallible, and are frequently the first to admit it.

One other thing I have needed to prepare me for my ordeals of being interviewed for radio and television, of coping with people of all kinds, and answering the interminable questions: this was experience in dealing with the general public which I acquired as a Counter Clerk in the Post Office. I worked at offices in many different areas, ranging from the impoverished to the wealthy, from residential to business in the City and the West End. This enabled me to meet people from all classes and backgrounds. I was also employed as a telegraphist until I moved on to writing and clerical duties, and this supplied yet another valuable acquisition which was nimbleness of fingers developed through many a long hour at teleprinter keyboards.

It was necessary for me to be reasonably articulate, too, so that I

66

could explain how the music was imparted to me by discarnate composers, and be able to defend myself if this was called for at any time. In this direction, I was fortunate. I won a scholarship from my primary school which took me on to a County High School, the equivalent of a Grammar School. We were so poor that I was awarded a grant to cover the cost of my school uniform, otherwise I would not have been able to take advantage of the scholarship. There is no doubt that my studies at this school gave me the tools of speech and penmanship, or penwomanship, to be pedantic. How invaluable these were to prove when I took on the world in my mission! As it was, I was often at the mercy of persons who had no scruples to restrain them from making sly inferences which were tantamount to libel but not sufficiently direct for them to be nailed down. At least I was educated enough to see how they were trying to discredit me without endangering themselves from the legal angle. It was wisest for the most part to ignore these despicable attacks, and to brush aside the more overt and often malicious onslaughts of the jealous, the ignorant or the fanatical.

One of our teachers used to give us advice regarding our future conduct in the world. I remember to this day just what she said:

"All of you here are almost sure at some time to be subject to defamation of character, however mild. When you find yourselves the victims of calumny, remember this is often the result of jealousy and can be regarded as a back-handed compliment."

I had to look in a dictionary afterwards to find out what "calumny" meant as it was the first time I had heard that word. I was to know only too well what calumny meant when I had left my school terms far behind, and launched into the psycho-musical work which made me the hapless target of any ill-disposed critic.

So, I was even prepared to some extent against the eventuality of slander and libel! Strange how the teacher's words lingered in my mind, as if they were a warning of the attacks on me and the in-nuendoes of the more underhanded.

It might seem I was being prepared throughout my childhood and girlhood both in body, mind and spirit. In body by the training for dancing which helped to put me at ease before an audience; for the piano through the constant use of my fingers as a teleprinter operator; in mind, through my home background and through my schooling; and last, but most important of all, in spirit through my studies of religion, and through meditation and prayer.

The stage was being set for my debut.

CHAPTER 7

Growing realization

The War was over at last. I left the Civil Service a few years after to get married. Perhaps it was essential for me to be a wife and mother to become sufficiently adaptable to work with the composers. For I have no doubt that marriage helped me to become fully mature, and motherhood, more than anything else, urges a woman to cultivate the utmost adaptability. Motherhood can also make one self-effacing, depending on one's reactions to it. I needed to be very self-effacing to work with the composers, since it meant I had to forget myself entirely and let them establish themselves.

I still had no idea what was ahead of me. I settled happily to being a mother, my delight knowing no bounds when I had first a beautiful daughter, then a fine son. My husband was equally delighted, and I am glad he had several years with them before he was taken into the Next Life. He adored them both. They were his joy and pride; but Destiny had decreed that he should be taken away. That is, taken away in the physical sense, for I know that he watches over them constantly, his affection for them undiminished.

My husband was a very versatile man with a brilliant intellect. He had travelled all over the world, and always tried to get to know the peoples of each country by living with them, sharing their ways of life, and learning their tongues. I would listen enthralled for hours as he described his travels and his encounters. My outlook was the richer for his narrations, and I learned a lot about other people's struggles, customs, and beliefs.

He was also a great philosopher. We talked into the small hours about the mysteries of Creation, God, and the Hereafter. He had a firm belief in an After-Life when he met me, and it was re-inforced by the communications that came via me from members of his family and friends who had already passed into that Life. He was very concerned because some people had already tried to destroy my belief in my psychic abilities on account of their acute jealousy. He coaxed back the confidence, which had been undermined by the attacks made on me. I must explain more fully.

For several years before we had met, I had been drawn into more than one Spiritualist group or Church. There was a small Church my mother and I both attended, and, at her suggestion, I offered my services free as a healer and clairvoyant. They did not want to know. It was so frustrating wanting to be of service and finding oneself rejected. We tried a larger Church. The same thing happened. As a matter of fact, the position was even worse at that one, as they seemed to practise a policy of deliberate suppression. They kept telling me the psychic path was not for me, nor the intellectual path. That did not leave much! It was futile to say the psychic path was not for me because I could not stop being psychic as I was born that way! As for the intellectual path, I have always believed that the Good Lord gave us our brains to use, not to neglect. What they did not have the insight to see was that both these paths could converge to lead to the Spiritual Truth.

Then there was the small circle held in the home of a Harley Street specialist. This usually comprised of the specialist, his wife, a seasoned "sitter", a psychiatrist, and one or two others. The specialist's wife was morbidly ambitious to become a trance medium, and soon became jealous of my psychic gifts, as I was to learn. Both the specialist and the psychiatrist encouraged me to give out any impressions which I received, and these often proved to be absolutely accurate. The psychiatrist, a lady, was very fascinated. In her own words, something was happening which she could not explain or explain away. This evidently inflamed the jealousy of the would-be trance medium still more and one day she slipped, apparently, into trance, then began saying very spiteful things to me. Whatever sort of spirit was possessing her, I wondered? The sequel was an unpleasant revelation.

After this circle, which was held weekly, we all trooped into the Drawing Room for refreshments, tea or coffee. This particular week, most guests excused themselves immediately after the circle ended. When they had gone, I found myself alone in the Drawing Room. The specialist was already giving one guest a lift to the station, while his wife and the remaining guest were closeted together in the seance room. There was a hush in the house, and I could not help hearing

69

their voices through the thin walls. The guest was remonstrating with the specialist's wife.

"Why did you do that?", she was demanding in a raised voice, "Why did you speak to Rosemary like that?"

She must have realised how cutting I had found the "medium's" remarks made during the supposed trance. The reply made it clear that the trance was a deliberate fake. The guest's wording of her question had already shown that she knew it was faked.

"I thought it might stop her giving messages. *I* want to be a medium. I don't want *her* to be a medium," the specialist's wife almost shrieked.

I was shattered to think that she, of all people, could stoop to deliberate fraud. I decided there and then to withdraw from the circle on some pretext so that the specialist would not be offended. But for all I knew, he may have been in collusion with his wife!

These experiences, and a few more like it, were enough to make me retire into a shell and become very wary of people – including those in the Spiritualist Movement. Had it not been for my husband's concern and encouragement, I might have stayed in a shell for the rest of my life.

"People are so bloody jealous," he said. He rarely swore like that excepting when roused to indignation. "You must not let them get you down. They are not worth noticing, although they will do their damnedest to try to get noticed."

Slowly and patiently, he restored my courage, although to this day, I have to screw it up each time I am called on to demonstrate or speak. Only my faith enables me to endure the ordeals, the sneers, and the setbacks.

My husband had helped me over yet another stile. I know he is often at my side in spirit, helping me over further obstacles. I was very fortunate to have such a fine man at my side for a few – precious few – years along life's hard road.

He worked as a free-lance journalist when we were first married. It was a precarious living, full of ups and downs. I typed out his articles for him, taking a joy in helping in his work. Then he said one day he thought it would be a good idea for me to write some articles. Good practice for the writing I was to do after he had left this life – but we were not to know that. To my surprise, some of my work was accepted, but when the children arrived one by one, there was no time to continue writing.

The next few years were tragic. My husband's health began to fail.

70

From the beginning of our marriage there was one financial set-back after another through the fluctuations in his work and health. He considered resuming scientific research as a possible means of a better livelihood, but we decided his health could not take the strain. Things became steadily worse, and the last year and a half of his life was sheer hell for him. The doctor had him hospitalised in a last desperate attempt to save him, but it was all in vain. It was a mercy, probably, that he did not die at home where the children might have witnessed his passing. Although he went peacefully in his sleep, I don't know what effect it would have had on them; they loved their father and had they seen his actual passing it could have been too much for them.

Parents must always be faced with a terrible dilemma when there is a death in the family, especially of someone close. What are they to tell the children? How can they explain, without being too harrowing, what has happened to the person they knew or loved? This was the second time I had had to cope with this kind of situation within a year. My mother, whom the children adored, had passed away a few months before, also in hospital. When they asked me what had happened to her and why wasn't she coming home from hospital, I told them as gently as I could that her body had got worn out as she was quite old, so God had given her a new body to live in and a new place to live in, a beautiful place in heaven.

"Lucky Nanny," commented my daughter, "Can I go and see her?"

"You won't be able to go to heaven until you have a new body as well," I explained, "But she will come and see us often. Her new body is so ethereal that most people won't be able to see it, but I think you might sometimes."

I had to try to describe the meaning of the word "ethereal", but my daughter had grasped that quite well, as she was also psychic and given to visions. My son, who was barely four years old at the time, seemed quite content with the idea of Nanny having a nice new body. I was surprised how well he seemed to understand.

"Did the angels take her out of her old body and put her in the new one?"

"Yes, dear, they did. They do that for all of us when our turn comes."

"Will I have a new body one day, then?" he pursued the subject.

"Yes, you will, so will your sister, and so will I. Then we will all be able to go and live with Nanny."

"Oh, good," exclaimed my son, looking very pleased.

71

Now I had to break the news of his father's passing. The sooner I told the children the better, I decided. They had to know in the end. We reached home, and the moment had come, I felt.

"You will both be glad to know Daddy won't suffer any more, and isn't ill any longer. He has gone to heaven, like Nanny did." My daughter was silent. I think she was numbed by the passing of her father only a few months after her grandmother. My son looked dismayed as he realised Daddy wouldn't come home any more. Then suddenly he said, "Now I want a new daddy."

That really choked me. I had been trying to be cheerful, because I didn't think it would be helpful to the children if I gave way to my grief. I had to turn my head away so that he would not see the tears welling up in my eyes.

He never was to get a new daddy. There are few men in the world who will take on a widow with two children. Why should they? They are not their children, they would argue. But anyway, I was no longer young nor glamorous, and I would have been very hesitant to re-marry lest their stepfather proved unsympathetic towards them. But for several years, my son seemed very conscious of his father's presence, and would often tell me something which he said Daddy had just told him. The psychologists might dismiss this as compensatory imagining, but whether it was that or not (I am sure it was real) it was a source of great comfort to my orphaned son.

I spent the next seven years working in school kitchens to eke out a living for myself and the children. Widowed mothers with young children were not given much help from the government, I discovered, either financially or in any other way. They would not even grant me the full allowance, although my husband and I had been married for over nine years, and we were both British by birth and parentage. A strange state of affairs in a democratic country which one would expect to care for its young even if it neglected impoverished widows! Fortunately, there were many kind friends who helped us along in various ways, otherwise we would have almost literally starved to death on the widow's lopped allowance and the pittance paid by the school meals service at that time.

Being a widow with two very young children to fend for taught me to stand on my own two feet, something else which was going to prove very useful when publicity burst in on my life with all its demands and clamour. Also when people tried to buy me, I recalled that I had managed for many years alone, having to exercise stringent economies, it is true, but managing nevertheless. So I knew I could

72

do without their questionable inducements.

I will only touch briefly on the War Years, because so much has been written about them already. Sufficient to say that I was retained in the Civil Service right through the War, stationed in London although having to be mobile from time to time. Anyone who was living or working in London through all those years knows how grim it was, how nerve-racking, and, in a way, how thankless. We were in the Front Line to all intents and purposes without getting much credit for our powers of endurance.

Everything came to a standstill excepting the War Effort – for most of us, anyway. We went to work in the blackout, and we returned home in the blackout; it seemed symbolic of the blacking out of the human spirit. We travelled through air-raids, and I had many narrow escapes personally during those shattering times.

If it had not been for that extra-sensory perception I have, in which so many disbelieve, I would probably not be here at the typewriter now. For I was warned by those very spirit beings whom sceptics try to explain away as hallucinations, warned not once, but several times, of imminent danger in time to avoid it.

Once, in the early days of the bombing of London in 1940, the nightly air-raid began while I was still at work, in Upper Tooting Post Office to be exact. There was an air-raid shelter there, but I always preferred to make my way home to join my mother and my father when he was not on night-duty. The Underground used to close when the air-raid warning wailed, and the buses stopped running, too. There was only one way left to get home – by foot, in total darkness, except for the fitful illumination of searchlights or gunfire . . . or the glowering blaze of fires caused by incendiaries and other bombs.

My route home was the most direct one I could take – straight along the main road until I reached my own road which turned off it. I had almost reached Balham Station which was near my road, when warning was given me urgently by a spirit voice.

"Don't continue along the High Road. Turn off by the Station and go round the back way."

I demurred because going "round the back way" meant making a detour which would take longer, and naturally, I wanted to get home as fast as possible. I had already had to pick my way over debris from a building which had been hit not long before I reached it.

The voice was insistent and grew more urgent.

"Take the back way! Take the back way! Never mind if it takes

73

longer."

So pressing a warning could not be ignored, I decided, and turned off the main road, hastily making my way home by the alternate route. Not long after this, a large bomb fell in the middle of the main road, blasting its way right down into the tunnel of the Underground. Many who were sheltering in the Underground were killed. I would have cleared that section of the road some minutes before the bomb fell, but the spirit who warned me did not want, perhaps, to take any chances, or could not tell exactly when it would fall although apparently being able to foresee the incident.

A similar warning came once during the daytime. I was walking down a road in the same district, when the sirens sounded. Suddenly I was told by spirit to get out of the road I was in as fast as my legs could carry me. I crossed from one side of the road to the other, feeling that side might be safer, but the warning voice told me that that was no help as either side was equally dangerous. So I fled as quickly as I could. I was in the next road but one before a bomb fell in the centre of the narrow street I had left, taking down the houses on either side.

It appeared that the presence of danger did not prevent the E.S.P. (extra-sensory perception) faculties from working, and that the deafening clangour of air-raids did not interfere with clairaudience. I have always been interested in trying to determine under what conditions E.S.P. can work, and in research into such faculties. On the whole, my faculties function best when I am completely relaxed, and tend to dry up when I am tense. It was a relief to discover that they could still function in spite of the uproar and stress experienced during the raids.

There were other dramatic instances of warnings which saved me from certain death. One morning, I was about to get on a bus to take me from the Elephant and Castle to Mount Pleasant where I was then working, when I heard a voice distinctly tell me to wait for the next bus. I was quite early, and decided I would wait as I had plenty of time to reach the office punctually. The following bus which I took gradually caught up with the other one. We had nearly reached Mount Pleasant when a flying bomb zoomed down and sliced the top right off the bus I had missed, just outside the offices of the *Daily Worker*.

Going home from work one day, I was about to get on a tram when a voice told me not to. By then, I had come to the conclusion that such warnings were to be ignored at my own risk. So I stayed

74

put and waited for the next tram which followed very soon. I got on, and we travelled as far as Kennington Park Road. To the horror of all the passengers, there, lying on the track just before the Oval, was the charred and flattened frame of the previous tram which a flying bomb had destroyed. The tram had been packed with homeward bound travellers. Had I been on it, my family would never have known what had happened to me. I would. have been yet another missing person presumed killed.

In my early teens, just before the War, I had made a deep study of various kinds of Yoga. I had practised many of the exercises assiduously, and carried out the breathing techniques carefully. Yoga was little known in the Western World in those days, and I practised rather secretly, realising that some people would consider it cranky. The effects were enormously beneficial to my health and steadiness of nerve, both of which needed to be preserved throughout the wartorn years.

When the War erupted, I was studying Buddhism closely, although at all times retaining the core of Christianity as an indispensable guide. It seemed plain that if everybody became Buddhists, there would be no war, no mass destruction, no trail of suffering triggered off by man's inhumanity to man. But there was the War raging onwards, having to be fought out to preserve freedom!

There was Christianity, there was Buddhism, there was a multitude of faiths, all urging man to live in peace with man.

In common with thousands of people, the desire for world peace grew stronger in me the longer the holocaust lasted. But what can one small voice do? What can a mere handful of people do? Not until the masses all over the world call a halt to warfare will they be spared the ravages of battle, and the possible danger of irreparable damage ot this planet. Until that day, we may find it difficult not to get involved in some way, bound by loyalties to one cause or another.

War interrupts life; it ends life; it may be directed to solving one problem, but it creates others. Will humanity ever abandon the use of force to gain its ends? One wonders as one watches sorrowfully yet another flare-up of hostilities. It is no use simply lamenting these catastrophies. Humanity has to think its way out of them.

This brings us to some of the conclusions I had reached which the war underlined starkly: that the solution of many of our earthly problems lies in a widespread change of outlook, in adopting new and different attitudes towards the whole gamut of our existence; that we have to live and let live, to use a very trite but very true expression, if we are to live at all.

During those war years, all the world seemed like a stage with a terrible battle raging upon it, while peace waited and waited in the wings. At last, peace was given a cue and made her entry, weary and limping.

My life, in its humble way, had seemed like a personal battle: a battle to find the truth; a battle to bear up against the burdens, tragedies, and hardships. I did not yet know that the time would come for me to limp wearily on to the world's stage, to speak in a rather halting tongue of some of the great but often unacknowledged realities of Life. For that is what my work seems all about; not only the writing out of music at the behest of master composers whom the sceptics think no longer exist, but all the implications, especially the spiritual ones, that follow in its train.

When Liszt began his work with me, when we were both still awaiting my debut, he warned me that to undertake such work would bring much suffering to me.

"Remember," he advised, "You will be doing battle, not just for us, but for God and Humanity. It is a desperate attempt to bring peace and enlightenment to the human race. Many will scorn you; even your own friends may turn against you; but we will never fail you. When you are belittled, do not lose heart for the everlasting arms of God are beneath you to uphold your soul."

I shall never forget his words. Since then, I have sometimes thought how foolhardy I was to take on such an overwhelming task. I am the butt for the ridicule of the ignorant and the learned as well. I have some wonderful friends who have stood by me through thick and thin; I also had friends who proved false, who wanted to be in the swim when things were going well, but deserted me when I was derided. The frailty of human nature has been brought home to me very sharply. This has served to make me believe all the more in the importance of trying to develop the human character in the light of the revelation that we are not flesh and blood alone, but spirit.

If we believe in matter alone, we are going to behave as if nothing matters but matter. To rise above our human limitations, we need to believe in something more. We need to believe in Immortality. We need to believe in the Infinite Spirit of Life. Religions teach us to believe in these two things. They do not offer us much proof, if any. The time has surely come for us to seek proof and make it known whenever we find it. Disillusioned by war, undermined by commercial exploitation, bewildered by the claims of conflicting beliefs, millions need something definite to hold on to in the midst of all the perils and evils. Can they look to Science to support their tottering hopes that there is something behind it all? That Life is more than a scramble to exist or survive? That this Life is only one chapter in the Book of Eternity?

If Science embraces parapsychology and metaphysics, there could be great hopes. If it turns its back on these things, denies their promptings, and goes hurtling on without thought for human values and needs, we have to fall back again on the religions. And so far, alas, these have not established peace between peoples and nations, or lifted us out of the mud of materialism. Perhaps because we have never worked at them enough, never applied them consistently to daily life. Perhaps because there is one thing missing from them: practical demonstrations that their promise of Life beyond Death (the fundamental justification for their teachings) is backed by firm reality.

We need the veil to be torn aside and I hope my work is helping towards this end, as I face both the brickbats and the bouquets which Sir Donald Tovey told Sir George Trevelyan through my mediumship would be forthcoming.

CHAPTER 8

Reaching the public

At the beginning of 1968, I was still labouring away in a school kitchen on weekdays, and struggling to maintain the outsize Victorian house which my surviving brother and I had inherited on my mother's death. At least the children and I had a roof over our heads, albeit a very leaky one. In my bedroom, where the leaks were very generous, I had to keep an army of buckets and baths to catch the rain. In our kitchen, I had to cook and wash up under an umbrella when it rained, and the water came through on to the gas-stove, the hissing of the gas being rivalled by the hissing of the rain dripping on to the hot plates. Rain also poured in at one corner of the room where the old piano stood. It seeped in through the ceiling of my daughter's bedroom; it seeped in almost everywhere: as if the old house was weeping at our plight.

I scraped and went without so that I could get some repairs carried out to the roof to try to make the home as dry and warm as possible for the children. It was a losing battle because the house was too big for me to be able to afford the heating it needed. We huddled together over one fire, and I heated the children's rooms with oil – totally inadequate for such large rooms, but all I could manage.

My brother lived out in Surrey. He commuted to the West End every day except Sundays, and could not find the time to visit us. He had his own life to run, his own family to look after, his own home to keep up. He could never have dreamt what we were having to contend with in what we jokingly called the "Ancestral Home", as it had been handed down from generation to generation. Little did I know that the "Ancestral Home" was going to be invaded the following year by a cavalcade of reporters, television crews, and all manner of interested or curious folk!

78

Before 1968, there had been what might be regarded as trial runs or rehearsals for the real thing. I had been introduced in 1965 to Mr. and Mrs. Hilary Wontner who in turn had interested a number of people in my musical work. Enthusiasm was growing, but no-one seemed to know quite what to do about it all. The Wontners introduced me in February 1966 to Sir George Trevelyan because of his membership of the Churches' Fellowship for Psychical and Spiritual Studies, and it seemed the work I was doing would fall into a category that would interest him. I was very excited when he showed keen enthusiasm, and said he would tell a colleague of his about it. The colleague in question was Mrs. Mary Firth, B.Mus., L.R.A.M., whom he felt was equipped to pronounce an opinion on the music.

This has been mentioned in my first book, but for those who have not read it, I must refer to it briefly. Mrs. Firth, whom I met in October 1966 for the first time, was also very enthusiastic, but at that time hesitant to tell her husband about it as she felt he might be unsympathetic. Meanwhile, Sir George kept exhorting me to be rather secretive about the whole thing. His secretary wrote me a strange letter saying that they could not "afford to be involved on outer levels with these astral-level phenomena-type things." This attitude, which was echoed by a number of other people, made me feel I was just something to be swept under the carpet! It did not seem very complimentary to Liszt, Chopin, Schubert, and Beethoven (the main communicators then) to speak of their work as "astral-level phenomena-type things". I mused upon the fact that the secretary would herself eventually become an astral-level phenomena-type thing! But, of course, one has to read between the lines, and try to determine people's intentions. In a further letter written a week later, on the 15th January 1967, she wrote, "It must seem to you that we made rather a sudden change of attitude after your visit."

How right she was! When I visited Attingham Park College in order to meet Mrs. Firth for the first time, and again to stay there for a New Year Course running from late December into the following month, all was tremendous enthusiasm and excitement. Plans were discussed to get something published in a suitable magazine about the music, and means of recording some of the music, possibly on tapes, were also examined – plans and means that were not put forward at my instigation, but at theirs. It seemed there was great promise that at last something would be done about the composers' break-through, and I was blissfully happy for their sake.

Then came the thunderbolt – a type of thunderbolt I was to meet again and again after people would be convinced of the genuineness of my work, but would "chicken out" when it came to giving any public testimony. A correspondent on a National Newspaper and the producer of the B.B.C. Woman's Hour had heard something about the music, and both wished to interview me about it. I wrote, naturally, to inform Sir George and Mrs. Firth since they had both shown such interest and great enthusiasm. Mrs. Firth wrote to Sir George:

"The idea of the *Daily Telegraph* and B.B.C. Woman's Hour fills me with horror; even though these are comparatively reasonable givers-out of news, the prospect of the kind of sensational stuff that could follow is unthinkable for both you and me."

I quote from Sir George's letter written to me, dated the 15th January 1967.

Of course, I could not expect them to take a public stand on my behalf, and I wrote to make it clear that I was prepared to "face the music" alone, to use an expression appropriately applied by Maurice Barbanell. But, alas, the way was now blocked because Mrs. Wontner, who had intended to introduce me to the *Telegraph* correspondent and the B.B.C. producer, thought it prudent to comply with Sir George's wishes for secrecy. How grateful Liszt and his colleagues must be to her that she relented eventually, and arranged for me to be interviewed at her house where a recording was made for a B.B.C. broadcast.

What had happened, so Liszt told me, was that Sir George had been "got at," to employ the modern idiom. The day after I left Attingham at the end of the New Year Course, a musician arrived to try to put into motion his plan to present some of his compositions at the College. Unfortunately for me, Sir George began to enthuse about the musical break-through from the composers in the Spirit World, and this induced so much jealousy in the musician – who had previously been one of my most ardent advocates – that he told Sir George that my work was regressive, the work of "entities", and a number of even less complimentary things. The Wontners, who had introduced this musician to me, were horrified at the complete volte-face displayed by this man. So the people who had given every indication of supporting me had deserted me or were wavering, and in a flash I knew this could happen all the time. I would have to be ready to hold the stage on my own, to fight a lone battle against enormous odds. If I did not have the courage to take a firm stand for what I believed to be true and to be of some possible value to

80

humanity, I would be failing in my duty. I vowed in that instant to go on steadfastly with the work, come what may. For the moment the stage was to be mine alone, though later others would come and go in supporting rôles of various kinds.

The first the public was to hear about my work was through a broadcast made in October 1967 as a result of the meeting arranged by Mrs. Wontner at her house with the producer of the Woman's Hour Programme for the B.B.C. This was the first tiny spark which I hoped would light a multitude of candles to throw a little radiance into the darkness of the world. It also sparked off a never-ending stream of letters which were sometimes to become totally unmanageable since I could not afford to pay for secretarial help.

The ice was broken. Reactions seemed favourable judging from the letters. Sir George and Mrs. Firth, perhaps a little reassured, began to formulate their own plans to present the work in a suitable form. They arranged for a meeting to be held at the College of Psychic Science in Kensington, carefully selecting and inviting the audience ... but carefully excluding the press, including Mr. Barbanell, the Editor of the Psychic News, who seemed the most obvious person to be present. The whole event passed off well enough, but did not promise to promote the work because the programme was one of discussion more than anything else.

The next scene in the unfolding play of events was one which placed me in yet another of the unending predicaments that the work presented. An expert in the Hi-fi field had been introduced to me prior to the College of Psychic Science affair. He offered very kindly to record the whole procedure on tape, and Sir George and Mrs. Firth deemed this an excellent idea. Immediately after the session had ended, and people were still gathered around, the Hi-fi expert came to me with another proposal, which was to form a company to produce tapes of the music and put them on sale. I replied that since Sir George and Mrs. Firth were by this time involved, I considered the matter should be discussed with them. Both of them thought the idea a sound one, and decided to go ahead, with Dr. Firth joining in since by then he knew all about the music and was an interested party.

As is my usual practice, I sought the advice of Liszt, because the music came from him and other composers, and it was only right and proper that they should be consulted regarding any procedure. Liszt advised me *not* to go ahead – which seemed surprising as the expert had asserted that he would sell the tapes like hot cakes. Indeed, the man had been in Hi-fi for some twenty years, and was skilled and

81

capable not only in that field but also as a promoter and salesman. But still Liszt said firmly, "No." It might be the composers only chance to have their music sent out to the world, I thought. "No," Liszt continued to say. I was now in a most awkward position. I had no wish to offend the Hi-fi gentleman, but if Liszt was so adamant, there must be good reason.

"Consult your solicitor, then you may understand," he ordered.

The solicitor opened my eyes to possible dangers in entering into the company as proposed. The expert, realising how poor I was, knew that I could not put money into the company. He suggested commencing with one hundred pounds' worth of shares saying that I could take out just one share costing me only one pound so that I would officially become a share-holder. Later on, I was informed, if I could afford it, I could take up further shares.

"Ah," said the solicitor, "You would be placing yourself in a very vulnerable position. Each time dividends were due, you, as the holder of only one share, would receive only one dividend. But those holding, say one hundred shares, would receive one hundred dividends. Also every time a vote was taken on any point, you would be entitled to one vote, but those with one hundred shares would have one hundred votes.

I began to see the snags. The solicitor said that no doubt my friend's intentions were to help me by getting the music on sale, but supposing anything happened to him . . . his shares would pass to someone else who might not be so honest and might decide to do something against my wishes. I would be helpless since I would be only a minor shareholder and could be voted out of the company.

Oh! how devious are the business aspects of the world. I could have been deprived of anything but a nominal financial benefit for all my labours. I was not doing the work for commercial profits, but I had sweated for years, straining every nerve and fibre, to take the music down from the composers. Was it morally right that others should make capital out of it whilst I, who had done all the donkey-work should be left out?

"No!" thundered Liszt, accompanied by an indignant Chopin, "You have borne all the burdens and taken all the rebuffs. If it earns anything, it is rightfully yours. To take it from you would be paramount to stealing and would be plucking the bread out of your children's mouths and your own."

I reasoned with Liszt that the company proposer would be doing all the work of forming and managing the company, and would be entitled to some reward.

"That is so," was the reply, "But a company is a precarious organisation because so many unforeseen contingencies can arise. Heed your solicitor's advice."

The solicitor's final pronouncement was that if I did go ahead, I must insist on having the casting vote.

"After all, "he concluded, "The shareholders would be making capital out of your brains and work. At least you should always have the final word in any decision and be able to carry out your own wishes."

The Hi-fi man refused to entertain the idea of my retaining the casting vote. That did it. I was trying at all times to comply with the composers' wishes and plans, and if I did not have a casting vote, not only could I be over-ruled, but so could the composers. My loyalty to them won the issue.

Many people came along with various proposals to do something about the work. But, naturally, they always wanted to do things *their* way which was rarely the composers' way. Some offered me fortunes, but you cannot buy those in spirit, so they could not buy the composers! Some merely wanted to get me into their hands to manipulate me for their own ends, or try to gain power. Some were very subtle, but Liszt often "tipped me off" regarding such people.

Dr. Firth came up next with a proposal which seemed to be made in good faith. This was to open a Trust Fund, as described in *Unfinished Symphonies*. He was to be the treasurer and joint trustee with Sir George, and the fund would be open to contributions from anyone interested. I would be paid a small allowance to enable me to devote myself more fully to the music, and give up my work in the school kitchens.

This seemed a fair chance for the composers to transmit more music without my running the risk of matters being taken out of my hands. Liszt seemed in favour. I accepted. All promised to be plain sailing, but storms were brewing. There was backing now from three people, Sir George, Dr. Firth, and his wife. It was not going to be a lone, bitter battle any more. Or so I thought. I resigned from the School Meals Service in May 1968. In less than three months, I was going to regret it.

The tempest that broke over my head was the result of an unfortunate misunderstanding. Sir George and Mrs. Firth now decided to brave the press on my behalf, a decision which I fear they must have rued. A meeting was arranged at the Wontners' home, and an

83

invitation issued to the *Telegraph* correspondent who had wanted for so long to interview me. This time Maurice Barbanell was also invited.

I sat there mutely while Sir George strove valiantly to put my case. Mrs. Firth seconded it with all her powers of persuasion and musical skill. Alas! It fell apparently on barren ground. The correspondent himself was manifestly attempting to keep the peace, and retain a sympathetic attitude towards me – even if he thought I was crazy. But his companion, a leading and brilliant music critic, dismissed the whole thing as utter nonsense, and stormed out. He was a Roman Catholic. Did this colour his opinion? Was it the way we presented it ? What had gone wrong? Would he have reacted any differently had he known that I have tremendous sympathies for the Catholic Religion?

Après le deluge ... the Firths announced that they were *not* convinced that the music was from the composers named. Puzzled, I wrote asking them to make things clearer to my poor, bewildered mind. The reply shed no light on my darkness, and brought no comfort. I thought they believed ... if they did not, why had they founded the Trust? Sick at heart and unable to comprehend, I wrote an appeal to Sir George. Before there was time for him to answer, I was scheduled to visit Attingham at the same time as the Firths. Meanwhile, my health had been undermined by some virus which caused me to delay my arrival at the College by a few days.

My son had been looking forward to the visit, and staying in the country for a few days. It would be our only holiday that year as we could afford no other. My daughter did not wish to come, and had a friend to stay with her. I was not really well enough to travel, but did not want to disappoint my son. So I pulled myself together, and off we went.

We were met at Shrewsbury Station by Sir George's secretary, who took the opportunity to assail me in no uncertain terms in front of my son for daring to bother "Sir" (as she called Sir George) and the Firths, who were all very busy people and had no time for me, she said.

My son was flabbergasted.

"Mum," he protested, when we were alone in our room. "We had not even got to the College before she started on you. And what are they doing, messing about with your music, if they don't believe in it? Let's go straight home again."

"No", I told him, "We can't do that. I must find out what has

84

happened, and whether it is true what she said about Sir George and the Firths."

Presently the secretary re-appeared, and told us peremptorily that Sir George and the Firths were ready for me in the Warden's Study. Sir George was at that time Warden of the College. We went to the Study, and my son was dismissed abruptly. I should have had the sense to insist on his remaining, but I was taken off my guard.

What happened next was like a nightmare. My friends, whom I thought were on my side, appeared to be ranged against me. The three of them sat in a solemn row facing me as if it were a court martial. Suddenly Mary – Mrs. Firth – said, "This isn't fair. It's three to one," She jumped up and came to sit beside me. By now I wondered whatever was coming!

Liszt – dear, kind, Liszt – had once again warned me before I set off for Attingham that something was amiss.

"Don't be too upset by what happens," were his words, "And don't let them push you around," he added, with his jaw setting in that firm line I was getting to know so well.

Now I began to understand his warning. Sir George started to accuse me of all sorts of things, all of which were quite unfounded. I tried to reason with him quietly – my mother had brought me up to try always to keep my dignity – but he seemed very incensed. He kept threatening to close the Fund and give everybody their money back. My spirits sank down into cold despair. I had resigned my post and it had been filled. I had the children to support, and unless the small wage I earned was replaced, we were really going to be in a terrible plight. I thought of Liszt saying I was to try not to be too upset, and held back the tears that were almost overwhelming me.

Sir George went on to accuse me of saying something in my letter to him which I knew I had not said at all. Liszt's instruction not to let them push me around flashed into my mind. With all the boldness I could muster, I demanded to see the letter, stating that I was sure I had written nothing of the kind. Rather reluctantly, on my insistence, Sir George produced the letter and said he would read it out loud.

I was conscious of Liszt at my side.

"Quick, take it and read it yourself," he exclaimed.

Trembling with righteous indignation, I almost snatched it from Sir George's hand, saying that I would read it myself. I looked right through the letter. I knew I had not written what he alleged, but had to ascertain whether the letter had been tampered with in some way. I passed the letter quickly on to Mary, before Sir George could re-

85

cover it. She read it through with careful deliberation.

"She did not say it, George," she said quietly to Sir George. Then she passed it on to her husband to read.

"I must have misinterpreted it," was Sir George's explanation.

He could not just have misinterpreted it. Either he had never actually read it, but had had its contents reported to him second-hand; or he had only glanced at it hurriedly, being a very busy person, and somehow had the allegation sown into his mind afterwards. Had someone maliciously tried to turn him against me? There were plenty of jealous people dancing attendance on him because of his position and rank.

However, he continued to threaten to close the Fund, but I knew Sir George's word was his bond, and could not believe he would carry out such a cruel threat. Plainly, somebody had been trying to make trouble, and he was still very irate. I knew I could not easily get another job at my age, but decided that I must do so as soon as possible.

There was worse to come. Sir George kept saying the music was trivial and unconvincing, and asking the Firths to endorse his opinion . . . which they did! Now I was faced with an even more shattering disclosure: either the Firth's musical judgement had been mistaken previously, or they had been letting me think their opinion of the music was high when it was nothing of the sort. The world seemed to be crumbling about me and my trusted friends failing me.

At last that terrible interview came to an end. I felt I could never trust anybody again. Mary was my last hope. She was a woman, like myself. I appealed to her when we emerged into the corridor.

"Mary," I begged, "Don't you really find any of the music convincing."?

"NO!" came her emphatic reply.

I had to try to find out if they had been fooling me. I had to know the truth, even if it was the awful truth.

"Not one single piece?" I entreated.

"No! Not one single piece," she answered.

I looked at her face, which seemed cold and severe. My last shred of hope vanished. Then I saw Liszt beside her, gazing at her with unbelievable sternness.

"It is not true," he said to me, his jaw quivering with outrage," It *is* convincing. But they don't have the courage to say so."

Poor Liszt. He was suffering, too, the repudiation of all his work.

Sir George must have repented his threats. He did not close the Fund, but the damage was done. I could never be happy about it again, or feel secure. He could change his mind again or have it changed for him. I set about looking for fresh employment, at the same time trying to keep my side of the bargain with the Trust.

Liszt begged me to hold on, prophesying new opportunities. My health was at its lowest ebb. Years of penury, of going without to give the children the best I could, of enduring the bleak heartache of widowhood, were taking their toll. I tried to continue the musical work, but often broke down in a flood of tears when on my own because I felt now that it was all so hopeless and that my friends, Sir George and the Firths, had no faith in me or in the music. Even the Firths said they did not believe the music was from the composers . . . and that they were not convinced, and for months went on saying the same thing. Dr. Firth, getting frantic, I suppose, for having put himself and his wife in the line of fire, was pressing for proof, music, information, and saying in his letters that he would drag it out of me like a dentist pulling a tooth! Meant to be funny, perhaps, but doing nothing to put me at ease.

Under such circumstances it was not surprising that the contact with the composers began to fade. Beethoven, deciding he was wasting his time if people were only going to deny that it was he communicating, disappeared for weeks on end. Liszt remained faithfully with me, together with Chopin giving sympathetic support to console me. I found that Chopin could be quite fiery with indignation at the treatment I had received. Once he seized my hand and wrote at great speed through it – I was holding a pen at the time to write some music. He wrote in French. When I deciphered it afterwards, translating as well as I could, I found he was raging about one particular man who was trying to get a finger in the pie, and saying he would not have this man interfering with *his* music!

Liszt was determined not to let his cause drop. I think he is one of the most determined people I have ever known.

"We will find ways. It is God's Will, and it cannot fail," he would say with his quiet assurance.

I was still trying to get fresh employment when I was asked to give a lecture-recital at Sutton Young Spiritualists Church. This was the first step towards real success. The flurry of events which followed as a result of Peter Dorling getting to hear of me through this landmark in my life (although I did not know at the time that it was) is described in my first book. Before I had time to recover from the surprise,

87

there I was on B.B.C. Television, looking a poor, broken-down old thing, I thought, but at last news of the work was going out to the world.

Sir George and the Firths had told me that I must never go on television. I would be made to look ridiculous, they said. But the composers indicated that I should go bravely ahead, so I did. When it came to the point, Sir George and the Firths decided to take part, although I had said I was prepared to stand my ground alone.

It was now 1969, and things really got moving. Press interviews followed, I was featured in further television programmes, Philips began to make a record of some of the music, and so it continued.

The B.B.C. Third Channel started to prepare a documentary on my work. Sir Victor Goddard, who had become acquainted with me at the College of Psychic Science, told me that I ought not to go on with this because he said the Third Channel was a highly intellectual one which would just pull me to pieces. Liszt said I *should* go on with it, and not worry as it would be a success. And it was largely owing to Liszt that it was a success, because he transmitted the piece called "Grubelei" to me – with the B.B.C. Third Channel officials watching part of the time. This was highlighted in the programme together with a very favourable analysis by Humphrey Searle, the Liszt expert.

Liszt certainly seemed to be doing his best to confound any opponents. But I often thought it was all right for him, comfortably out of reach of the critics' tongues which were sometimes very barbed; I was the one who was bearing all the brunt – a thankless task. He would keep telling me that it was all worth while, and that it would help a lot of people, so I took him at his word and struggled onward.

"There will always be sceptics," he would often say, "But it is God's plan and cannot fail."

But there were still people *trying* to make it fail! People whose motives were often self-interested or even malevolent. It is a battle against human nature more than anything else; yet, paradoxically, it is a battle FOR human nature.

88

CHAPTER 9

The lone crusade

The year progressed, and things did not ease up at all. The demands being made upon me were tremendous and at times absolutely unreasonable. I had become an object of curiosity to many people; they forgot, apparently, that I was also a human being with limits of endurance. All this had to be gone through as part of the work's development and presentation to the public.

It seemed as if all the world was on my doorstep, clamouring for something or other. Much to our dismay, many people tracked us down, and gave no peace to myself and my family. The cranks turned up, all too many of them; the would-be hangers-on turned up; people who had not wanted to bother with me suddenly saw me as a desirable asset. We had to give up answering the front-door in order to preserve the last remnants of our privacy. Fame had arrived, and I did not like it at all. It was another thing to be endured as part of the mission. But all the frequent intrusions upon us, all the demands – often selfish ones – were interrupting the work with the composers, for which I needed peace and solitude. I wished with all my heart to be able to move, and move to a secret destination. . . .

Some of the most distressing incidents were caused by men who saw a widow as a possible target for their attentions. Some had "honourable intentions" and wanted to marry me. Some had intentions that were anything but honourable. One man, quite advanced in years, whom I discovered later was a married man, sought me out, claiming to be a friend of Leonard Bernstein. I did a little checking on him, and found that he had been associated for many years with the Spiritualist Movement. But I was unable to check on his Bernstein story which proved untrue, until later. He said Bernstein had asked him to try to get some information about a composer from me, and that it seemed I was the only one who might be able to obtain it. So, foolishly, I realised eventually, I agreed to see him. Slowly, it dawned on me what sort of man he was. When I admitted him to my house, I let him know that my daughter and her fiance as well as my son were there. I had an unpleasant intuition as soon as I set eyes on him, and felt it wise to let him know I was not alone. How true this was, became plain when he tried to become familiar with me. He kept saying he had no inhibitions, and as my mind does not run along the lines that his obviously did, I did not realise for a time what he meant. At last the ugly truth came home to me, and I got him out of the house as quickly as I could. He continued to pester me, calling at my house, and writing to me, so I had no choice but to write and say bluntly that I never wanted to see him again. Still he persisted, and finally I had to go to the police and appeal for their help.

After this incident, I was unlikely to allow any strangers to meet me. Even less likely to allow them into my home. It does seem ridiculous that abolute strangers should see fit to turn up on my doorstep unheralded, and expect me to invite them in! Yet this still happens. Would they invite someone in, not knowing anything about them, or their motives? Not knowing for sure whether they would be entertaining undesirable people, snoopers, or even mentally deranged people? Often callers have a good yarn to spin, or a tale of the old iron pot, as my mother used to say. It is quite common for them to say they have travelled half across the world to see me (would they really be rash enough to do that, not knowing whether I would be at home or abroad?). The next piece of stratagem, also common, is the news that they are leaving that night or next morning for the U.S.A., India, China ... or Timbuctoo, and MUST therefore see me there and then! Does it not occur to them that I could be – and usually am – already engaged in some activity? Some of them may be genuine callers who just do not stop to think. Some of them are, no doubt, spurious types who just wish to force themselves upon me. The genuine people will, I hope, understand – if they have been turned away – why we refuse to admit casual callers. Funny that they do not seem to think of writing first.

Pressures had been too much. Too much sheer spite had been vented on me by ill-disposed critics, and by the acid-tipped pens of some sections of the press. Why are people so beastly? Because someone does not believe in something, that does not give a justification for sinking to the level of maliciousness; there must be an ulterior motive:

90

jealousy, bigotry, or some kind of perverted instinct. One day, perhaps, they will know better! Until then, pioneers such as myself must endure the sneers and jeers of the ignorant and the venomous.

At least by that time, the Firths had written to state that they were "now convinced, and wished to convince others". But it seemed too late to counteract the first impression given by their denial. I had to try to live down all the distasteful repercussions that had ensued. I would have it flung in my face many times that the Firths, – who were my friends, it would be pointed out – were life-long musicians, and if I had not convinced them, what could I expect from people who were not my friends? I would strive gallantly to defend the Firths and myself, mumbling that they had their musical reputations to think of, which only seemed to make matters worse with some people.

There had been another attack from an unexpected quarter. Sir Victor Goddard had typed out a long document about my work and circulated it amongst a circle of his acquaintances. I was the last to hear about it. In this document he stipulated that I should never be permitted to play the compositions, and that the Trustees, to whom he sent copies, should not countenance any more publicity for my work. I had thought he was on my side as a fellow-believer in Life after Death; that, too, was shattered as I realised with horror that his actions could have the effect of undermining my work.

I wrote immediately to the Trustees to say that if they followed his advice and did not countenance further publicity, I would resign forthwith. My contention was that if one had a light, though it be the tiniest candle, one should not hide it under a bushel. I stated – as I had many times to Sir George – that I was absolutely certain that my work should be made known to as many people as possible to give them whatever help it could. I would not, of course, have risked exposure to more reviling had I not believed with all my heart and mind and soul that it was my duty to speak out about my work. Any attempt to withhold my work from humanity was wrong in my eyes; people had a right to hear about it, even if they could not believe in it.

With so many people ranged against me including those from whom I mistakenly thought I would receive sympathetic support, I felt more and more the bitterness of my lone crusade. My faith in God alone kept me going. But my body, never completely robust, could not take the strain. I succumbed to severe cystitis, feeling at the end of my tether. I fought my way back to health, only to get stricken with the influenza epidemic that was rampant, which was complicated by bronchitis. Dr. Firth was wanting me to undergo further tests of my E.S.P., tests of a psychometric character to be carried out by a friend of his, Professor Beloff. I was being battered by adverse critics, pestered by cranks and crack-pots, inundated with interminable demands and questions, and was in no fit state to cope health-wise. Feeling I could not do justice to the Trust, since it was impossible for me to comply with the requirements, I came to the decision that I must resign.

I withdrew as tactfully as I could from the Trust, expressing my gratitude for what they had done, and saying that I hoped it would make no difference to our friendship. I was willing to go on sharing what Dr. Firth called the "musical phenomenon", and wrote to that effect. It was not a question of wanting a change, but of needing a break from the rôle of guinea-pig which seemed more or less to have become my lot. It gave me a claustrophobic feeling of being type-cast.

May, 1970 brought the release of the record from Philips of some of the piano music. It also ended my connection with the Trust Fund, but not with the Trustees and Mrs. Firth. In the Spring of 1968, Mrs. Firth had made a recording of some of the piano pieces at the Craighall Studios, Edinburgh. A batch of five hundred records had been made privately from this recording, and acted as a preliminary sample. Dr. Firth informed me that no royalites were payable on this batch of records since they are not paid on privately made records – but all that mattered was that a little of the music had been recorded. I was grateful that Mrs. Firth had undertaken to perform a few of the compositions for this private presentation. Now, with the Philips record coming out, I was paid in advance on royalties, and immediately there was an outcry in certain press publications – including *Time Magazine*. There were allegations that I was "doing it all for the money", and the advance was flaunted as if it was a small fortune. It was not pointed out that I would receive nothing further unless the record sold in excess of the advance. It was all so ironic; there I was, with both my children still at school, having some recompense for all my exacting work, yet there were people mean enough to begrudge me the hard-earned royalties! People who probably earned far more than that in a few months or perhaps even a few weeks! There were plainly those who would distort the facts or stoop to almost any trick to try to discredit my work.

In October of 1968, it came to the notice of Mrs. Firth that tapes of some of the music were being offered for sale invoiced at four pounds each. These tapes contained some of her performances of the music and some of my own performances, but neither of us had been consulted, and the tapes had been circulated for about eight months entirely without our knowledge. It was, of course, a breach of the copyrights, and we had to have warnings sent to the people responsible to stop their illegal activities. It was another complication, another betrayal of my confidence in human nature. I was to wonder more and more whom I *could* trust. In fact, I was beginning to feel that the only people I could trust were my spirit colleagues and friends!

The rewards for all the work were few. I was certainly not doing the work for money, and the money was little enough when it came because a lump sum such as the advance on the records was liable to have to last for a very long period of perhaps years. I got more kicks in the teeth than anything else, and had to endure suggestions that I was a fraud, charlatan, and God knows what else. People hinted that I was unbalanced, and some of my so-called friends deserted me for fear of being associated in the public's estimation with something that was controversial. There was an enormous amount of stress and strain to bear, due to the unceasing pressures of the demands made on me by many members of the public. The almost total disillusionment in human nature that inevitably grew from the denigration heaped on my head, and the betrayal of my trust, as well as attempts to exploit me for gain or other ends, tempted me to wonder whether it was worth going on with the work. But I decided that it was all the more reason for trying to contribute something to help other people.

There were compensations such as opportunities to meet celebrities in various fields. In May 1970, I was invited to Dublin to take part in a live broadcast. Sitting right beside me, also taking part, was the champion racing driver, Jackie Stewart. I marvelled at the quiet courage and good humour of this great driver, and thought how my brother, who had been a member of the Junior Racing Drivers' Club at Brooklands in his young days, would have been thrilled to have met Jackie. This was the first of many meetings with great and famous people on my travels. Some of them would discuss my work with me, and give their views. When I met Colin Davis, the distinguished conductor, he told me that he had always thought death meant complete annihilation, but that I had made him think again. For some people, annihilation is not so terrifying as it sounds for it could mean an end to all their troubles!

The public gets to know one aspect of a person; Jackie Stewart,

93

driving champion – what else do they know about him, except that he has a brave and charming wife and children? Colin Davis, conductor – probably a complete mystery to people apart form his appearances on the rostrum. How little we really know about public figures. How type-cast they are! So it is with me: I have become known as the housewife who gets music from out of the nowhere, a parapsychological curiosity, a musical mystery. People pass judgement on me without having so much as met me, without knowing a thing about me; and all public figures probably have to put up with the same ill-informed judgement.

Once I was at a social gathering – a large party – and I was amused to hear a group of people summing me up. Must be daft, said one man. A lot of rubbish, commented a lady. How could anyone be expected to believe that stuff? queried yet another. One of the group, glancing over his shoulder, saw me standing there alone in the midst of the throng. He drew me into the conversation, perhaps feeling a little sorry for me being on my own.

"What do you make of this woman, Rosemary Brown, I think her name is?" he invited my view. I thought it best to confess who I was.

"I *am* Rosemary Brown," I murmured rather meekly.

There were exclamations of dismay from the group who had been running me down, followed by apologies.

"Don't worry," I reassured them, "I am used to being criticised."

They talked with me for some time, asking lots of questions. Now that they had actually met me, they said, they had quite a different impression. I hope they meant it, and were not just trying to gloss over their previous comments!

If nothing else was happening, I was getting to know human nature more thoroughly which is an important thing when you are seeking the truth about the human race, as I am. The vast mistrust of the "Unknown" which is a natural and common factor is a barrier between us and knowledge. Yet it is a barrier that most of us may be wise to retain, unless we have minds that are prepared to consider ideas which are strange to us. Most of us like to cling to that which is familiar to us both in our surroundings and relationships as well as in our thoughts. When anything new is presented to us, we have to make an effort to understand it, which will not deter us if it is something we really want to know. The territory which I encompass in my work is unknown territory; if our scientists and parapsychologists can explore that territory, they will without any doubt be able to dissipate much of our apprehension towards it. They could help to

94

conquer the fear of death and so make this Life far more enjoyable.

It may be impossible for me to escape being type-cast in the public imagination, but my real role is that of a seeker of truth and a researcher. Whatever view people take of my work, perhaps it can throw some light on the subject of E.S.P. Perhaps it can open up new worlds, and help to link us with the Next World.

To simplify life, we type-cast a great many people. We say so-and-so is "nice", somebody else is "bossy", etc. We pick out what is to us the main characteristic of a person, and classify him accordingly. This can be very misleading, and is very vague. Human beings are a conglomeration of different ingredients, and all of us have our "nice" facets and our less attractive ones. In the next world, people are the same – at least, when they first pass over: which is something that appears to be instinctively recognised by interviewers sometimes. More than once there has been a suggestion made that because Liszt in this life was a womaniser, he might be after me – an idea so ridiculous that it is laughable. I am a middle-aged, ordinary person, with no feminine allure as far as I am aware. Even if I were young and pretty, it is ludicrous to think of a spirit chasing after an embodied soul; they are in totally different dimensions. If Liszt were still of the same nature as he was on earth, and wished to continue his pursuit of the fair sex, he could and would surely track down a desirable quarry in his own world.

So I have found that even souls who have passed on to the Next World remain type-cast in our eyes. Liszt's ardent attentions towards women caused him to be a topic of scandal, according to reports. His behaviour, like many men's, was governed by the physical appetites to which he was subject. Having shed one's phsyical body, one cannot any longer be subject to its desires, hungers, weaknesses, or aches and pains. To retain the identical image of a person, no matter how long he has been in the Hereafter, is to create a falsely static picture of his character. In this world, we are likely to change some of our views and likes and dislikes, and are liable to alter our behaviour patterns, especially if there is any revolution in social values and standards. How much greater or faster such changes may or may not take place in the Life Hereafter, we cannot determine, although we can surmise that the changes will still be controlled by the individual's effort and response.

It is the same with Beethoven. People talk of him to this day as a disgruntled man prone to outbursts of violent temper. I doubt whether this picture of him is anywhere near the truth about him

95

now, and I have myself never once witnessed any show of bad temper, only the occasional display of impatience when he is unable to communicate clearly or quickly in order to convince an unbelieving world that he is still alive in the World of Spirit. The old adage about giving a dog a bad name does seem to hold true. When a soul has been released from the physical burdens and material pressures which may have been the breeding-ground of certain undesirable traits, one would expect it to be relatively easy for it to eradicate those traits. Remove the cause, and the effect should wear off in cases where it could only continue as long as the perpetuating cause continued.

Several times I have been contacted by a well-known psychologist who is now in the Spirit World. To avoid any argument over his identity, I will simply call him Professor Y. Once he wanted to impress on me the dangers of falling into the habit of classifying people into fixed categories, and keeping them permanently in these pigeon-holes.

"Human nature is full of surprises, although it seems to change little on the whole. You will find unexpected good in the bad, and unexpected bad in the good. It is impossible to tabulate with exactitude any one person. We can only get a general idea of someone's nature and tendencies, and must remember that we have not yet discovered ways of assessing all the possibilities of the individual. We may see someone in a temper once or twice, and conclude that he or she is bad-tempered. To look at the situation more accurately, we should rather regard the person as having an experience of bad-temper than as being actually bad-tempered. The experience of bad-temper may be repeated a number of times, and confirm our impression that the person is of a bad-tempered disposition. We might be more correct in diagnosing the person as one who is subject to fits of temper in the same way as we diagnose someone who is subject to fits of depression."

This was, perhaps, a round-about way of saying that Beethoven was the victim of bad-temper which was in all probability engendered by the circumstances of his life and by his indifferent health and his tragic deafness. I was thinking that this kind of outlook seemed to condone bad-temper and other faults, but Professor Y evidently read my thoughts, for he added:

"Being the victim of bad-temper or some other weakness is no reason for not making every effort to cure it, any more than being the victim of a physical complaint is any reason for failing to attempt

96

a cure."

It is manifest that Professor Y considers that there are disadvantages in practising rigid type-casting in the field of psychology, which is something that many psychologists may do for all I know. A lot of us may unconsciously make little moulds and try to fit the people we meet into them, and be tempted to become exasperated when they just don't fit those moulds!

As I had not studied the composers' lives, and knew very little about them, I met them with an open mind, and grew to know them from my own direct impressions rather than from any existing accounts of them. Just as well, for after all, most of them have been over in the Next World for a long time, and have naturally modified in some ways. To think of them exactly as they were must be harbouring false ideas about them. Liszt I have found to be a devout soul, generous, straight-forward, always ready to help others, and have seen no sign of his still being a Casanova. Chopin has proved to be gentle and sympathetic, and a great wag, but always gentlemanly even when roused with indignation at some injustice. Beethoven's presence can be felt to be vibrant with power, yet he has a noble simplicity that helps put one at ease with the sheer majesty of his soul which could be overwhelming; there has never been any hint of the disagreeable temper which is attributed to him. These three and some of the other composers with whom I have been in touch failed to match precisely with the hackneyed portraits of their personalities. I would say that all that is finest in them has been perpetuated; that any imperfections they had have faded away.

In time, in the Hereafter, we can perhaps attain perfection through the grace of our Creator. Then, possibly, we shall be type-cast as saints!

CHAPTER 10

Happiness for all mankind

"Is happiness for all Mankind an impossible ideal? Perhaps it is, but that should not deter us from cultivating it as widely as we can."

That was what Bertrand Russell said to me on one of his astral visits. "To begin with, we must allow for the contingency that human nature is not always arable, just as the soil is not always arable, to stretch the metaphor a little. Land can often be made arable or more arable than it was. Human nature, too, can be treated to make it more fertile by feeding the imagination, by implanting good sillage to enrich the foundation before hopefully sowing seeds that will bring forth a good harvest in the person of a happy member of society who will in turn give happiness to other members of society.

"A great amount of time and energy has been spent in the pursuit of happiness by a great many people since time began. Given the fundamental prerequisites for bodily health and well-being, happiness would seem reasonably easy to obtain, so one might presume. But we know from the high number of depressed individuals and the increasing percentage of suicides, that this is plainly a fallacy. What is it, then, that will assure happiness for us, all obvious causes of discomfort and pain having been ruled out?

"There can be no universal panacea for happiness which is obvious to anyone who has studied, as I have, the root causes of happiness and its opposite. Happiness is a state which is created within us by a very large and very varied number of factors. One man is happy with nothing less than a luxurious mansion and estate and a fleet of fast cars; another man is happy in a monk's cell with the minimum requirements of life. It would seem, therefore, that it is not what we actually possess which provides us with happiness, but our reactions to what we possess. The secret of happiness, like the kingdom of heaven, must be within us, and the key to it is our attitude towards life and especially towards our own personal life.

"Can we teach people to be happy in the same way as we can teach them to add, subtract, multiply and divide? To do that, we would need to teach them to read their own selves just as we teach them to read literature. This would mean beginning with the alphabet of self-analysis which could not easily be taught to children since standards of comparative behaviour need to be studied before self-analysis can effectively be undertaken. Children would not have had sufficient experience in these standards to be able to absorb the significance of self-analysis. If we teach children to stop and think Why am I behaving like this? at every stage in their daily work and play, they might be in danger of losing all their spontaneity which is the very well from which their natural gaiety springs.

"We have travelled the full circle, and returned to the point under consideration, namely, whether we can teach people to be happy. Our observation of children would incline us to think otherwise, and to believe that happiness can best occur as a purely involuntary event. Is this the nearest to the solution that we can reach, that is, the inference that happiness is something which just happens to a person and cannot be induced? We can think of many things which are calculated to bring pleasure as distinct from pure happiness, and we know that pleasure can result in happiness but that they are not always one and the same thing. An alcoholic drink, for instance, can bring pleasure to the palate, but does not necessarily convey any joy to the brain or ease to the body. We can have all the wealth in the world, and still be miserable although that wealth is more than sufficient to buy all the pleasures that the world can offer. Yet the idea that wealth furnishes the means of purchasing happiness persists with obstinacy in the human mind, and is the breeding-ground of capitalism." (See Appendix I for a further message from Bertrand Russell commenting on current trends.)

"Happiness is to a large extent dependent on our disposition. We say that someone has a happy nature and that someone else is nothing but a miserable worm. We need to discover how to bestow a happy disposition on people and at what age this can best be achieved. Childhood would seem the period of life in which to create a happy disposition because in most individuals the disposition developed in childhood remains with them throughout the rest of their life. The question is whether children in general possess an intrinsically happy disposition, which certainly seems to apply in the case of healthy

99

children. If, then, they appear to be born with a happy disposition, it would seem a natural tendency, a tendency which oft-times becomes despoiled as they grow up.

"If happiness is our natural tendency, all we need to do is to discover how to retain this tendency or to avoid having it impeded or destroyed. This brings us to the questions of environment and upbringing, education and general experience, a galaxy of considerations which cannot adequately be covered in this essay. In any case, these questions could only be discussed in a very broad sense as individual histories differ so widely and present so much complexity.

"Some environments are obviously not conducive to health and therefore not conducive to happiness. The same applies to upbringing, and extends also to the matter of education which aims to inculcate knowledge without concerning itself with anything as unintellectual as the pursuit of happiness. General experience is something over which we do not have much control, and we have to take what we get and make the best of it. The attitude of an individual can enable him to rise above great personal tragedies and still find happiness in living, demonstrating that general experience, in whatever form it comes, need not deprive us totally of our inner serenity. Our reactions and our attitudes, the former being largely dictated by the latter, are key factors in our search for happiness, It therefore appears that the influences which determine our attitudes are of paramount importance. We have to admit that our attitudes for the most part are determined for us by others, at least until we reach an age when we can reason and think for ourselves.

"Health, which might be termed bodily happiness, depends on a varied and adequate diet, a healthy environment, and sufficient exercise and rest. The health of the mind, which one would take to be synonymous with mental happiness, must depend on similar conditions. The mind needs variety to avoid boredom which is one of the main causes of unhappiness, and it certainly needs a mental climate which is propitious to its well-being. It also needs to be exercised to keep it in good form so that its interest in life can remain keen and ward off the onslaught of boredom. Rest for the mind is probably one of the most essential requisites for its happiness, for tiredness and zest cannot go hand in hand, and happiness calls for zest."

Zest for living, interest in life – essentials to happiness. That certainly makes sense when we remark how often a person loses his zest for living upon retirement *unless* he has something to interest

100

him apart from the job he performed. When we are off-colour, we have no appetite for our food; similarly, when our minds are jaded, we have no enthusiasm for life. Our own approach to life can give us greater or lesser access to happiness according to our outlook.

Children play with zest and are enthusiastic in their wonder – at the world about them. Perhaps we grown-ups deem zest to be a childish thing since we seem to shed it steadily as we grow older. We cultivate a more sober demeanour, we become deadly serious (deadly, because it is the wrong kind of seriousness which has a deadening effect), and if we appear too light-hearted, other adults may frown upon us, even accusing us of being flippant and irresponsible. Perhaps we do indeed need to become like little children in order to enter the kingdom of heaven or in other words the state of happiness.

Those beings with whom I am constantly in touch in the spheres of the spirit tell me they are working ceaselessly for the happiness of Mankind. When I was pondering about this one day, Liszt, the main spokesman, said this is not because they are trying to be virtuous, but because they recognise that happy people are more likely to be kindly to others, and that kindness will assist in the establishment of good relationships. This in turn, he went on, could help in the creation of world peace which it is necessary to promote so that Mankind can evolve satisfactorily. A great deal could doubtless be said in support of Liszt's statements. Educationalists do know that happy, healthy children are able to learn more successfully than those who are miserable or unwell, hampered by poor health. The theory advanced by Liszt, that we can evolve more advantageously in a state of peace or happiness, seems feasible according to those observations. This does not set aside the cases where individuals have learnt through suffering to display courage and endurance, and, in some instances to become more compassionate towards others. We can always learn if we are willing to make the effort, so he says, but will evolve best in conditions of harmony and well-being.

Liszt says that he and many others are working for our happiness in this world; but what are our prospects in the next one? It was Sir Donald Tovey who gave me an answer to this query.

"Life for most people in the Hereafter holds no problems other than themselves, problems which are accentuated by the fact that we are face to face with reality and can neither deceive ourselves nor others as to our natures, intentions, aspirations, beliefs, attitudes, and limitations. In the world of matter, it is possible to escape from one's inner self by pursuing a round of fevered activities, by procuring the

101

pleasures of the flesh, or by rendering oneself stupefied with drink, drugs, and other mind-paralysing resorts.

"There is no avenue of escape here, and the truth about ourselves stares us unblinkingly in the eye. To see ourselves exactly as we are, and not as we wish we were or as we might make ourselves out to be, can be a most disconcerting and humbling experience. There is a measure of consolation, however, in knowing at last just where we stand and precisely what qualities we possess or lack. It is always better to know definitely rather than to surmise or speculate. We can then set about the task, if we are so disposed, of making good our deficiencies. In this after-life, some power has given us the gift to see ourselves as we are, not merely as others on earth saw us; for it must be borne in mind that others do not always see our true selves since they cannot know us thoroughly from within. There is a strong propensity amongst human beings for them to misjudge each other, and their opinions of each other may be entirely false. The truth about oneself comes direct in self-revelation activated by the Infinite Spirit, our Creator."

As the question of our prospects in the Next Life has arisen at this point, it is appropriate to quote further from Tovey on the subject.

"Funeral ceremonies are seldom so conducted as to convey to the mourners any glimmering of insight as to the whereabouts of the departed soul for whom the aforesaid ceremonies are being performed. Indeed, it is doubtful whether many ministers possess anything more than a vague idea of the state in which the newly-deceased might find himself or herself after having passed through the inevitable portal of death. Church officiants of any denomination would, one must surmise, be partial to a solemn belief in a further existence of some nature to follow after life on earth, perhaps believing that it is available only for those subscribing to the views of their particular Church.

"Some religions stipulate specific requirements as necessary qualifications for entrance into Eternal Life. We are all familiar with the doctrine that we must be 'saved' before we can inherit Eternal Life. This doctrine of selective survival after death must have been the cause for much distress of mind, both amongst those about to die, and amongst the bereaved. It is often used as a weapon to make unbelievers conform, which to my mind is pointless, since conforming through fear is not true conversion.

"Those who believe that a distinction is drawn at death, with only the chosen entering into another life, should pause to consider how

102

anomalous this would be in comparison with entrance into the material world. When a soul incarnates on earth, there seems only one apparent requirement: that two persons of opposite sexes should come together in a conjugal relationship resulting in the development of a human foetus and its subsequent birth. This provides the necessary physical vehicle which the soul can inhabit during its earthly sojourn. The Supreme Law creates individual lives on earth which do not have to meet any categorical requirements apart from the provision of a material body. Why, then, should we presume that the commencement of life in other spheres or dimensions should depend on anything other than the furnishing of a suitable body or vehicle in which to function? The assertion that the Infinite Spirit practises a system of discrimination with regard to admission into Life after Death appears at variance with the laws governing entrance by birth into the Life before Death. The logical mind perceives the inconsistency of this line of thought, and would question the implication that at one stage the Law of Life inaugurates existence unconditionally, only to inaugurate it conditionally at a later stage. stage. This, to the logician, would indicate that the Law is subject to fluctuations of an unpredicatable nature, which would mean that the Law is unstable. The scientist informs us that Law is stable, and we cannot, therefore, lend credence to the idea of an unstable Creation."

In our world, religion and science often clash. Religion is inclined to urge us to believe without providing ample substantiation for belief; science urges us to accept only that which can be scientifically proved. In the next world, they seem able to reconcile religion and science. They have the advantage of knowing that there *is* Life after Death; we can only surmise that Life goes on, unless we are amongst the fortunate few who have received irrefutable evidence that it does. Because they know in the Next World that Death is not the end but a beginning to a new life, they naturally develop a different attitude towards Death. To them, it is not the final and awful tragedy that it seems to many on earth. It is a release from physical suffering and material burdens, and a joyful reunion with dear relatives and friends who passed on before us. Sir Donald had quite a lot to say about the happiness of the new life.

"Let me give an account of an event which I have witnessed on many occasions since my own departure from your world. We observe from the sphere in which I have now taken up residence that considerable uncertainty and no little apprehension arises in the human mind concerning the experience of death and transition to

103

another life. Countless numbers of people have no notion at all of the process by which a soul leaves its earthly garment, the physical body, and travels to its heavenly destination. I say 'heavenly' destination since the vast majority of people do proceed to a state which to them constitutes a heaven.

"I could not myself believe that I had passed through death's door upon my arrival here: the entire experience is so natural, so automatic, so serene, and so imperceptible from the soul aspect. Those who fear some strange and unnerving passage might await, following the actual moment of decease, may dismiss their apprehension as totally groundless. At the moment of death or prior to that instant, consciousness is suspended, and the soul, released from the corpse, floats freely to its new abode. I have watched the coming of souls to my spiritual surroundings, and have seen that they appear to rise through a sea of light, gently and slowly and effortlessly, borne securely in their new bodies which are provided for their souls upon cessation of their physical existence. In actual fact, those new bodies already existed although merged with the physical bodies and linked to them by the silver cord, as it is known. At Death, this cord is dissolved or severed, and can be compared with the umbilical cord which is also dispensed with after birth. Death, after all, is like another birth into another world, excepting that one's new body is a counterpart of the lately vacated physical body. When you are born on earth, you enter a body provided by your parents; when you are born into the World of Spirit, you emerge in the counterpart of that body at whatever stage it has reached, excepting that it is without defect for defects are characteristics of the world of matter and not of the world of spirit. Does that sound too far-fetched for some to grasp? You will understand one day that spirit is whole, therefore nothing lacks in its manifestation; but matter is incomplete and consequently subject to many imperfections.

"When the arisen soul regains consciousness, it awakens in peaceful surroundings where it finds friends or relatives waiting to greet it and make it feel at home. I am speaking of the average soul, and not of those whose consciousness has become clouded by the shadows of a wildly mis-spent life or darkened by sinking into the murky depths of questionable activities. We recognise here that the average person is not of an evil nature, although few of us pass through earthly existence without committing a few errors of some kind which are for the greater part minor offences, occurring as a result of our lack of knowledge or because circumstances have driven us willy-nilly

104

to be rash or thoughtless.

"After a soul has adjusted to its new life it can, if it should so wish, then take stock of its past life and extract the good to carry forward, leaving behind that which it now finds valueless. This sounds a simple process, but it is not easy to abandon the habits of a lifetime or to re-orientate speedily a misinformed outlook. Indeed, there are some who cling tenaciously to their old beliefs even when it should be obvious to them that they are false; fear of letting go or false pride will hold people back from progressing into enlightenment.

"One thing does become rapidly clear to newly-arrived souls; that is, the divine order of the nature of things. Each and every soul meets here with its just deserts, not because they are dispensed by a presiding deity, but because it is literally true that one reaps what one has sown. If one has endeavoured to make the lot of others easier in earth-life and sought to promote the welfare and happiness of one's fellow-beings, then one finds oneself in a pleasing environment amongst congenial companions, and able to adapt without difficulty to the new mode of living. But those who have deliberately deprived others of their material rights and human needs, or have wantonly caused suffering, will find themselves in turn deprived and also imprisoned by their own meaness of outlook. This does not mean that they are trapped for ever in a self-made hell; the moment a soul sees and confesses its past misdeeds and attempts to rectify them, the way opens for it to evolve into the light. True repentance, as the Churches teach, is the key to forgiveness and salvation.

"This exposition is in danger of becoming a sermon, and not one of us has the right to sermonise to another. We believe here in learning together, and none dares set himself or herself up as superior to others; for we realise, if we had not already done so on earth, that we are all equal in the sight of God, and that it is only by His Will that we possess our individual talents. We witness that it is true that as a man thinks in his heart, so is he; we see each other precisely as we are which can cause not a little consternation in the first instance. All the polite or misleading lies people tell become transparent tissues without any power to dissemble. We can see at a glance, almost, whether we have misjudged or failed to appreciate others or whether we have over-rated them. This is indeed a world of Truth and Reality, of which the material world is a distorting mirror."

Sir Donald went on to describe the happiness which can be experienced in the Next Life.

105

"The greatest joy for most risen souls is to find that there is full scope for the harmonious development of self-expression. All the bitterness of frustration dies away as each one unfolds his or her own gifts becoming capable of giving happiness to others by their use. I myself could never peruse enough during my life on earth although I read very extensively; I have been an avid reader here in the splendidly equipped libraries that are established on various planes of consciousness. I found speedily on my reading excursions in this domain that many fabled stories are based on fact, and that not a few things solemnly held to be actually true are, conversely, figments of the imagination.

"I believed, for example, that a man is a man not solely by virtue of the male body he inhabits, but also by some undefined quality or qualities of his nature, and that a woman is a woman by the same precedent. Since my arrival here, and prolonged study of this matter, I have with some bemusement altered my ideas concerning the differentiations. It is becoming understood in the world, perhaps with reluctance in some male preserves, that the line of distinction between the two sexes is in many respects not as marked or as constant as formerly believed. This is drawing much nearer to the fundamental truth than can be imagined. Only now am I beginning to comprehend the truth of the matter, that is, that every human being, irrespective of sex, is of identical essence though manifesting in differing forms.

"Those who have incarnated in feminine guise are usually happily surprised to discover that in the World of Spirit there is no distinction whatsoever drawn between female and male, because these are recognised to be simply aspects of physical existence bearing no relationship to the eternal nature of the soul. They are happily surprised because they find themselves in a world or sphere where they will no longer be discriminated against or deprived of various rights and opportunities on account of their sex. In the Hereafter one is estimated according to one's innate qualities and cultivated merits, and the question of sex does not enter into account.

"Those who incarnated in a male guise are sometimes disconcerted to find their traditional male superiority, if they so regarded it, without any continuance in the after-Life. Intelligence, character, and even physical strength so patently vary irrespective of sex on the earth-plane that it should be a matter of no great difficulty for the perceptive to deduce that a male physique does not necessarily guarantee possession of superiority in any of these respects any more

106

than a female physique necessarily disqualifies superiority. One is limited, it is true, by the form one takes in the world of matter: but a male can be a physical weakling or a mental defective, and a female can be endowed with muscular power and intellectual ability. So the masculine and feminine roles are not to be so categorically defined as our predecessors might have held, that is, not with regard to their physical and mental capabilities.

"Humanity squanders much of its female resources, or has done so until recently, by retaining the male prerogative with regard to the vast majority of issues, which has thrown the burden of the world's business on to masculine shoulders. My contemporary, Bernard Shaw, suggests quizzically but not quixotically that this status quo is due to femine guile having prevailed on man to carry the responsibilities of business and state thus relieving woman of these loads.

"Opportunities for all to develop their abilities and put them to use in the service of the community should be available irrespective of class, colour, creed, nationality or sex, if the world is to benefit fully from its human resources. There is such a deplorable waste of ability in all sections of society. This adds to the attendant miseries of a planet populated by peoples of which a large percentage is underprivileged and over-exploited. With the network of communications and travel facilities drawing the world's inhabitants into increasing contact, the need to ensure that no group or nation is deprived or oppressed becomes a vital issue which will tolerate no further procastination or neglect."

Sir Donald referred to the state of our world in much the same way as Bertrand Russell, showing an interest in current developments, and commenting on some of the present-day problems.

"We watch with admiration your great scientists and philosophers and psychologists applying their energies to penetrate the unknown realms of the material, the abstract, and the mental worlds. Vast discoveries have been made during the past century, pushing forward the pace of living and widening its scope. The tenor of life on earth has changed from a series of ostensibly disjointed and isolated events into a more closely-knit, interacting pattern which appears to be getting daily more entangled in its own undischarged commitments and unresolved conflicts.

"The intricacy of modern politics renders it increasingly difficult to comprehend the purposes of national and international federations and confederations. So many groups are divided against themselves in a free-for-all where each seems concerned only with his own

107

immediate benefits; few appear to have the foresight that would enable them to realise that no individual person or separate section can obtain complete satisfaction of their needs and wants unless they are compatible with the integral life about them.

"Mankind tends to use its intellect as a weapon of destruction against others rather than as a constructive force, and its strength to strike fear into all and sundry, rather than as a power to protect the interests and welfare of all human beings, especially the helpless, the defenceless, and the underprivileged. The destructive element has become preponderant and erupted into demonstrations which often deteriorate into disorder and violence and which seldom achieve anything except an aversion towards such methods by all law abiding citizens, and damage to the image of their case, be it sound or unreasonable. No lasting result of estimable standing can ever be obtained by the use of pragmatic persuasion or tyrannical tactics since this unfailingly provokes resentment in some quarters where it will smoulder in an uneasy threat to the continuation of the practices or principles which have created disaffection."

Sir Donald then turned his attention to the problems of young people nowadays:

"Children today are becoming more aware of their parents' uncertainties, and by the time they attain their youth are liable to have sought their own solutions prematurely before their judgement has had the opportunity to develop through experience! So we have the young agitating against conditions which are not always as inacceptable as alleged to the mature judgement, in which case their elders are at a loss to grasp the over-emphasised character of the problem. Some of the less discerning amongst the younger generation wish the use of certain drugs to be made legal, although these drugs are known to carry a medical risk in escalating addiction. It is a sad verdict on the present-day prevailing climate that there are people who feel they have to resort to drugs to enable them to cope with the pace of life. We seem to be losing our spiritual backbone.

"There are, of course, diverse real and urgent problems and flagrant injustices affecting people of all ages and groups. Humanity is in a melting-pot of its own overheated emotions, and the heat may inflame many a normally cool customer into searing speeches and feverish efforts which sometimes prove regrettable and go up in smoke.

"Far beyond the turbulent tide of strife and struggle, there lies an era of promise where many existing grievances will have become

108

obsolete, and many new ways of coping with individual and mass problems will have been discovered and put effectively into practice. In the scramble for self, countless numbers are overlooked and neglected, permitting hideous discrimination and victimisation, in some instances against those least able to press their own case or give a coherent account of their straightened circumstances or frustrated rights.

"There is another way of looking at life which is all too seldom viewed by humanity as a whole. It is doubtful whether a completely satisfying state of existence can be obtained by attending only to immediate needs such as the bodily requirements of food, water, shelter, warmth and similar necessities to healthy life. Man cannot live by bread alone, in spite of the fact that many assert that they can, taking bread to signify material needs. Man does have a spiritual need, however much this is disputed. Most people will agree that there are needs for recreation, relaxation, and non-commercial interests. These are just as vital to total health of mind and body as basic nutritional specifications. With increasing leisure becoming available to increasing numbers in the later part of the Twentieth Century, these additional needs must be catered for to ward off the growth of boredom and discontent.

"Most important of all, although believed by the materialistically-minded to be of no consequence, are the intrinsic spiritual requirements of each individual. However, these can only be met by personal discovery through coming to satisfactory but not self-satisfied terms with oneself, and finding a harmonious orientation to the world, to life, and to that Infinity which we call God. God can do without Man, but Man cannot do without God."

CHAPTER 11

Tovey talks

It is sad to think that the general public is unlikely to know the name of Donald Francis Tovey; sad because he was not only a brilliantly gifted musician and composer, and an equally gifted lecturer and scholar, but also a remarkably fine character of great sensitivity and wit. I myself never knew him or even met him in this world, but have had the rare privilege of getting to know him in his "discarnate capacity", as he puts it.

He first made himself known to me in 1966, although I suspect he had been sizing me up long before then and planning to utilise my psychic awareness. His name was unknown to me, and I knew nothing whatsoever about him. When he first put in an appearance, Sir George Trevelyan was engaged in a tête-à-tête with me about my musical spirit compositions. Having announced himself simply as "Tovey", he asked me to tell Sir George I could see him, and to describe his appearance to him. This I duly did, but Sir George said he did not know what Tovey looked like, and that he would have to check with Mrs. Firth who was one of Tovey's last pupils. The description was found to tally exactly with Tovey's appearance. We were satisfied that I had seen clairvoyantly a spirit who resembled Tovey in every detail. He was able to convince Dr. Firth – a sceptical scientist – by his verbal communications that he was indeed none other than the Tovey he claimed to be.

Since Tovey is a person of great verbosity, and this book has to contain mention of a number of other subjects as well as the Tovey communications, it is not possible to quote everything he has said on the "heavenly telephone" as he jokingly calls it. One particular remark is worthy of special mention, as it seemed to be the deciding factor for Dr. Firth.

110

This remark, made by Tovey to me and passed on to Dr. Firth, was as follows:

"Mine was an exploratory mind both by inherited trait and diligent cultivation."

Dr. Firth wrote to tell me that this was absolutely true though no-one could have been aware of it. To quote from a letter of Mrs. Firth's, dated the 27th October 1973, "The point is that Miss Weisse always gave the impression that Donald's abilities (genuis – what you will) covered every aspect of being a musician, which she recognized from an early age and trained, and that he came from a family which was totally unmusical and uncaring."

I must explain that Miss Weisse was not only Tovey's teacher, but became something of a foster-mother to him.

Mrs. Firth's letter goes on to explain that her husband's researches into the background of Tovey's life uncovered the information that "Donald's mother's family was large and brilliant in intellectual powers, all the sisters speaking many languages, keen on nature, keen on astronomy, keeping up with literature and philosophy; some writing books, one becoming a Welsh bard – and so on. Donald's father was not only a hard-working parson, but *the* authority on the poet Thomas Gray, on whom he wrote a book; a classicist, and not only learned in Greek and Latin, but the examiner on Shakespeare for Eton – and so on."

Dr. Firth also discovered that ordinary days in the Rectory had Father in his study coaching students or writing his own works, and Mother in the sitting-room reading and conversing in French, German or Italian with someone or another (or playing chess); and every letter to her Dearest Don speaks of his playing, or his compositions, and every day's entry in her diary notes his playing after the evening meal when he is at home. His Father never missed a concert at which he played, and listened to him every evening if both were together – and by far the best poem he wrote in a little published book of poems was "D.F.T."

Mrs. Firth concluded, "The important thing is that both parents were incredibly proud of everything he did in music – far from being uninterested, and Donald's vast knowledge of languages, literature, philosophies, etc., etc., came very much from his parents' families as did his quality of mind – his sense of humour and his goodness."

She added that most of what she wrote to me is revealed in the family letters and papers, and they have only come into the house (the Firth's house) during the past year or so. My communications

111

from Tovey came to me long before these letters and papers had become available to the Firths, having been previously locked away inaccessibly in the University. Mrs. Firth's letter is dated the 27th October, 1973.

As an interesting side-light, I will go off at a tangent here to relate an incident of healing confirmed in the same letter from Mrs. Firth.

In May, 1968, I paid a visit to the Firths in their Edinburgh home. Mrs. Firth asked me if I would give her husband some healing while I was there. I attuned myself by silent prayer to the Divine Source of Healing, and found that the prayer had evidently attracted the attention of Sir George Scott-Robertson, a "deceased" relative of mine, who was an army surgeon in this life, and often gives help when I am healing.

Sir George stated that Dr. Firth had a large lump at the back of his neck, and that he wished me to treat it under his direction. I informed Dr. Firth of this, and he said he would remove his jacket so that I could see whether there was any lump there – and sure enough, there was the lump where Sir George had indicated, on the nape of the neck. It could not be seen while Dr. Firth was wearing his jacket. Point number one: I could not have known there was a lump as it was imperceptible before the jacket was taken off.

Sir George then directed me to cup my hands over the lump, palms facing it. The lump began to diminish in size before our very eyes. Sir George then told me that was sufficient for him to maintain a contact and continue the treatment without my keeping my hands over the lump any longer. Mrs. Firth's letter of the 27th October, 1973 confirms that the lump had been there for a number of years prior to my treating it, and that immediately after the treatment, it looked as if heat had been applied, and WITHIN HOURS THE LUMP WENT! Five years later, there was still no sign of it, which demonstrates that such healing is not a mere flash in the pan.

Now that I have covered the contents of Mrs. Firth's letter, let us return to some of the other communications from Tovey. He seems to have a gift of being able to make himself heard clearly, which does not apply to all spirits. For some reason, it is difficult or even impossible for some of the departed to communicate; perhaps they do not wish to, or have nothing in particular to say – like many people in this world. My own experience in spirit communication has shown that as a rule the extroverts can get across the best, or the more reticent ones can be successful with determination. There are obviously a great number of conditions influencing communication, since it

112

varies so much in clarity, sometimes being almost indistinguishable, and at other times clear as crystal. The same problems can rise in these communications as occur in telephonic contact: conversation may be muffled, there may be a poor connection, and there can be all kinds of interference of crossed lines. Also the communicators themselves, like people on the telephone, may not possess very clear diction. Hence, there can be errors in transmission, and a word or number can be mistaken for something else. Tovey has probably succeeded in impressing the gist of his conversation to me with remarkable exactitude, in spite of the fact that he uses a mode of speech to which I am unaccustomed – 'high-flown", my mother would have called it.

On the 29th February 1968, after the discussion of my work had been held at the College of Psychic Science that month, Tovey evidently decided he should explain the aims of my musical activities from his point of view and that of his colleagues. Here is what he said:

"It is high time that a statement was issued by the incorporeal corporation for the edification of those interested in the musical processes taking place through a certain individual. This, then, represents our first attempt to dictate an account of the origin and purpose of the scheme. The greater part of this account is the work of myself, Tovey, who is known in the "Other World" as "Tacitus." Do not too narrowly analyse the sentences which are to follow: often a form of précis is used in view of time limitations.

"You may wonder why I should associate myself with the so-called phenomenon with which you are becoming ever more closely linked; and you know that I would waste no time in a direction that I did not consider amply worth-while.

"Attempts have been made from time immemorial to communicate with your world. These attempts have frequently met with failure or rebuff; at best, success has been half-baked and not considered worthy of assimilation by those who deem themselves shrewd. Even the half-baked successes have been doomed to be exploited by Man for his own ends in many instances.

"Prophets and holy ones, saints and sages, have sought throughout the centuries to bring humanity into synchronisation with the higher levels of consciousness. You will agree that there has been little success in this direction. What more can be done? We need new approaches, we need to break new ground and present the Cosmic Laws in a new light. Our theme must be broad enough to include the

113

whole of humanity and powerful enough to withstand the disrupting influences of inflexible creeds.

"Music is the language of all people, the language which can come from the heart and go to the heart without the need of a single word. With this in mind, we plan to utilise music in our efforts to establish communication. By trial and error, by experiments and experience, we are learning many of the pitfalls of two-way links with earth."

This communication was intended primarily for the Firths, who were by that time both taking a keen interest in the music I was receiving from departed composers. Tovey had apparently introduced a partly hidden point of evidence in this outpouring, when he said he *is* known as "Tacitus" in the next world. Dr. Firth informed me later that Tovey had studied Tacitus at University; the reference to the name, I reflected, could have been an indirect way of revealing that he recalled his University studies.

Occasionally, Tovey will communicate in epigrams or very tersely. While the discussion was under way at the College of Psychic Science, he appeared to be noting all that was taking place. Suddenly he remarked to me that "Genius is the most effective channel for the Creative Source", and when I passed this remark on to Sir George Trevelyan there and then, we were struck by its originality and its intepretation of the nature of genius. At the time, the discussion had turned to the question of genius, which drew Tovey's apt analysis.

Some wit – or dimwit might be more appropriate – on hearing that I believed myself to be in contact with composers of the past who were transmitting new music to me, suggested that Tovey was at the bottom of it all, and perpetrating a huge joke at our expense. This brought the following response from Tovey, on the 5th June, 1968.

"Far be it for me to lead you up the garden path, however lovely the garden. We, too, have our 'spoofers' over here on the lower levels, but you can be sure that I will shut the door firmly against such intruders. When on earth, I could readily detect the musical and social spoofers, or so I congratulated myself, and I was sometimes amused by their inane antics! Here, it is even easier to detect these types, and deal with them according to their deserts.

"Our earth channel" (referring to me) "is constantly on the watch herself for the deceiver and the self-deceiver, and we try to guard her when she is unaware of the imposition and interference of misleading (although not necessarily destructive) influences."

Tovey continued, addressing himself directly to Dr. Firth:

"Now, dear sir, how can we best express our appreciation of your

114

trust and assistance? We can do this most truly by responding with a concentration of our contact and communication. Speech is limiting; there are ideas we wish to convey which are difficult to clothe in words. We range in ranks from the immature souls to the highest developed ones who are consciously and constantly in the presence of God. From the heights the Light streams down, entering into the souls of all receptive to its Power; this Light is an energy-force, a life-essence, which is very real and factual. We need energy to communicate with you; we need to harness and direct it; you need to learn to receive it without distortion or oscillation. The human mind is such that it interprets all things according to its own scope of understanding."

Later in June, Tovey spoke at some length about the Other World view of our world. Here is an extract:

"Mankind as a whole has been isolated from the Godhead as a result of its folly and selfishness; but a time has come when it is no longer prudent to leave Humanity to its chaotic thoughts and violent emotions; it has had, as it were, enough rope to hang itself, and has almost succeeded in so doing. Time now to call a halt and assist Humanity to re-orientate its outlook before it is lost for ever. These, you will say, are words of grave portent, but we do not speak idly. There is growing concern over here regarding the present state of your world which appears to us to be growing *less* civilised. It would be easy for us to turn our backs and leave Humanity to its own ends, but so many innocent ones suffer and so many cry out for help that we would have to be deaf indeed not to hear.

"One of the greatest sins on earth by far is the *laissez-faire* practice; the other extreme is the over-officiousness which spells interference with the rights of the individual. True, the individual cannot be upheld to the detriment of the masses, but to sink individuality into a morass of herd consciousness (we should, perhaps, say unconsciousness) is the beginning of the end. Those who indulge in the repression of the individual are sometimes groping blindly towards a class of communal consciousness in which all become one by virtue of their unification with the Great Common Factor – I come back again to the mathematical systems, always fascinating to me, and often the most logical demonstration of the Life Everlasting."

Tovey told me one day that he would like to write a book and dictate it to me if that were possible. It was a fascinating idea, but one that so far has not been possible to accomplish owing to the

115

many demands made on my time in other directions. There is so much to do – running the home, attending to correspondence, taking down new compositions from various "dead" composers, having to give some interviews and do some broadcasting and filming, trying to cope with the endless demands on me. There is rarely time for me to practise at the piano, although I need to desperately for the occasional public performance which is required. I do not think anyone would envy me my lot if they realised the long, tedious hours of hard work that is involved, coupled with the continual buffetting by sceptics who can be very hostile.

I do have quite a lot of material from Tovey which could be used in a book when and if time permits. He gave me a foreword on the 13th March 1969, intended to preface his book which he said would be on the subject of Immortality. Here is the foreword, announcing his intentions:

"Read this, and you may be none the wiser. You may already know most of that which is set forth in these pages, but I guarantee that even the most knowledgeable person will glean from herein a few new ideas, if not facts. At least it shall be, if my intentions are fulfilled, a book which holds the attention of even the most blasé peruser and the most kangaroo-like skimmer. I shall sweeten it with lovely thoughts, spice it with wit, colour it with humour, heighten it with drama, and, not least, ornament it with such learning as I have gathered throughout my time.

"I came to the decision to write this book, as come many of my decisions, slowly, ponderously, yet with a growing certainty that it must be created to my satisfaction were it to be created at all. I never was one for half-measures, nor am I now that I am in a non-material world. If I am blunt at times, this is due to my desire to be quite clear in my statements so that there need be no quibbling over my meaning; at the same time, I have no wish to offend any section of the public. If offence is given, it is accidental and accompanied by my profound apologies for not having the good sense nor the good grace to expound my experiences and views in a more congenial context. This sounds as if I anticipate trouble, and suspect that I may give cause for it in that which follows. I hope for no trouble, but long, and sometimes painful, experience has taught me that in a dense population of varying types of people, there lurk the inevitable trouble-makers, the fussy fault-finders, the caustic critics, and the tortuous twisters of words. To these sundry stirrers, I can only proffer my condolences for their being the unfortunate victims of

116

some kind of warped inner sense which compels them to indulge in such destructive practices.

"To all those who give my book a fair hearing, or reading, may there come some bright revelations to cheer them through the rest of their earthly lives, and help to conduct them serenely through the experience of physical death into immortality."

The announcement by Tovey that he wished to write a book about Immortality could also have been his way of imparting further evidence of his identity. For when I wrote to Dr. Firth and told him of this development, he wrote back to say that it seemed to him as if Tovey was harking back to his University days when he wrote a thesis on "Immortality". I found that Tovey did not often speak of himself, but of his many and varied interests, and sometimes about music. He was often humorous, so that I would find his presence not only invigorating on account of his cultured, fine, mind, but amusing and cheering.

Tovey's humour never took the form of getting a laugh in an unkind way at someone's expense, although he showed that he could see much that is comical in human nature. One day, after I had been set upon by a lady who seemed to believe that she alone had access to heavenly wisdom, Tovey came to console me for the personal attack she had made on me in connection with my work.

"Poor, dear, Mrs. X," he declaimed, "She trots round dispensing truth like ice-cream, and like ice-cream, it just melts away."

Once I had been working with Tovey for about three hours, concentrating hard as he spoke, in the effort to hear him distinctly and get his words down correctly on paper. It is no easy process, often like straining to catch someone's conversation on a bad telephone line. Tovey saw I was tiring, and decided to give me a break.

"Take a rest," he said, "I will retire to gather fresh blossoms of wisdom from the Elysian Fields."

His words conjured up a vision in my mind of the broad form of Tovey tripping lightly through some heavenly meadow as he plucked flowers in a carefree mood – which was, perhaps, the very vision he wanted to create in order to relieve the heaviness of my brain-fag.

In September of 1968, he dictated a little homily on the path to truth which may seem surprising on first examination because of his reference to the importance of what he calls "the intuitional mind". Here it is abridged:

"The world at the present time can scarcely see God for 'isms' and 'ologies'. Until the Creator is placed first and foremost before

117

ideas, humanity is going to continue living in confusion and chaos.

"Man thinks he can think out the Truth – the Eternal Truth – with his brain; this is not so, as we speedily discover upon entering the Life after Death. Man's brain, when wisely employed, can perform many noble and useful tasks, but it is solely through his higher mental powers, the intuitional mind of the God-self, that he can reach the Eternal Truth. This is plain fact, not a meaningless statement unsuitable for application to everyday life.

"It is reasonably clear that, had Man's brain been the instrument which could conduct him to the Truth, he would have reached it long ago; for Man has sought for centuries – nay, for thousands of years to gain access to the Truth. His brain has helped him to understand many of the laws governing the material and physical planes, and given him a little insight into the psychology of the individual; but nowhere along the line of evolution has it brought much light to bear upon the nature and function of God, or revealed much concerning Man's soul or immortal self.

"It can be deduced that the brain is not constructed in such a manner as to be capable, on its own, of penetrating into the inner and less tangible planes. Yet Man, in his pride of intellect, sometimes believes that spiritual enlightenment can come only through the expansion of his intellect.

"Now I would lead you along a different path conducting you to levels of consciousness which, although linked to the intellect in many cases, by far transcend the powers of perception of the physical brain. To avoid confusion, we refer to the intellect of the body as the brain, and to the higher mental faculty as the mind. The brain perishes with the phsyical body, but we have demonstrated our continued powers of thought and imagination and recollection after we have vacated our physical bodies. This shows that immortal Man functions independently of the physical brain, and that he possesses ethereal organs which are imperishable and continue to operate after physical death. It is reassuring to know that we can continue to expand in consciousness after we have left the earth plane, and extend our development beyond the limits it had reached during our earth life.

"As with all organs or faculties, neglect of the higher mental faculty or mind or intuition, call it what you will, brings about a state of atrophy. Mankind as a whole has for so long neglected or ignored this faculty that it has fallen into gross disuse; indeed, as often as not, he is not even aware of its existence, and may even strenuously deny it.

118

"Part of our task from our celestial realm is to foster an awareness of this faculty and to encourage its resuscitation. To impart the knowledge which can teach Man to use this dormant faculty will be a lengthy and delicate task; we need to provide examples of the working of this faculty to give a glimpse of the magnificent achievements which lie ahead in this field for those who will devote themselves to the cultivation of the higher mental powers. We are endeavouring to use many channels to indicate the scope of these powers, and to give the parapsychologists openings into the investigation of their functions. Our endeavours often have to be sustained in the face of blind disbelief: blind, indeed, for there are none so blind as those who will not see. We are striving to eliminate errors and misunderstandings in transmission, which are sometimes caused by factors on our level and at other times by conditions surrounding your world or the channels we select. Until effective apparatus has been invented and constructed in your world to receive our transmissions, we have to rely on human channels with all their variability."

CHAPTER 12

Tovey's commandments for musicians

One of the longest communications to come from Tovey was a set of essays which he entitled, "Ten Commandments for Musicians."

These essays may offer interesting reading to musicians and to non-musicians, so I include them here in an abridged version. I believe these commandments are intended to be taken quite seriously in spite of the suspicion that Tovey speaks at times with his tongue in his cheek.

"1. The first and obvious law regarding music is the necessity for absolute single-mindedness in its pursuit. This does not mean that you should not follow other interests currently: these are also a necessity to lend relief between periods of concentration, and to enrich one's mind in other respects, enabling one to bring to bear upon music itself a greater measure of mature judgement, keener awareness of its values, and deeper appreciation of its beauties of structure and sound.

"I say unto you that if you intend to be a full-blooded Musician, you must give your all to music, your whole self, loving it with all your heart as ardently as a young swain loves his first sweetheart, probing it with all your mind as meticulously as a biologist dissecting the object of his study; and, above all, worshipping it with all your soul in its highest expressions which are like unto the mighty tongues of angels speaking, the dulcet voices of heavenly choristers, the veritable echoes of the majestic tones of the Almighty.

"My love of music is profound, and I listen to it not only with my ears, but also with heart and mind and soul. I find all things in it, enough to satisfy the musician in me, the scientist in me, the dreamer in me, and the pilgrim and seeker in me; it satisfies every facet of my being. In no other subject can I discover all in all; it is complete, yet many-sided; whole yet divisable; speaking one language yet rich in many dialects. It can soothe a fevered brow with a touch of infinite balm, as the old song says; it can comfort a saddened heart, and assuage fear and anxiety; it can cheer the desolate, rouse the lethargic, quieten the violent, heal the sick, and uplift us into the very Presence of that Great Being we call God.

"A thing of such wealth and wonder indeed merits our attention; and the reward for our attention is endless and increasing joy, new raptures of sound, and fresh marvels of its inherent architecture. I am extolling that which I personally term music in which I do not include all the latest hotchpotch of noises masquerading under that name. This brings me to the second commandment:

"2. Thou shalt not make false images of music and bow down before them or before those who begat them.

"Many are fooled nowadays by a strange species of current snobbery into accepting almost any new noise as music. Where, oh where, is thy discrimination, oh generation of deceivers and deceived? How many, puffed up with conceit at their own vain imaginings, describe themselves as composers: of what are they composers indeed? We can all compose something in sound and produce some noise: the child clanging upon a tin drum; the older child strumming on a guitar; even the old crone crooning away with cracked voice; it is conceivable that they all form a new series of sounds or compositions. But a clutter of sounds does not make music, and a multitude of notes upon the musical staves, like a flock of starlings on telegraph wires, frequently produces only noise of a most unpleasing nature. A composition does not automatically guarantee music unless the composer is creating not only with his brain, but also with that mysterious part of himself or herself which is the mind of the soul as distinct from the mind of the body. I hold the belief that all musicians of true insight will know exactly what I mean. True music comes not from the stuff of your world, but from the stuff of heaven and from the angelic realms, and at times betokens a quality which fires the soul with splendour and kindles the spark divine within the human breast.

"3. Speaking of the third commandment in relation to music, this is to be illustrated by quoting the parable of casting pearls before swine. In other words, it is wise (if you desire a successful event and good ovation) to assure as far as possible that any programme of music drawn up for presentation to the public shall be calculated to call forth their appreciation at whatever level they are equipped to respond. Never think to take upon yourself the rôle of a messiah whose mission it is to convert the heathen to worship what you deem to be good music. We have to remember at all times that one man's meat is another man's poison, and that that which makes good listening to one person can be quite unpalatable to another.

"Try to assess your audiences' likely tastes and ability to absorb various types and styles of music; give them something they can feast upon with delight, a banquet not so rich as to cause musical indigestion, nor so frugal as to foster under-nourishment. It is equally harmful to over-eat as to starve, and this applies to music no less than to food.

"You will indeed take the name of music in vain if you insist upon delivering a programme which is totally unattractive to your listeners. Usually they have paid good money for their listening experience, and are therefore entitled to obtain some value for their ticket. If their ideas of value differ from yours, this does not give you the right to foist upon them your own particular standards, no matter how right they seem to you.

"Introduce with the greatest care and in minute doses any brand of music the reception of which is doubtful: that is, if you wish to preserve the pearl untrampled for those who will know its true value. If you fear not to have the pearls trampled underfoot, nor to be turned upon and rent, then you may boldly experiment and risk the outcome.

"4. We proceed to the fourth commandment. It is my solemn opinion that all persons, whether makers of music or listeners thereto, should have intervals of absolute abstinence from music of any kind. Never to give oneself a rest from indulgence in music may well blunt one's senses and detract from the quickness of one's responses. I know that many will disagree with me, and tell me they can never tire of music or have too much of it, but, as Beethoven proclaims, music is composed not only of the notes produced, but also of the silences intervening; a subtle stillness between sounds, or the flagrant and dramatic pauses between passages. We can truly appreciate things by contrast; we can the more easily know light by its opposite, darkness; we can best savour food by the intervals between meals; we can only soar to the heights of joy by plumbing the depths of sorrow.

"Let us bear this well in mind, and grant ourselves a complete rest periodically from all listening and partaking in music. We will then find our musical appetites sharpened, our ears rested, our minds renewed with zest for fresh contact with music. We need a holiday from music, a Sabbath, in a manner of speaking, in order to keep ourselves really fresh for it. Over-rehearsing without any break may make the performer stale and defeat his or her end: namely, to attain perfection; and over-indulgence in listening may similarly make the appetite sicken and die, or at least, take the edge off it.

"So remember the Sabbath and observe it in appropriate measure towards music.

"5. The fifth commandment in the Bible exhorts us to honour our fathers and our mothers. In relation to music, who can we regard as the father and who the mother? Each musical work requires two sources to create it:

(a). The score supplied by the composer, the mother, let us say, who conceives and brings forth the child.

(b). The performer or performers who unite with the score to produce the offspring in audible form. Thus the performers signify the active, outgoing, male principle.

"Until a work is performed, it lies virtually dormant in the score. There are those who, like myself, can happily dispense with an actual performance of a work, and extract its essence like a bee sucking the nectar from a flower, by merely reading the score in question. This visual grasp gives birth to an inaudible yet realistic sound. Most people, however, need a full-scale delivery.

"We should honour, therefore, not only the composer (though doubtless he or she should receive the initial and greater part of the honour since without his or her creativity there would be nothing to acclaim), but also the fine interpreter who gives a faithful rendering of the composer's ideas.

"These, then, we can regard as the parents of the music world. The more closely identified the performer is with the composer in understanding, and the more completely consummated the composition and the performance in aesthetic marriage, so in accordance is the issue a beautiful and perfectly formed creation, and a true reproduction of the composer's conception.

"6. The sixth commandment says, 'Thou shalt not kill'. It is all to easy to kill a musical work by giving a bad performance either through lack of attention to the composer's intentions or through inadequate rehearsal. Truly it lies in the hands of the performer to make or mar a piece; I speak of those persons who have acquired ample technique to enable them to render a good interpretation through intelligent study of the score concerned, coupled with careful practice.

"The standard of playing at present, especially in pianoforte, is remarkably high, due partly to keen competition in the working musical world, and partly to a wider and deeper appreciation of music in general.

"There is still much unnecessary waste of talent because full training is not always made available to the latent virtuoso or composer. Many gifted persons are swept aside by those who have financial or influential advantages; many more fall victim to the sheer obligation of finding a reliable means of securing a livelihood.

"Music, I aver, is a necessity, not a luxury, as I will expound in a later commandment. So, on the musical path, as well as in all walks of life, let us not allow a budding talent to be blighted and lose the glory of the full bloom; neither let us wantonly nor carelessly bamage or destroy meritorious creations, since such are comparatively rare.

"7. The next commandment, 'Thou shalt not commit adultery', links with the previous one. A poor performance can adulterate a musical work; can spoil the untouched beauty which the composer intended to convey; can cloud the pure vision which was meant to be imparted. The aim must be to give the finest possible performance under the finest possible conditions, in order to demonstrate true musical integrity.

"There is another, more subtle form of adultery committed by serious students of music: that which occurs when the aspiring composer or performer dallies with distracting diversions to such an extent and in such a manner as to ruin his or her proposed partnership with music by sheer lack of fidelity. There must be other interests and other activities, as I have asserted elsewhere, but one who aims to be a composer or performer of the first water must grant music the first fealty. Those who are not prepared to devote full allegiance to the cause of music would, if sensible, become non-starters unless they intend it to be solely a hobby.

"When musical interpretation is prostituted to technique or vice versa, this is tantamount to an adulteration; there should be a fine balance between the two as in a perfect marriage where both parties give equal delight to each other, and fully observe each other's rights. By wedding a superb technique to a sensitive interpretation, we have a thing of beauty, the specific brain-child of the composer being delivered true to life.

"8. 'Thou shalt not steal,' states the eighth commandment. Possibly this is the worst crime of all. One breaks the sixth commandment,

124

through destroying a life by murder or neglect; one is at the same time stealing a life in a sense, thereby breaking two commandments simultaneously. One can steal others' goods or property, or their rights, or even their health by acting in a manner that is detrimental to it. To take away others' peace of mind or ruin their happiness is also stealing something from them.

"Composers often borrow from each other openly or by stealth; where to draw the line between flattering imitation and actual brazen theft is difficult. Motives and subsequent handling of the musical material borrowed may possibly decide the moral aspect.

"Liszt was well known for giving his own interpretations and transcriptions of other composers' work. Frequently (I concede this somewhat begrudgingly) he produced finer effects than the composer had in the first place, and this sometimes assisted to establish the composer in question, enhancing his musical reputation and perpetuating lasting fame. Liszt's motives were no doubt varied; often, as he would admit, he poured out these transcriptions to exhibit his own supreme mastery of extemporization and pianistic technique; but, more often than not, he performed these feats in open admiration of the composer involved.

"Those who deliberately pick another's brain, and try to pass off the material extracted as their own work are both thieves and deceivers; fortunately, they are in the minority, and are unlikely to pull off their schemes very successfully. To offer a new presentation as a tribute to the originator is another matter, and an exemplary effort if well carried out.

"This brings me to the subject of Rosemary Brown's unusual task. This is not an attempt on her part, either consciously or unconsciously, to create transcriptions of old works or to produce what has sometimes been given the misnomer of 'pastiche': she is, indeed, completely incapable of achieving an imitation of old compositions, both through lack of training and knowledge and lack of any personal flair. Her work does not comprise of a borrowing from music of the past, but is a flow of genuine new inspiration from the composers co-operating with her. We are glad that there are some musicologists who are discerning enough and courageous enough to pronounce their opinions that the music flowing from Rosemary Brown's pen carries a ring of authenticity. We do see that she is not always able to receive full transmission, and that there happens at times to be a blurring of the fine edges: but, with constant application, her capacity to receive accurately and at greater length is increasing. We

125

are frankly amazed that she has accomplished so much under our guidance, and this fires us with enthusiasm to carry the work to greater heights, expressing ourselves in more complicated and advanced works. But I digress, so onwards to the next commandment which tells us that we must not bear false witness against our neighbour.

"9. This commandment I would refer largely to music critics, since this essay is an adaptation of the ten commandments to music. We understand that musical criticism is the critics' chosen means of livelihood in many instances, as much their bread-and-butter as the road-sweeper's equally necessary, or even more necessary, job. But alas and alack, some of these gentlemen occasionally abuse the power with which they are entrusted, and deliberately mislead the public. When they write an account which expresses their honest opinion, however warped that may be, there can be no question but that they have followed their calling faithfully according to their own standards. They will protest that they are only doing their job, even if personal issues are at stake and reputations lost by their reports. If a man's engagements are curtailed and his wife and family suffer through the ensuing loss of earnings because he was given a devastating review, the critic may claim that he is not morally responsible for this catastrophe. What is so often forgotten is that the criticism merely represents one man's opinion which can be very far from a proper assessment of its victim. We have only to examine various derogatory criticisms uttered in the past about composers and artists who have since become highly successful and highly acclaimed to see just how wrong the critics can be. If their criticism was an error of judgement, we must draw the conclusion that they may not be sufficiently qualified for the function of critic. If, however, they have allowed their criticism to be coloured by prejudice, they are guilty of a betrayal of moral principle, and have surrendered their integrity by their wilful misrepresentation.

"It is laudable that most critics take a pride in their work, and that honour is, on the whole, maintained. There can be a temptation for the critic to play God and expect his word to be taken as final, or for him to grind an axe of his own. The critic bears a great responsibility towards composers, performers, and the public in general. To be a true critic, he must do justice to all three bodies; if he tempers his justice with mercy, then we are blessed with a critic who is not only downright but also upright.

"10. We come to the tenth commandment which exhorts us not to

126

covet. This is the last commandment in the Bible, but I could invent more than a few further commandments for musicians which would most probably prove tedious or even aggravating. I am aware by now that I can be over-fastidious in my expectations from students and professionals, so I will confine myself to the same number as the Old Testament.

"Music, as I claimed earlier, is to my mind not simply a luxury but a pressing necessity in the noisy, discordant world as a means of restoring some harmony and beauty. It is becoming apparent that music possesses great potentialities to heal the sick of body, and more especially the sick of mind or of heart – speaking here not of the heart as the physical organ, but as the vehicle of the emotions. Music of an appropriate kind may relieve or even mend the broken conditions existing in some people's inner beings.

"Now, what, you may ask, has all this to do with convetousness? If you look around the world today, you will see that a large proportion of the suffering that exists is the result of covetousness on the part of certain people. There is a continual covetting of the property or possessions of others, or of their state, or of their position, or of their income, and so *ad infinitum*. Covetousness causes misery to those who covet for a covetous person cannot be a happy person. It can also cause suffering to those towards whom the covetousness is aimed, since it is liable to result in friction, strife, and even violence.

"The old, outworn precept that people (especially those in lowly circumstances, note you) should accept their lot, and know their station, and so forth, I hold with not at all. I believe that people have a right to improve their lot as far as possible providing that in so doing they are not harming others. There was a time when music was almost solely the prerogative of the rich, when only the rich could afford to indulge in the hire of musicians. How fortunate that the masses now have far more access to music by virtue of the introduction of broadcasting, and through the invention of various recording instruments. Even those who are infirm and confined to their own homes or to institutions may be able to enjoy listening to music as freely as more mobile persons.

"Music is something which can be shared by millions, and unite people from all walks of life in a common interest. It loses nothing by being shared, therefore one need not fear that a fellow-listener will take more than his fair share: the music flows freely on the sound-waves without favouring a single member of the audience. It is impartial; it is democratic if we like to regard it in that sense. It does

127

not make a different sound for a peer or a commoner, as many sycophants and snobs are guilty of doing. It harbours no discrimination, knowing no barriers of language, nationality, class, belief, rank, age, or sex. Bestowing itself equally upon all who can and will listen, it contains the essence of brotherhood, and speaks in a universal language. Beethoven must have realised this when he wrote his great choral symphony: '*Oh ye millions, I embrace thee!*'

Let me end by paying tribute to music, and giving thanks to the Creator without whose beneficience there would be not one single note."

CHAPTER 13

Shades of Shaw and Shakespeare

Amongst my ghostly visitors there arrived one day a tall, thin, bearded gentleman with carrot-coloured hair and sharp blue eyes. He told me that he was George Bernard Shaw.

"Prove it if you can," was my prompt response, thinking that there are probably dozens of spirits resembling Shaw.

"You will have to take me at my word," he retorted.

"As for the rest of the world, even if I appeared to them in person some would say that I was a hallucination and others would say I was the devil, no doubt."

Could be Shaw, I thought. Certainly looked like the newspaper pictures of him. The only way to try to find out if it were actually Shaw was to engage him in further conversation, so I tackled him with another question.

"Why have you come to see me?"

"I know that you are writing a book, lady, and it is my plan to add to the interest of that book."

Naturally, I welcomed the idea of having a contribution from Shaw. I was wondering whether "lady" could be regarded as a compliment or whether he was being patronising, when I realised he was speaking again.

"Never thought I would be a ghost-writer, least of all in this sense."

I don't expect he thought he would ever be a ghost, I reflected.

"There are comments I wish to make on the world situation," he informed me, "And a short play, a condensed version of a much longer one, that I will dictate for your pen."

I prepared myself to listen attentively. Shaw placed his hands behind his back, threw his head up slightly, and began.

"The title of the play is 'Caesar's Revenge,' and the characters are

129

taken from Shakespeare. Are you ready?" he asked, suddenly shooting a piercing glance at me.

"Yes, I'm ready. Go ahead, and I'll do my best to follow you," I promised: (During the sessions that followed, he sometimes used the present tense, sometimes the past, but for consistency I have mainly used the past tense.)

Act one, scene one, he announced, was set in one of the lower grades of the Hereafter, one which is rather like a kindergarten: a place where immature souls remain until they have evolved sufficiently to move up to a more advanced grade. Two characters take part in this scene; Brutus and Calphurnia. But let me quote the adapted version given to me:

Brutus was in a very thoughtful mood that fateful day. There he was, resting in the Elysian Fields whilst Calphurnia sat beside him, twining the heavenly daisies into garlands, when he suddenly made up his mind.

"Calphurnia", he addressed her. Then he stopped, wondering how she would react to his decision.

"Yes?" she inquired idly, her attention still on her daisy-chains.

"I've decided to go back to earth," he blurted out.

"What?" shrieked Calphurnia, dropping her daisies, "Go back to *that* place? You must be mad."

"Didn't think you would approve," muttered Brutus.

"It is not a question of approval," retorted Calphurnia somewhat icily, "Just that I can't think what gave you such a stupid idea."

"Well, you see, I'd like a bit of action or something of a challenge," he explained, "Everything is rather dull here."

"That's your own fault, Brute," she said sharply. She always called him "Brute" when she was annoyed.

"You could make your life much more interesting here if you made the effort," she continued, "You are far too lazy, that's all."

Brutus frowned. He hated being called lazy, perhaps because he knew it was perfectly true.

"All right, so I'm lazy," he admitted, "All the more reason for me to go to a place where I can't be lazy. Anyway, we've been here for so long, must be hundreds of years."

"Oh, Brutus dear, don't go," cajoled Calphurnia, changing her tone, "Please don't go. Think how lonely I'll be here without you."

"But I would not be gone for ever. Even a long life on earth is a

130

mere moment out of eternity. And you have plenty of friends to keep you company. I dare say old Julius would be glad that I'm away for a while, too."

"Bet that is why you want to go," commented Calphurnia.

"What do you mean?"

"You know how he annoys you by dropping in to see you every so often, and harping on about the way you murdered him."

"Well, it's enough to get on anyone's nerves. After all, I have apologised to the chap, and it was all so long ago. You would think he would try to forget it now."

"He would have forgiven you if it had really been patriotism that made you listen to that smooth-tongued Cassius, but you know very well that when he got here, he soon found out that you fancied me, and wanted to get him conveniently out of the way."

"You fancied me, too, don't forget. You must have been sick of being tied to that physical weakling who was incapable of making love to you, and tried to kid the populace that you were barren."

"Yes, he was a real bore – and still is; that's why I don't want you to go. It would be simply awful stuck here with him gloating because you had left me."

"Darling, I would not be leaving you, only going off for a little adventure. You can watch over me if you like, and try to send me a few heavenly messages now and then. You might be able to tip me off about things I ought to know while I'm on earth."

"That's just like a man, always thinking of himself, and making use of a woman in any way he can! I can sit here, pouring out sweet nothings that you will probably never be able to hear, whilst you gallivant around on earth forgetting all about me. Oh, how could you! You brute!"

"Don't get cross, darling. You know I love you. It's just that I want a change."

"All right. Go and have your change. Go back to earth. And if you think I'm going to sit here meekly watching over you, you are mistaken."

"What do you mean by that?"

"If you are going, so am I. You don't think I'm going to let you go there alone, do you? And very likely find some other woman in my place? Besides, if you are not here, Cassius might pester me – you know that he seems to be getting tired of his male cronies. I could not bear it if he turned his attentions to me which he might decide to do if you're not here to protect me."

"You could soon choke him off. You're very good at turning the cold shoulder when you want to, you know."

"I don't believe you want me to come with you!"

"It's not that, darling. Just that I don't want you to have the awful bother of going through all the red tape and filling in all those application forms to get an earthly passport. You know you hate all the tedious rigmarole of officialdom. You didn't enjoy your last visit to earth at all, so why go again?"

"The same applies to you, Brutus dear. Remember how tormented you felt after helping to do Julius in? And what a nuisance Portia was with her injured party act when you wanted to come and live with me? And how guilty you felt when she took her own life because she became so demented over the whole affair? Then when you found out that Cassius was just playing you along for his own ends, you became so bitter that you were simply impossible."

Brutus groaned.

"Let's forget all that. Perhaps this time it will be different. After all, things have changed a lot on earth now there is all that permissiveness. No end of men and women live together without marrying. Even Cassius would be more tolerated – they have actually passed a law to legalise his kind of indulgences providing they are practised in private."

"I think that is terrible. And there are still assassinations and murders taking place. Think of all those ghastly bombs they make nowadays, and the horrible wars they keep having. Really they haven't advanced much in some ways. Human nature is still the same. Oh, Brutus, they might make you fight in one of their wretched battles, and you could get killed."

"If I got killed, I'd be zoned back here, wouldn't I? So that would end all right because I would be back with you."

"Worse than that, you might be frightfully maimed and have to live for years like a mutilated cabbage. I couldn't bear that, Brutus dearest. Don't go, for goodness' sake, for my sake. It can't be any fun there. Let's try to brighten things up here instead."

"How can we, Calphurnia? You know we don't qualify for the Realm of Eternal Bliss or even the Secondary Plane of Semi-Permanent Heavenly Joy. We cannot escape our consciences until we have purged our souls, and we cannot purge them until we have achieved something to make up for our misdoings. Really we are in a vicious circle here, one we have created ourselves. Our surroundings are quite beautiful, I know; but we are imprisoned with the memories of our mistakes, even if we had good intentions when we made those

132

mistakes. I must find something to take me out of myself. Something to help me find God. He must be here somewhere. It's so tantalising; here we are on the threshold of real Paradise, but never able to gain entry because our passports aren't quite in order. I must do something about it."

There was a faint fanfare of distant trumpets.

"Hark at that!" exclaimed Calphurnia, "Every time you mention God, those trumpets sound a fanfare. They must know when we talk about Him. Sometimes I wish I could meet Him, but, of course, we have cut ourselves off from Him. It isn't really unpleasant here, Brutus, but it does get dull at times, I must admit. Feeling shut out from the Heavenly Presence is so miserable, and it is rotten not being able to visit some of our best friends because they were drafted to higher planes than this. I know they come to see us now and then, but it is quite humiliating to think we can't visit their homes, even if they invite us. This one little heavenly meadow we were allotted is so small it becomes claustrophobic. But remember, Brutus, we can do what we like here, although it is so confined."

"That is just it. I want to move around, to go to other places, to do new things instead of dallying here century after century. Can't you understand, darling? Don't you ever feel the same?"

"I suppose I do, to be honest. But our only alternative is to return to earth, and I don't want to do that." Calphurnia sighed.

"If we did go . . ." mused Brutus.

'Well?"

"And we lived really good lives, never hurting anybody else, we might earn the right to go to the Fields of Divine Expansion where you have plenty of scope to develop. I've heard it is very interesting there. Or, if we tried really hard, we might be given permits to enter the Halls of Sublime Meditation."

"Huh! I would not want to go there. It must be even more boring than here, sitting for ages in contemplation."

"Cinna, the poet, says he has been there, and that he found it very peaceful and beautiful. He wrote a sonnet about it: now, how did it go?

> *Temple of peace where light enfolds the soul*
> *With iridescent, softly-shining wings:*
> *'Tis here eternal bliss puts time to flight,*
> *And inner harmony resolves all things.*

"Oh, I expect it is a marvellous place for poets and dreamers,"

133

interrupted Calphurnia, "But I don't think it would suit you at all. You know you can't bear to sit still for long. You don't like thinking very much, either, and they must be practising some form of thinking there."

"Cinna said it is not like that at all. They don't *think*; they just empty their minds and let the Supreme Peace fill them."

"You ought not to have any trouble doing that," teased Calphurnia, "Your mind is empty most of the time."

"If you are going to be rude, I'm leaving", Brutus announced with an air of offended dignity.

"Oh, my pet, don't be offended. I didn't mean to be rude, really. But you can be scatter-brained, and I adore you when you are like that, just like a happy-go-lucky schoolboy. That was one of your main attractions for me. Old Julius was such a blue-stocking, so formidably clever, and always so serious. The moment I first saw you, so manly, so strong, and heard you roaring with great gusts of laughter at some joke, I fell madly in love with you. Julius couldn't laugh if he tried; he never seemed to see the funny side of anything."

Brutus had suddenly fallen silent.

"What's the matter, darling? Have I said something you don't like?" asked Calphurnia.

"No. A horrible thought has just struck me. Suppose I make a hash of my life on earth, and finish up worse than I began? I might be sent to the Regions for Reformation when I leave earth!"

"But you would *not* make a hash of it, because you intend to live a good life, don't you?"

"Of course I do. But I'm afraid that once I get to earth, I might forget that, and get carried away by all the temptations and pitfalls. Suppose someone like Cassius came into my life with a devious plan which involved me –"

"Oh, Brutus, I'm sure you wouldn't let anyone talk you into anything rash again, not after that experience with Cassius."

"No, I don't think I would, but sometimes I am haunted by Cassius's own words: 'Who so firm that cannot be seduced?' That makes me feel unsure of myself."

"Just before you are born again, tell yourself firmly that you will not be led astray again," counselled Calphurnia, "The mind doctors here believe that what you determine in your thoughts immediately before you go off to earth imprints itself in the prenatal cipher and is set to trigger off a subconscious memory reaction."

"I only hope those mind doctors are right. They don't know much

134

yet about the connecting links between this dimension and the earth dimensions."

"Perhaps if you waited a few years, by then they might have found how to bounce the memory beams down into earth consciousness. Then you would be quite sure to remember."

"But it might be ages before they discover that, and we can't be sure they will ever find a way."

"There must be some way. After all, a lot of people here manage to communicate with people on the earth, don't they? Remember Lucius said that when he was playing at a Celestial Concert not long ago, someone in the orchestra told him that Saint Cecilia herself was sponsoring experiments to transmit music to the earth? Very difficult, naturally, what with all the harsh vibrations of the world, and the muffling effects of matter."

"Yes, I remember. And I heard that Sophia the prophetess predicts a major breakthrough before very long when the earth's atmosphere becomes less dense after some new Cosmic Ray is concentrated on it."

"Sophia could be right. Our scientists are working hard to find foolproof ways of communicating with people on the earth. When we can communicate more easily we will be able to warn people that they will find themselves in the Wastelands here if they waste or misuse their lives on earth. But communication is still so far from being perfected, so much a case of hit and miss. . . ."

"It doesn't help that we are having to do all the donkey work over here. If only the people on earth would make more effort to build communications with us," interrupted Calphurnia.

"Well, they are handicapped on account of opposition from misguided people who think it is wrong to attempt communication. They don't think it wrong to telephone a relative at the other end of the world; they don't think it is wrong to communicate by radio or television; but they think it is wrong to get in touch with us. So illogical, human beings."

"They will become more logical as they evolve, I expect. And we will become more logical, too, won't we, Brutus?"

"I thought I was being logical when I was in the world. But now I can see that I wasn't really logical at all. Emotions get in the way; situations develop that are so involved that logic is clouded by conflicting issues and loyalties. If logic were a simple thing that everyone could understand and apply, I'm certain the world would not be in such chaos."

"It seems to get worse there every day. Why go there, Brutus? There is so much turmoil and unrest, and far more violence than there was in our time."

"I know. But if that is the only way to make progress, I had better take the plunge. Here comes Cassius. I wish he would keep away. Every time he appears, it reminds me of my misdeeds."

Cassius drew near to them, then struck a dramatic pose and began reciting:

"What is this rumour that I hear, breathed soft upon the heavenly air, that one named Marcus Brutus seeks earthward to fly from out our midst? What hope has he upon the earth the clamour of conscience to escape? Will not the ghost of Caesar still cause his quaking soul to gape? For Caesar will his soul pursue and never let him cease to rue that evil day and evil deed that made the mighty Caesar bleed."

"Go away, you beastly little man!" cried Calphurnia "It was really you who murdered Caesar, anyway, you know that very well. You were cunning enough to get others to join in your dirty work, that's all. Go away, or I'll call Caesar at once."

"Ill words do not my feelings move, nor empty threats a danger prove. If thou call'st Caesar, then will I, quick as a flash, to Portia hie, and fetch her here to stay a term, with righteous wrath to make you squirm," countered Cassius.

"Be quiet!" shouted Brutus, "You're the one who should squirm, you worm."

"Ha! That's quite good: squirm and worm! I'll use that rhyme in my next verse," sniggered Cassius.

Brutus turned to Calphurnia.

"That settles it. I'm definitely going back to earth, if only to get away from Cassius."

Calphurnia wheeled on Cassius in fury.

"See what you have done! Driven Brutus out of here. Driven him back to earth."

"Such ire, your countenance becomes my dear, your fiery eyes my very soul would sear, were I susceptible to female wiles, and. . ."

"I'm not going to listen to any more," Calphurnia broke in, turning her back on Cassius.

"Neither am I," said Brutus.

"Let's go straight to Earth Passport Control and apply for World Re-entry," suggested Calphurnia.

"Right," agreed Brutus.

And off they went.

136

CHAPTER 14

Shaw thickens the plot

The second scene of Act I takes us back to the World of the Hereafter. Caesar was sitting twiddling his thumbs, and gazing thoughtfully into space. Cassius, who was seated nearby, knew better than to interrupt his train of thought. At length, Caesar spoke.

"So, Cassius, Brutus has decided to make an earthly come-back. Good of you to let me know because it has enabled me to make a few arrangements of my own. I may despise you, Cassius, but you do come in useful as news-carrier."

Cassius smirked ingratiatingly.

Caesar continued.

"I suppose you are trying to make good for inciting my erstwhile friends to kill me when we were on earth. If you really want to atone for your sins, you can do something for me."

"Anything you wish, noble Caesar," promised Cassius in slightly faltering tones.

"This is what I want you to do."

Caesar paused for a moment as if ruminating.

"That chap Brutus needs to learn a thing or two before he can graduate to the next plane. And so do you, of course, Cassius."

"Yes, yes!" agreed Cassius obsequiously.

"First go to Passport Check Office and substitute Brutus's papers for Calphurnia's. You will have to do it at the last minute before they are due for departure, so that there is no time for the substitution to be noticed by any official. Make an excuse that I, Julius Caesar, wished to have it confirmed that Brutus and Calphurnia are leaving at the same moment, but that I am too busy to see to it myself. Any details I require, or any confirmation I seek, cannot be denied me at Passport Check Office, since I have certain rights I can exercise over

137

both Brutus and Calphurnia until they have expurgated their debts to me."

"But, illustrious Caesar, that will mean Brutus will incarnate in Calphurnia's place, and vice versa."

"How discerning of you, Cassius. It is all part of a plan I have conceived to coerce them into discharging their debts. What is more, I have arranged for you to return to earth to clear your debt, also, and you can collect your own papers and documents which you will find waiting for you at the Passport Check Office together with a duly authorised passport."

"But I have not said I will go back to earth!" cried Cassius, horrified at the idea.

"You don't have much say in the matter, Cassius, since you forfeited your life to me when you brought about my death. I am claiming my right to over-rule you by having you returned to earth. Death in reverse, you might say, since to be born on earth is like dying to this world."

Cassius blanched, and opened his mouth as if to speak.

"No use protesting if that is what you were going to do. I have let you remain here in the World of Spirit for a long time, and given you plenty of opportunity to repay me for your crime. But you have made scarcely any effort to make reparation, so I have decided that you must go back to earth. It has all been agreed to by the Lords of Celestial Justice, and they have signed and sealed my application. It is useless to appeal for, as you know, no appeal is allowed to one who took another's life or deliberately caused it to be taken through motives such as yours."

"What sort of life is decreed for me?" queried Cassius with an apprehensive expression.

"You will see when you get there," answered Caesar tantalisingly. "Now, off you go. After all, it will be a relief to you to settle your debt to me, won't it? Farewell, Cassius. I shall be watching to see how you progress."

"I suppose I have no choice," said Cassius ruefully, "Oh, well, I'll be on my way, then. Farewell, Caesar."

Cassius left Caesar sitting on a heavenly hammock smiling to himself, and rubbing his hands in satisfaction.

The second act, first scene of *Caesar's Revenge* is set at the Launching Station for World Flight. Shaw continued with the story.

138

Calphurnia and Brutus sat side by side in the World Departure Lounge, waiting for the Angel Gabriel to sound the signal on his ceremonial trumpet for boarding.

They had been allotted all the necessary documents to permit them to return to earth, parents had been duly appointed, and all was arranged for their respective lives in which they were programmed to meet at an early age. As soon as the documents had been finally checked and given the seal of approval by the Frontier Guardian Angel, they would be on their way.

Two chariots, yoked to flying horses, stood ready to transport each of them. The horses pawed the heavenly pavement impatiently, eager to wing their way earthwards on the flight that could be watched by heavenly eyes but could not be seen by earthly eyes because their lightning speed rendered them invisible to the slower world vibrations.

"They are a long time with our documents," remarked Brutus, "I hope they find them all in order."

"Of course they are in order," Calphurnia reassured him, "But you know how slow officialdom can be, even in the heavenly spheres."

"We are due to leave in a few minutes by earth time. I do wish they would hurry."

"Don't worry," Calphurnia tried to calm him, "It will be all right. Oh, Brutus, I shan't see you for twenty years – twenty long earth years!"

"The time will soon pass, and they have arranged for you to have a very happy childhood and girlhood," said Brutus, "Besides, when we have crossed the River Lethe, we will forget everything until we pass back over it."

"I know. But that worries me a little. I don't want you to forget me, and I don't want to forget you."

"Calphurnia, remember, it is only the earthly part of us that will forget. Our souls will never forget."

"Yes, that's true. Oh, I'm getting nervous with the suspense of waiting."

"Time is getting very short. I can see Gabriel raising his trumpet to his lips to blow the farewell fanfare."

"Oh! Oh! Our chariots will take off without us. What shall we do?" wailed Calphurnia in dismay.

There was a sudden stir in the Passport Check Office as a clerk came bursting out, and rushed towards them with their documents.

"Hurry!" he urged, thrusting the documents into their outstretched

139

hands, "No time for the drivers to look at them before you leave. They must examine them *en route*."

Calphurnia and Brutus grabbed the documents, and ran towards the chariots.

"Farewell, Brutus, my love, until we meet again," called Calphurnia as she climbed into one of the chariots.

"Farewell, my darling. See you on earth," responded Brutus.

Tah-rah! Tah-rah! sounded Gabriel's trumpet. One blast for each chariot, thought Brutus resignedly. The drivers tugged the reins and SWOOSH! Off the chariots flew, shooting their way at a rate faster than anything that can be timed on earth.

Having set the horses on course, the drivers took the documents and began to peruse them carefully. By now, the two chariots were on widely diverging paths, one destined for London, the other heading for Dublin.

"Oh, lord!" Brutus's driver suddenly exclaimed, "I've got the wrong passenger."

"What!" cried Brutus, "You mean I'm on the wrong chariot?"

"Afraid so, sir," replied the driver, "And what is more, we can't do anything about it. Can't change chariots in midstream, if you know what I mean."

Brutus was aghast.

"That means," he said slowly, "That means that I'll be born a girl in Ireland instead of a boy in England."

"That is exactly what it means, sir. I'm very sorry. It's not my fault. I was instructed to zero in on Dublin, and can't alter course. They let you get on the wrong chariot."

"Oh! the idiots!" groaned Brutus. But just then the chariot forded its way through the River Lethe. He forgot everything as his mind was washed clear, and drifted into a deep sleep.

Act Two. Scene Two.

Some twenty years have passed. We find Caesar twiddling the controls of an Astral Television set. At last he gets it to the desired frequency, and a picture of a suburban dance-hall on the outskirts of London appears on the screen.

"Ah!" exclaims Caesar, "The hour of vengeance is at hand. Now I can watch as it strikes."

The dance-hall is crowded with young people, many of them in their late teens. A pop group loudly amplified, is playing a lively

140

tune, and all the dancers are flinging themselves about in time to the rhythm.

Amongst the dancers are three people whom we must introduce under their new identities. First, there is a young Irish nurse named Marcia McManus. She was born in Dublin, but has come to London to work. She is, of course, none other than the one-time Marcus Brutus. Dancing with her is a young man who is a student at the same hospital where she works. His name is Calvin Gray, nick-named Cal for short, and he is – or was – Calphurnia. The third person with whom we are concerned is a certain Caspar Smith who is a porter at the hospital. This porter is the notorious Cassius that was.

Caspar is jigging about in time to the music, partnering a rather plain, insipid girl. He is making no attempt to hide his boredom. Suddenly he spots Marcia nearby.

"Hey! Marcia! You didn't tell me you'd be here," he shouts.

Marcia turns and sees him, "Didn't ask me, did you?" she retorts.

"You told me you don't like dancing."

"No, I don't really. But Cal asked me to come with him."

Caspar suddenly realises whom Marcia is dancing with, and reddens with fury.

"What are you doing with him? You're my girl."

"I'm not you girl, and you know it. I've told your enough times," Marcia protests.

The music stops abruptly. Cal puts his arm round Marcia's waist to lead her off the dance-floor. That is the last straw for the jealous Caspar.

"Get your dirty hands off my girl," he bellows at Cal.

"Who says she is your girl? Didn't you hear her say she's NOT your girl?" Cal shouts back.

"I said get your hands off her!"

There is a scream from Marcia as she sees that Caspar has drawn a knife from his pocket.

"Caspar, don't! You must be drunk or something. Drop that knife!"

Marcia tries to get the knife from Caspar, and Cal joins in the struggle. Between them, Marcia and Cal manage to disarm Caspar.

"Phew!" exclaims Cal, "What a temper the chap has. Let's get away from here."

He turns away from Caspar, and motions to Marcia to follow. Marcia is standing rooted to the spot with shock, her eyes still fixed in horror on Caspar. With a sudden swift movement, Caspar draws another knife from his jacket, and lunges at Cal who is completely off his guard.

"No! No! Leave him alone," shrieks Marcia frantically. She makes a clumsy effort to pull him back, but fails, and in one last act of desperation, plunges the first knife which she still has in her hand into Caspar's back. Caspar gives a terrible gasping, gurgling cry and falls.

"Oh, God! I've killed him!" cries Marcia.

Caesar, who has witnessed the whole episode on his Astral Television, lets out a sigh of satisfaction.

"At last, Marcus Brutus, you have avenged my death and slain the instigator of the plot that led to my murder. At last, Caius Cassius, you have paid the penalty for your crime. Now I await the return of the soul of Cassius. Justice has been executed."

Act Two. Scene three. The final episode.

Caesar, together with the Celestial Committee for Re-assessment, are waiting in the Hall of Return for Cassius.

The President of the Committee speaks.

"Word has just come that Caius Cassius, lately Caspar Smith, has now passed through the Memory Restoration Channel, and is on his way here."

"Ah! He will have had his memory of his life as Cassius re-instated by now," remarked Caesar.

"That is so," replied the President," Now we can assess his new position. His debt against you has been cancelled, of course, but otherwise we do not consider that he has made much progress."

"Pity!" exclaimed Caesar, "I thought a lot of him at one time – before he plotted against me, that is. He was a remarkably clever man then. But, of course, he had quite a percentage of his cleverness with-held while he was Caspar Smith as a penalty off having misused it during his life as Cassius."

"As you know, he blamed his brilliant intellect for his downfall during his incarnation as Cassius, and entered a petition to be invested with a more simple brain in his following life on earth. He therefore placed himself voluntarily within the operation of the penalty. It must be borne in mind that every man and woman is granted the privilege of exercising his or her free-will within the limits to which they have become entitled through progress already made."

"It appears from the reports now prepared by the Celestial Computer Records that his duller brain did not result in his living a better life. This proves that the Sages are right when they maintain that goodness does not necessarily coincide with a brilliant intellect or accompany dull wits."

"Your clever idea of switching the sexes of Brutus and Calphurnia led to the accidental avenging of your murder. If Brutus had incarnated as a man again, he and Cassius would have been drawn by their old links to become friends making it unlikely that Brutus would have freed himself from Cassius's harmful influence over him. Brutus and Calphurnia remained attracted to one another through their previous association, so that when Cassius attacked Calphurnia in her guise as Calvin Gray, Brutus, although in the form of a woman, naturally sprang to Calphurnia's aid. With honourable motives, as of yore, Brutus slew Cassius, thus throwing off the insidious hold the latter held over him. In this way, Cassius, who once brought about your death, brought about his own death by inciting Brutus yet again, but this time to his own detriment."

"In truth, I had not foreseen that all would turn out so. My aim was simply by a reversal of sexes to disentangle Brutus from the wily Cassius."

"Well have you succeeded, Caesar, and your ruse unintentionally discharged the outstanding debt of Cassius. Your assassination has been avenged. He who instigated the crime, he who struck the first blow against you, has now been cut off by Brutus."

"To know that Marcus Brutus has won back his honour by shaking off the power of Cassius is good news indeed. Truly this knowledge makes sweet my revenge."

When taking down the story of *Caesar's Revenge*, I noticed there seemed to be surprising twists in the plot. When Shaw began by saying that Brutus and *Calphurnia* were assembled together, I thought for a moment that he had his Shakespeare characters confused. Dim recollections of having read Julius Caesar at school came to mind, and I recalled that Portia was the wife of Brutus if I were correct. I ferreted out a copy of Shakespeare's play, and hurriedly looked up the characters: sure enough, I was right.

On my next encounter with Shaw I murmured rather apologetically that I must have been mistaken in thinking he had said "Calphurnia". He replied that I had made no mistake, and that neither had he, as I

143

might see if I followed through to the end of his tale.

At one time, perhaps I became a little huffy with him because I seemed to detect a continuance of his old anti-feminine attitude. This huffiness on my part hindered communication temporarily, until one day when he persuaded me to listen to him.

"If you did but read my works, you would discover that I had a generous measure of appreciation of the various qualities and talents of womankind in general. However, I saw that they were for the most part incapable of realising or putting to good use their talents because they had allowed themselves to become mere shadows of their real selves. They had accepted for too long the subordinate position imposed upon them by their more cunning male counterparts, and needed to be shaken out of their apathy. With this aim in view, I appointed myself to stimulate them into thought, to sting them into action, for it could not be left to men to unshackle their womenfolk unless the women themselves clamoured to be set free.

"I would not work with you if I were not strongly on your side, and an implacable champion of equal rights and opportunities for all people irrespective of sex, class, birth, and all the other contingencies exploited to deprive certain sections of the community."

After this revelation on Shaw's part, I felt much happier working with him. He told me quietly that he admired me, and when I raised my eyebrows disbelievingly, he added that my suspicion of flattery was a symptom of my general disillusionment with my fellow-beings! I said that I could not but help being disillusioned with some, at least, of my fellow-creatures. When criticism of my work was adverse, and many a busybody was trying to disrupt it, and still others were trying to belittle the music, a number of people (including so-called friends) cold-shouldered me and treated me very badly. Then, when the mantle of fame fell upon me, and the music began to be acclaimed by experts, most of these people changed their tune. Suddenly, they wanted to cultivate me, whereas before they had not wanted to know!

"Well, I am not cultivating you because of your fame, you can be sure," Shaw observed, "I have struck up an acquaintance with you because I see you as a channel to increase knowledge in the world, or at least as a means of setting people thinking. There is so much apathy in the world, and so much taken for granted. Worst of all, so much is overlooked. People just look at what is immediately in front of them, and do not look around. They are afraid to look in case they see something different from their neighbours or their countrymen or

144

their fellow beings. It would make it so awkward for them if they saw something that others did not see! To feel secure, they conform, excepting in things which they can flout with impunity. Only a minority dare to entertain different ideas from the rest when it comes to vital issues. New avenues of thought have few to tread their paths at first, but in time, those avenues acquire the respectability of age, and crowds stampede along them willy-nilly."

Does this really apply nowadays? I myself would have decided that most people had the courage to hold whatever opinion they chose in the last decade or so. Yes, in many matters, Shaw agreed that was true; but not in relation to spiritual evolution and psychic evaluation.

What about the comments he said he wanted to make on the world situation? He said that the chaos and unrest is due to changing values, not only changing material values, but changing moral values. What did he mean by moral values? Nothing to do with sex, but with the recognition of the rights of all peoples to live in the best conditions that can be made available, and to share in all the resources of the world. This recognition is growing, but all too slowly, he concluded. Only world-wide co-operation will establish world-wide peace and prosperity.

"And that is surely what you all want", was his parting remark.

145

CHAPTER 15

Soul-searching and Jung

By far one of the most delightful characters in the Hereafter with whom I have had the privilege and joy of becoming acquainted is Carl Jung. His gentle presence, his kindly humour, and the quiet depth of his great soul, communicate a profound feeling of serenity.

He did not attempt to establish his earthly identity with me at first. He told me he had recently been in our world, and practised psychology, and when I asked for a name, answered somewhat whimsically, "Just call me Joe."

Naturally, I became curious as to his identity, although respecting his apparent wish to remain anonymous. He would often talk to me about psychology, knowing perhaps my strong conviction that we must come to know ourselves as fully as possible if we are to make the most use of our inner potentials. The longer I live, the more deeply I feel there is a pressing necessity for us to develop greater understanding of others, for only in this way, perhaps, can we learn true tolerance for the other person's point of view, forbearance for uncongenial behaviour, and an increase of the give-and-take that is so indispensable in the cultivation of good relations. As Shaw wishes to point out, if we cannot build good relationships between employer and employee, between governments and unions, industry and commerce will fall into chaos and possibly grind to a halt. And a great deal of this good relationship depends on an honest and consistent effort to appreciate the problems of others, and to co-operate in dealing with them effectively in a manner that is not detrimental to either party in any dispute. But these are complicated matters involving running costs, standards of living, costs of living, solvencies, and so forth. This chapter I wish to devote to the problems of human nature, so we will leave the matters of economy and the questions of the demands made by employers on their employees and vice versa.

We can often be puzzled by the behaviour of others. Even when we have known people for years, they may suddenly do or say something that seems entirely foreign to their nature. It dawns on us that here is a side of them we did not know. Our relationships with other people in this world tend to be very shallow affairs based on a knowledge formed through a desultory observation of their appearance and manners, speech and actions. We often form an opinion of someone very hastily through one or two short conversations with them. In fact, our judgement of others is based on such fragments of knowledge about them in most cases, that we can be sure our judgement more often than not is incomplete or totally erroneous.

We have a habit of presuming things about people when we do not really have the faintest idea of what they are like. In my own experience, I have found that people have taken it upon themselves to pronounce judgement on me when they have not so much as met me once – a ridiculous and dangerous practice on their part. Many people seem to take a fiendish delight in disparaging other people, perhaps because they themselves possess an acute inferiority complex and seek to compensate themselves by trying to belittle others. This may be the result of our heritage of ancient primitive instincts which drive us, if we let them, to try to establish superiority over others. In fact, it could be this very same instinct which is the root-cause of all our wars.

All in all, we do have an abysmal ignorance of our own inner selves and of others, but as Jung has persistently reassured me, there is an element in human nature which urges it continually towards the acquisition of knowledge, understanding and insight into the very heart of Creation and its purposes. What troubles him is that we do not appear to have the tools to chisel our way out of the prison of ignorance in which we seem to be almost perpetually locked. First, he says, we must make the requisite tools which we have to fashion out of our consciousness. Before you can make music, you have to make instruments on which to perform; before you make poetry, you have to select words on which to play; before you contemplate the inner nature of Man, you need to know something about the psychological ingredients which contribute towards this nature. In other words, he says, you need to have some idea what to look for and how to seek it.

I asked Jung if he would enlarge on this, and his reply was quite simple. Basically, he stated, we display one of two reactions towards

147

everything which comes into our experience: we either go towards the experience or draw away from it, figuratively speaking. We can guage our reactions at first, to determine whether a particular experience causes us to turn towards it or away from it; then we can penetrate into the mysteries of our reactions by trying to discover why we reacted as we did. We must not over-simplify this rule and apply it to obvious situations such as those presenting a threat of danger, in which case the normal reaction would be to reject the danger either by flight or by overcoming it in some way, where both actions, or even a freezing into immobility, would constitute a withdrawal from the experience. But in the more obscure cases of acceptance and rejection reactions, once we have been able to decide which reaction applies, we have made the initial move which can set the inquiry going.

He told me once that he was much in favour of dream-analysis providing it is conducted in a thorough and understanding way. When I asked him why, he said that during confrontation analysis, a laborious and sometimes impossible task presents itself in the process of removing all the layers imposed by the conscious and subconscious mind over certain facts that the patient would not desire to be brought to the surface. In dreams, he pointed out, the censor or suppressor steps aside and allows the mind complete freedom to function as it wishes; although careful and informed interpretation of dreams is essential to an understanding of them, the truth is revealed in them without resort to any subterfuge other than symbolism in which to express something that cannot be directly expressed.

"You know," he said, smiling a little sheepishly, I thought, "Some of the dreams I related were, in fact, waking experiences which I had undergone; but I realised that I would be regarded as a wool-gathering mystic if I revealed that to the psycho-analytical world."

He said that he would be proud to be called a mystic if we were using the word to denote a rapport with God.

"You live in a strange world," he remarked, "where in everyday life people are all the time hiding their thoughts and feelings. Every now and then the whole business of concealment becomes too much for the individual, and sets up excessive stress causing a breakdown, like an overloaded cable blowing a fuse. Then the individual may consult a psychiatrist, who tries to encourage the reverse process: that of exposing the hidden feelings and giving them a good airing. If people were not so artificial in their everyday behaviour, there would be far fewer patients for the psychiatrists' couches."

148

I visualised people going round saying just what they thought and making no attempt to preserve polite restraint. A horrifying picture, it seemed to me. As if he had picked up my thoughts, Jung said, "There is no need for people to practise aggression or become arrogant while pursuing a policy of natural rather than artificial manners. It is all a question of being honest with oneself. For example, if, for some reason known or unknown, you dislike a person intensely, there is no need to tell him so to his face – after all, he may be a perfectly harmless and very sensitive person who has given no cause for your dislike – but to try to persuade yourself that you *do* like him, perhaps because we are told we must love everybody, will set up a conflict in your mind and confuse your subconscious mind which will not know whether to register like or dislike."

I thought I began to get a dim idea of what he meant. There are, perhaps, a great many things which we do not admit to ourselves, especially if they are likely to offend the natural vanity which many of us must possess in some degree, even if very small. Most of us like to regard ourselves as people who are just, and we must know in our hearts that some of our attitudes towards others are not the result of a fair appraisal but of an impulsive or instinctive reaction. This kind of reaction comes to light very clearly in racial prejudice, where dislike is expressed simply because another human being has a different coloured skin from one's own; we know that this cannot be justified because the colour of a person's skin has nothing to do with character and qualities, yet some people will still have an aversion which may sometimes be accounted for by an inherited fear of aliens – an inherited fear which may date back to primitive times when a stranger to the tribe was naturally regarded with suspicion or fear.

To return to Jung. Again trying to simplify matters, he stated that we register a dual reaction more often than not to other people and to situations. This is speaking in relation to the relatively civilised sections of the world, where education has taught us to try to use our reason. In this case, our minds may be employing reason while our instincts are pulling in the opposite direction towards an apparently unreasonable reaction which arises from racial memories and other hidden factors. In the less civilised sections of humankind, you will not come across so much inner conflict because the primitive self has not an intellectual self to oppose it; reactions will be uncomplicated by any process of attempted analysis or interpretation by the conscious mind. Mankind, in advancing, creates new problems for himself, and

149

has to overcome many difficulties as he does in his development in any direction. When these difficulties threaten to become overwhelming or unbearable to the individual mind, there is an attempt to revert to the primitive state where reason does not function. It is an attempt to escape into the past from a present which is less attractive or, rather, apparently less attractive.

Jung continued by saying that to him it seemed that the evolution of Mankind's reasoning powers illustrated the meaning of the allegorical story of the Fall in Eden. The primitive mind would know no difference between what we term good behaviour and bad behaviour: for the primitive creature would simply react instinctively to any situation without applying any moral sense which at that stage of evolution he would not possess. The primitive creature just exists and has not consumed the mythological fruit of knowledge which would endow him with powers to reason out the merits and demerits of his own and other creatures' behaviour. In this sense, he is innocent. With evolution he loses his innocence and has to compensate for it by inventing codes of behaviour. With the formation of behaviour codes there develops a sense of responsibility, but this sense of responsibility can be an uncomfortable thing, therefore he seeks to shift the burden of responsibility on to someone else or something else. This attempt to shift the responsibility, this attempt to appoint a scapegoat, gives rise to many legends and fables, such as the story of Adam and Eve and the Serpent. It is interesting to note that according to this particular fable, it was Womankind who took the first step towards the founding of a moral code, and made the first move towards the acquisition of knowledge. In fact, instead of making her the scapegoat which apparently the irresponsible Adam tried to do, he admitted her to be the pioneer of truth, the pilgrim on the pathway to self-knowledge. Perhaps he felt somewhat guilty at trying to pass the blame for his actions to her, and was compelled to try to make amends by inventing yet another scapegoat for her: the mythical Serpent, more easily excused for its actions on account of the fact that it was a mere creature of the earth or the ground, and could not be expected to aspire to moral stature. There is no doubt that all this is highly allegorical, and men of science nowadays will not be disposed to accept this Old Testament account as historical fact.

It is easy to trace the repetitive pattern of this inborn tendency to pass responsibility and blame to others. By nature, we seek to justify ourselves, and by nature, we try to pass any blame to others. For a scapegoat, we will either deliberately or unconsciously select a victim who seems weaker than ourselves so that he cannot throw the responsibility or blame back to us. Only persons who are blessed with a sense of humility as well as a sense of justice will accept blame when they believe themselves to be culpable.

Jung said that his studies and cogitations led him to the conclusion that every mind is linked to an Over-mind, as though the individual is usually unaware of this link. This Over-mind is the Supreme Intelligence which might be termed God. It directs the automatic functions of the body, constantly at work to try to maintain the body in a state of health, endeavouring to counteract the effects of an unhealthy environment, to heal its wounds, and compensate for any loss of faculties. The mind of civilised Humankind, as it develops, becomes self-governing, setting itself up as a separate authority; if this authority isolates itself from the Supreme Intelligence, it acts in a self-willed fashion which can be very destructive to others and ultimately to itself.

I inquired what Jung meant by the mind setting itself up as a separate authority. Broadly, he replied, this involved any self-engendered competing authority such as can be exercised through the wilful or careless misuse of the body either as a result of deliberate and harmful indulgence of some kind or as the effect of simple neglect. It is as if the body has a self-repair mechanism built into it, but this mechanism cannot function correctly if interfered with by forces at variance with its programme. Here, it seemed, Jung was speaking more of the body than the mind which he had mentioned in connection with authority. Hurriedly, he explained to me the theory of the inter-action of mind and body. It is, he pointed out, the mind which determines the behaviour of the body in most of its activities, the conscious mind and the subsconscious mind combining to govern these activities. This might not apply in cases of total disorientation of the mind, he continued, and would apply within certain limits only in cases where the body, through damage or deterioration, cannot respond to the impulses signalled to it. To express it more plainly, he referred to the natural authority of the Over-mind in its rôle of maintenance and repair agency, the natural authority which assists medicine and surgery in the recovery of patients' health.

In the past, Jung reminds us, the body and the mind were treated as separate entities. Now that we are realising more fully the interconnections between the two, we can more easily recognise the causes of certain disorders and stand a better chance of making a

151

correct diagnosis which is, of course, the key to successful treatment. These are straightforward comments which can be understood by all.

Many of the truths which are gradually being uncovered by the advances of medical science have been expressed in symbolic terms through certain rites and ceremonies associated with religion. The Book of Exodus illustrates the deeply felt need to escape, not simply from a geographical situation, but from the tyrannies of the temporal world, from ungodliness, and from the restrictions of unspiritual authorities. The same need, perhaps, that leads some souls to enter monasteries and nunneries. The battles described throughout the Old Testament can be read to be struggles between the power of good and the power of evil. These bear a parallel to the inner conflict between our desire to conform with the best in human nature and the opposite desire, to behave in a manner that undermines the best.

Jesus himself spoke often in parables, knowing that the majority of his hearers were incapable of perceiving the deep spiritual significance of his teachings; he knew that a multitude of the people could only trust and live by blind faith without real understanding, a case which still applies to thousands or possibly millions today. So that the masses could grasp the meaning in some way, symbols, parables, and simple formulations of the truth had to be represented.

The Communion Service holds a profound meaning within the simple act of taking the bread and the holy wine. The mystery of communion is unveiled as the need for us to identify ourselves with the higher nature, to remember that flesh and blood must be spiritualised, that is, lifted out of their instinctive, animal character, in order to become the vehicle of the higher nature. It also indicates to those who seek to become true Christians, that they must become one with Christ, they must allow His Spirit to enter into them, and must absorb the very life-stream of His Being. The Infinite, the Supreme Wisdom, the Absolute Power, are in a sense continually offered to us, but we can only avail ourselves by acceptance, by partaking of their substance, by actual absorption of their attributes. In other words, we are ignorant, not because there is nothing to know but because for some reason we do not or cannot acquire knowledge. We are cut off from the Life-Stream of the Creative Force, not because the Creative Force does not exist, but because we do not identify with it. To overcome the narrow limitations of our egos, we have to combine with the Great Intelligence, and this must be the goal of every true mystic, every sincere pilgrim, and every dedicated seeker. This is a teaching expressed in many religions.

152

Jung said he did not rule out scientists, even the most atheistic amongst them, from this allusion to Communion. They, too, are searching for the Truth, and trying to digest the mysteries of Life. Their aim, if they are worthy of their calling, is to attain the life more abundant, to increase the nourishment of the mind, and to expand our consciousness.

The outer processes of life are reflected within us. We are, each one of us, worlds within ourselves. To know our own world and to build a constructive relationship with it is to know in miniature the balance of spirit and matter. To look deep into the mind, beyond the personal ego, is to catch a glimpse of the Divine, to see dimly that Great Self of whom we are all a part. The difficulty lies in attempting to reconcile our minute beings with a Being so vast, that the most it seems we can hope to do in our present state is to touch the fringe. We can but stand upon the threshold, yet from that threshold we may be blessed with a vision of the immeasurable interior, the hall of wisdom, the kingdom of infinite understanding.

Two things became plain to Jung, so he stated; one was the need for Humankind to find a meaning behind life, and to invent a meaning if it could not discover one. But meaning, if any, lies all the time within oneself and cannot be revealed in external things. If meaning cannot related to oneself it is without meaning. Over and over throughout his life, he asked himself, he said, what was the meaning of it all. There could possibly be many meanings or none, yet the process of individuation, the development of the human psyche, appeared to aim at a meaning. He reasoned, rather imaginatively he admits, that it is impossible to aim at nothing, therefore the force of evolution must be directed towards some achievement. A force which seeks to achieve an end must have a determining power to motivate it. The thought of the evident existence of a determining power encouraged his feeling of an underlying purpose, and a unifying principle. This, in mental terms, was the nearest, he thought, that the scientific thinker could approach at the moment to the recognition of a God-power.

Blessed are the real mystics of the world, he announced in conclusion, for they are able to dispense with the laborious and endless contrivings of science and psychology and merge with the intangible, omnipresent Self of which we are fragments. Yet both science and psychology point in the same direction towards the perception of a complete concept of life and the place of the individual within that concept.

153

Before ending this chapter, I must describe how I came to know Jung's identity. In 1970, Columbia Broadcasting Services made a film about my work under the direction of Jules Laventhal with David Dimbleby acting as interviewer. Between takes, sometimes during a coffee break or over a meal, Jules conversed with me on many topics, including religion and psychology. He remarked that I displayed ideas very similar to Jung's in many respects, and I told Jules that I was in touch with a spirit claiming to have been a psychologist in a very recent life in our world. I had never, at that time, read anything at all of Jung's, and when Jules discovered this upon questioning me he brought with him at our next meeting one of Jung's books 'which carried a photograph of the author. The photograph showed a man with the same looks as "Joe". I recognised the same kindly features, the same quiet gleam of humour in the eyes, the same gentle strength of character and I felt sure it was none other than the same person.

On my next contact with Joe, I inquired whether he was, in fact, one and the same as Jung. He admitted that this was so, explaining that he had not felt it necessary to give me his earthly identity which he said was "only a facet of his total self".

I was left wondering why he had decided on the nickname of "Joe", and he said that one of his colleagues on earth had once called him "Holy Joe" because of his absorption in religious matters and his strange hypnogogic visions. He had dropped the appendage "Holy", he continued to explain, because he was no holier than others.

To this day, I address him as "Joe", which may seem a gross familiarity on my part towards a man whom Liszt hails as one of the greatest to have lived in our word. But since it was at his own request that I address him thus, I hope that he himself is not in any way put out by what others might say regarding my approach to him.

He is to me, not only a great psychologist, but a real mystic whose penetration into some of the mysteries of religion has given me a deeper understanding of these matters. I am especially grateful to him for making acceptable to me certain of the Christian dogmas and rituals which were previously not only incomprehensible but almost repellent, since my reason could not equate them with the principles of justice and good common sense. Through his help, I am now able to discern a deep, hidden significance in the creeds and ceremonies of Christianity, and instead of seeing through a glass darkly, to see face to face the glorious image of the Godhead interpreted into Christian terms and symbols.

As Jung adds at this very moment, we can measure God only in our terms, and not in God's terms, hence we can only obtain a telescopic view of the great and wondrous reality. Since we insist on looking through many different telescopes, we are apt to get dissimilar images and to view the Almighty from one narrow aspect. One day, he says, we will realise we are all looking towards the same Shining Truth which is beamed down to us on many rays and through varying densities of "the clouds of unknowing". As we grow in understanding, we will learn to rise above these clouds of unknowing, and behold the Truth in all its brilliance, clear and undistorted by the mists of human ignorance.

This chapter is a personal tribute to "Joe", and a gesture of deep gratitude to him for helping me to understand myself and others more fully; for helping to restore my shattered self-confidence when others had belittled me or denigrated me, and for bringing me a vision of the Absolute that has given me the key to that freedom of the soul from its little self which enables it to enter into the Whole.

CHAPTER 16

Chopin gives me support

In February 1971, when my first book was published in France, the publishers arranged for me to pay a flying visit to Paris to mark the occasion. There must be many people who have visited Paris or would like to because even the very name has a magic about it. I set out for France with great excitement and filled with happy anticipation, although it was to be very much a working event.

It turned out to be a whirlwind affair. Scarcely had I stepped on to French soil before I was whisked off by car to commence a non-stop programme of activities which included radio broadcasts, television appearances, press conferences, and so forth. Now and then I was required to play the piano at some function or other, and, naturally, I chose most of the items from the music that Chopin had given to me, alternating with some of Liszt's new compositions.

There was hardly a moment to breathe in between the various engagements, During one of the intervals, I asked Monsieur Jean Major, the publishers' representative, whether there would be time for me to visit Chopin's grave.

"I cannot be in Paris without going to visit his grave," I said.

"A H!" replied M. Major, "We have arranged for all that already. We wish to film you beside Chopin's tomb."

I was delighted to think I would have the chance to pay tribute to Chopin's memory – though for me, of course, he is not just a memory but a living soul.

"That is good," I expressed my approval, "Now I must buy some flowers to place on Chopin's grave. Will I be given time to buy some for him?"

"But we have arranged all that also," answered M. Major, "There is already on order a beautiful sheaf of flowers for you to take to his

156

grave."

I thanked M. Major, reflecting on how everything had been thought of and carefully organised.

We were very fortunate with the weather which was dry and quite warm. A week later, when I was back in London, the weather in Paris turned bitterly cold, and I joked with Chopin that he must have arranged fine weather for my visit!

We wound in slow procession through the Cemetery where Chopin's body was laid to rest, and when we reached the tomb, I found myself full of very mixed emotions. I had never thought I would have the opportunity to visit his grave during my life which had been so dogged by poverty that the cost would have been beyond my pocket.

It is a beautiful tomb. There is a small garden plot which is carefully – and lovingly, I have no doubt – tended, and in the midst is a statue of a young girl seated with her hands in her lap, palms uppermost. Someone had placed in her hands a small bunch of violets – Chopin's favourite flower together with roses. I suddenly felt very moved. Here lay the earthly remains of a great genius who had died so young before he had had time to pour into the world more of his beautiful music. Thoughts of his suffering overwhelmed me, and the past seemed to well up and engulf me. Although it was a fine day, unseen rain seemed to be falling like tears, and I had to remind myself that he lives on and still makes lovely music to be heard in heaven or here on earth by those who will listen.

With a start, I came back to the present as I suddenly saw that Chopin himself was standing beside his own tomb. He smiled gently, sensing, I think, the sorrow I was feeling. He watched me lay the sheaf of flowers tenderly upon the grave, then he spoke in French as he often does – remarking how lovely the flowers were and thanking me for them.

"I don't know why you feel so sad," he continued, "I am here, not in there". He pointed to the tomb.

"Ah, well, I suppose it is a grave matter," he joked, speaking this time in English and making a pun of the word "grave". He is trying to cheer me up as he so often does, I thought. He is so full of sympathy, and hates to see anyone sad.

When I had returned to England, Chopin gave me a new piece of music, a little nocturne, in commemoration of my visit. It is a poignant piece in A minor reminiscent of the falling of raindrops or teardrops. He can even make sadness beautiful.

Later during the schedule, the publishers arranged for me to visit the Polish Museum in Paris where many souvenirs of Chopin's life are displayed. The authorities in the Museum were very kind, and allowed me to handle the death-mask of Chopin, and the casts taken of his hands. This gave me the opportunity to check up on something Chopin had said about his hands. He told me one day that my hands are very similar to his own; in fact, he stated, they are exactly the same size. Measuring my hands against the casts of his, I found that this was so.

Portraits of Chopin do not always resemble him very closely, and the colouring is often wrong. I have gazed intently at his eyes, which are a beautiful grey-blue, sometimes looking very blue indeed, and sometimes melting into a misty soft blue-grey. His hair, which I have observed carefully, is a light brown, rather on the fair side. I have had people argue with me over this, maintaining that he was dark-haired. I was very pleased to be able to satisfy myself that I had seen the colour of his hair clearly, for there was a lock of his hair in the Museum, and it was of the same hue.

Also in the Museum was an armchair, said to be the last chair in which Chopin sat before he passed away. I was given permission to sit on the chair – in fact, I was invited to sit there – and I felt strongly an impression of heavy suffering, both mental and physical, as I sat with reverence where Chopin had once sat.

It gives one a strange feeling when one looks at the relics of a departed person, knowing that the real person, the immortal soul, is quite likely to appear at any moment! The transient nature of earthly existence is all the more sharply emphasised in these circumstances, and the fact that it is so transient is thrown into relief by the vivid reality of the Life Everlasting.

If only we all had eyes to see, and ears to hear! But perhaps this would merely complicate matters for some people, and others would be scared, of course, if they were not accustomed to such things. Fear of the unknown is a natural thing which is bound to grip us all at some time. When we know more about Life after Death, when we realise it is a wonderful reality, let us hope that the fear of Death, the fear of the actual transition, and the fear of what is to come, will be dispelled.

Once, I remember the spirit of a recently passed man appeared, and I listened to him clairaudiently as he mourned the fact that his wife now regarded him as some kind of strange bogey just because his phsyical body was dead.

"Can't she realise," he asked me, "That I am still the same person,

158

and that I love her just as much? If only she didn't shrink from the thought of me, and think of me as a mere ghost! I am real, I am alive, I am the man she knew and loved."

I tried to explain to the man's wife, or, rather, widow. She said she understood what I was saying, but that it was so difficult to visualise her husband as a living being.

"Tell him," she begged me, "That I am trying to understand. It is just that he does not seem to be there. But I do believe there is another life, and I do still love him."

This seemed to console the man's spirit.

"I'll be waiting for her when she comes over," he said, "And I'll be watching over her until then. Tell her she always did need watching."

I repeated all this to the lady, and the bit about her always needing to be watched obviously meant something, for she managed to laugh.

"He always used to call me a little flirt, but, I wasn't really. I just liked to be admired. He used to say 'I'm watching you'. You have made me feel he really is alive. I shan't feel he is just a wispy ghost now."

It is strange, perhaps, to see the spirit of a 'dead' person beside his or her grave. Still more strange to see one beside his or her coffin at the funeral service! This is what happened when my father died. He had asked, long before his death, long before he was taken ill, to be precise, to have his body cremated. I don't think he minded the idea of his body being buried, but he had a belief that his soul would be freed all the more quickly from the body if cremation took place. According to his wishes, my mother and I arranged for a cremation service.

I stood beside my mother, trying to enfold her in comfort during the brief service. Although my mother sometimes "saw", I think she was too absorbed in her natural grief to notice that my father was standing right beside his own coffin. Rather surprised to see him at his own funeral, I gazed at him transfixed.

"What's the matter?" he asked, "You look as if you are seeing a ghost, and I'm not a ghost, I'm your father."

This made me a little worried as it seemed he did not know he had passed over, but his next words reassured me.

"As for that", he said, pointing to his coffin, "Blow that! Thank God I'm out of that old body at last."

I was relieved to see that he knew, and that he felt no qualms about

159

the disposal of his body. He told me he had come to be near my mother and try to cheer her, and he confessed that it gave him a lot of satisfaction and a sense of triumph to see his outworn body, which had caused him to suffer so much, being "finished off!"

During his life, my father had to wear boots to support his ankles as one of them was weak after being broken when roller-skating. He had always wanted to possess a pair of patent leather black shoes, and to have clothes like a "real toff". We were too poor, of course, for him to have anything other than one working suit and a second, cheap, suit for best. When he appeared to me after his demise, he was dressed in a beautiful Savile-Row style suit and wearing, not surprisingly perhaps, shiny black patent leather shoes! His wish had been realised at last. He told me to write and tell my brother what he was wearing, and said he would go to my brother and show himself to him in the same outfit.

My brother was in Burma at the time in the Royal Corps of Signals. He wrote to me to say he knew that our father had passed on as he had seen him. Our letters crossed in the post, and the one from my brother described the clothes my father was wearing on his "spectral" visit, and the shoes on his feet . . . which were shiny, black patent leather! My brother has some degree of psychic ability, but wisely keeps very quiet about it as he sees no reason for enduring the jibes of the disbelievers. He is a regular Church-goer and perhaps fears that his Church would frown upon such abilities. But if one has these abilities, one has them, and one cannot help being made that way. Of course, they are not wrong in themselves – how can anything God made be wrong? But he knows as well as I do that there are people who think it is wrong to have such faculties, so he holds his peace.

Strange how the whole of the Bible, both the Old and the New Testament, is full of stories of the supernatural, of visions and voices, of prophets and angels, and happenings, that defy or appear to defy natural law, and yet the emergence of anything that hints at the supernatural has since been frowned upon and those connected with the supernatural condemned by narrow-minded bigots. If they can accept, lock, stock and barrel, all the events related in the Bible, and never turn a hair at the fact that it bristles with the supernatural, they are hardly logical in their rejection of present-day manifestations of the supernatural or apparently supernatural. Their motto seems to be that in the Bible it is O.K., but outside the Bible it is not. This is indeed dislocating a great Book from reality, and it does not need

160

much sense to realise that anything out of touch with reality is likely to fall out of use and lose regard. We may need to look at the Bible in an entirely new light in order to benefit from its fountain of wisdom and understand the lessons about human nature which it contains. And what about all the other Sacred Scriptures of other religions? How much have they been correctly interpreted and how much understood? How often have errors and omissions occurred in the processes of translation and copying? Our safest course seems to be to live by the spirit rather than the letter. It complicates matters if we try to trace the precise meaning of each book and each text, but if we are sincere in our search for truth, we must continue to examine, analyse, and get as close to the truth as we can. No God could ask more of us – or less.

Chopin once gave me an interesting talk about his studies in the Hereafter of some great volumes which he said are called "The Chronicles of Human Evolution". These chronicles, so he told me, record the development of the human species on earth from its beginning. They cover, not thousands of years, but millions. The animal form was first evolved slowly to become a suitable vehicle for human intelligence. I noted that this infers there was primarily an animal form which was limited to an instinctive intelligence. Chopin confirmed that this was so, and that there was a passage of time, long in duration, before the animal form had been sufficiently prepared to receive the first spark of human intelligence. This process of the introduction of human intelligence, according to Chopin's account, is repeated in each human birth, the human baby constituting a mere animal on its first arrival, with the spark of intelligence being kindled throughout its growth. In Mongoloids the spark cannot be properly struck because the tinder, to pursue the analogy, is not sufficiently inflammable. Nevertheless, so it is recorded, even in such cases, a soul is linked to the infant in question; but the soul under such circumstances is unable to make full use of the earthly vehicle, and can only make a partial manifestation. I thought this must be very frustrating for the soul, but Chopin said there are a variety of reasons for such lives, and that lessons can be learned from them both by the semi-incarnating soul and those who care for it.

This perpetual process is a conditioning of matter, and a stimulation of its responses without which it would remain inert. Why all this preoccupation with matter? Why not remain in the spiritual state, in the allegorical Garden of Eden? Because conscious knowledge comes only through experience of opposites, which spirit, in

161

its original pure form, cannot distinguish, since contrasting conditions such as heat and cold would have conveyed no meaning until they had been actually produced in Creation. It is all a question of the Unmanifest being made Manifest, and the realisation that the Manifest existed in the Unmanifest before its emergence. Very thought-provoking, yet we continually have witness to this process of the Unmanifest materialising in the cycles of life, in the seasons, in the coming of Spring, in the growth of tiny seeds into plants and flowers, and in the slow transformation of an acorn into a mighty oak tree.

It is not that we do not know, so Chopin postulated, but that we do not know that we know! Does the acorn know consciously that one day it will be a great tree? Yet the knowledge necessary to its growth is inherent in itself. This is a different kind of knowledge from that obtained by the intellect through learning; one is an intrinsic but unconscious knowledge; the other is an acquired and conscious knowledge. This is the difference – the enormous difference – between the Eden State and the "Fallen" State; in the Garden of Eden we existed in the bliss of ignorance, obedient to the laws of Creation because we knew no choice. The acquisition of knowledge gives us a choice: we commence to learn the laws and either live in accordance with them or break them as a result of neglect, defiance, or lack of sufficient understanding. It is obviously important to work for the fullest possible understanding of the laws and complete co-operation with them in order to live in harmony. Having taken the first bite of the apple, we are obliged to consume it because a portion of knowledge – a limited understanding – has committed us to increase that knowledge or remain partially ignorant at our own risk.

Where will all this endless course of evolution lead? Chopin said that the aim is for spirit to conquer matter, and that the human race is learning gradually how to control, influence and direct matter or the material world. Eventually, after an immense era of evolution, this will bring about the reconciliation of matter with spirit. As far as he is able to determine, states Chopin, there are no short cuts in the process of evolution, but it can be considerably speeded up as Mankind's awareness expands. Once Man realises he is spirit here and now and that he does not have to wait until some distant time or until physical death to become spirit, he will begin to recognise his own real nature, and this will make it possible for him to give expression to this real self. Man limits himself by thinking of himself as mere flesh and blood, and fails to draw upon the great resources of his

162

spirit derived from the Infinite Spirit, the Universal Source of all Life.

All this seems very ponderous, and can present an overwhelming picture to us in our finite moment of time and place. It can make one feel very small and insignificant. Think of yourself as an intrinsic part of the whole, Chopin advised, in fact, a vital part of the whole as we all are, no matter how unimportant we feel; for each soul is a facet of the Great Soul. There is no need to feel lost in the great scheme of things, for we all have our part in it, and we are all part of the evolving consciousness. We often feel ourselves to be so separate, so isolated, but we are all enfolded in the One Great Spirit, and we are all included in the Divine Plan for self-chosen transmutation into perfection, for conscious union with the Whole or Absolute, for transfiguration into the Immortal Spirit. The process is slow because we are slow to awaken and slower still to make the choice.

What we must bear in mind, I was told, is that each part and particle of Creation, and each person and soul has to evolve individually, with the individual evolution assisting in the advance of the whole. The onus for our evolution rests largely with us; no-one can hand wisdom to us on a plate; it has to be attained. The pace of evolution can be speeded up by individual efforts or, regrettably, slowed down by the absence of them. In a way, the whole depends on the part, and the part on the whole, so we can assist the forward movement or retard it.

Our responsibility, therefore, is not to ourselves alone, but to our fellow-beings. A solemn thought which should shake the complacency of those who do not care about others.

"For I, if I be lifted up, will lift all men," are words attributed to one who tried to point the way. This, Chopin intimates, is an aphorism which can be applied to each and every one of us. By lifting our consciousness, by raising our standards, by aspiration, we will be helping to lift world consciousness. Following the example displayed by one before us, we can help in the salvation of humanity, by good thoughts and deeds, and by kindly words of encouragement and understanding.

I have written all this because Chopin himself asked me to convey his message to people. If it is too heavy-going for some readers, let them pass it over at least for the time being. But I hope it will make others feel that their efforts to live a good life are more than worth while, not just for the blessing it may bring them, but for the blessing

163

it may help to bring to others. It often seems that the wicked prosper, and that there is no reward for goodness. To know that no effort towards the light is wasted, and that each endeavour, however small, is a contribution towards evolution, towards growing understanding and happiness, is an idea to fire us anew when we begin to feel we are fighting a losing battle.

I hope Chopin's words help to kindle within us a new zeal to make the world a fine place to live in, full of fine people, and a joy to the Creator.

CHAPTER 17

Identity, its roots and its meaning

The title of this chapter has been suggested by Bertrand Russell, but it will not consist entirely of quotations from him.

I will begin by repeating his opening remark on the subject.

"Identity is a far more complex matter than the casual observer believes; it has its roots in Man's distant past, and its ramifications are so diffuse as to defy total analysis. There is the question of personal identity which is of paramount importance to the average individual. To lose one's personal identity is to become non-existent to all intents and purposes: one is a non-entity in actual fact under such circumstances, a mere object, and an exile in the land of the living.

"The need for a sense of identity is easily recognised in the human being. Hence the struggle for the infant to draw attention to himself, not only for the satisfaction of his bodily requirements, but to be acknowledged *per se*. In later life, if an insufficient degree of acknowledgement is demonstrated, the individual may react by cultivating a persecution complex, or delusions of grandeur, which are possibly to be regarded as two sides of the same coin. There may be attempts to over-dramatise one's self, or one's situation, and we are all familiar with the type who always has something wrong with his health and expatiates at great length on his symptoms. Attempts to draw attention by those who feel that their identity is overlooked or submerged can take on so many different disguises that it is not possible to elucidate them in detail. The most common form of defence is portrayed in the over-self-centred person, who may be feeling that he is ignored, and compensates by focussing his attention on himself."

Now that Russell has set the ball rolling, let us pause to think for a moment just how much a sense of our own identity means to us, and how much a sense of the identity of others also means to us. The whole of human life revolves around this question of identity and relating identities with other identities. It is identity which gives meaning and shape to life, and a sense of continuity through posterity without which life would become unintelligible and disjointed.

If we go into the highways and byways of civilisation, we will find that this sense of identity varies widely in its quality. In the Twentieth Century, thanks partly to the birth of modern psychology, the sense of identity can become marked by a high degree of self-awareness, and the tendency towards the practice of meditation can enhance this sense.

Jung has asserted a precept to me which he says many a religious teacher has also postulated: that is, that to become absolutely aware of one's identity is to become aware of God. But this awareness of God can only come about when all the false aspects of the personal identity have been shed. The process of self-awareness is one demanding continual vigilance, he warns, because negative ideas, like weeds in a garden, are constantly being thrown into the mind or self-engendered; they must be systematically removed to make way for the true growth of self-awareness which is a self-less condition as opposed to its counterfeit condition, self-aggrandisement.

The continuance of life after death without retaining one's identity would fail to be a bona fide continuation. If identity were not retained, one would become something or someone else – a different entity, not one's self. Perhaps this is why those who communicate from beyond frequently display a wish to prove their identity in any way they can demonstrate, by referring to their own past life and characteristics, to their memories and feelings, and trying to show that they have remained the same person. They can, of course, progress and modify, it must be reminded, just as we can progress and modify in this our present world.

It is obviously of great importance to the Christian Religion that Jesus demonstrated after his death that he was the same person, that he was essentially the same character the disciples had come to know and love. It was this that made such an impact on them; had he appeared in a different guise, they would not have known him, and would not have been able to cry in exultation, *"He is risen."*

It is notable that major religions usually revolve round an individual, illustrating the recognition of the significant rôle of identity. And large numbers of people can only conceive of God as an indi-

166

vidual, as a person they can identify.

The second significant statute in most religions is the exhortation to link or merge one's identity with the God-identity. It is Mankind's humble admission that his own identity is limited, isolated, and insufficient, and he seeks to overcome the limitations by identifying with that which he regards as greater than himself, that which he believes to be all-sufficient, that which is whole. He becomes aware, so some religions teach, that he is separate from God, cast out from the Garden of Eden where he lived within the sphere of God's influence; and, having become aware of himself as a separated identity, he is driven, more often than not, to seek reunion with the Absolute Identity. If he does not himself seek this reunion, he will be liable to be urged or coerced or even bullied into seeking it by some of his fellow-beings.

So it becomes apparent that there is in human nature, generally speaking, a basic need to be recognised as an individual, and a secondary need, perhaps more fundamental than the first, to join this identity with another or others. We identify ourselves throughout life with various people, with all kinds of beliefs, movements, with the family we were born into, or else with an outside group which is after all a substitute for the family. Even the Buddhist, seeking non-attachment, is attaching himself to something: to his beliefs; he is still identifying with something although this something may be an abstract idea. The normal person is bound to develop self-consciousness (consciousness of self) as he grows; in fact, self-consciousness unfolds to a certain extent without any apparent effort on his part. But the step out of this separated consciousness into a consciousness integrated with a fuller, or absolute consciousness, requires an effort which in some cases seems almost insurmountable.

Human consciousness, as Jung describes it, can be likened unto a tide which flows out of the deep on to the shore of the earth-plane, and then appears to be drawn back again into the mighty depths. But while lapping the shore of earth-life, it is still part of the great ocean of consciousness, or of the fuller expanse of the spirit-life. This is where the "meeting of the waters" of the spirit takes place with the shore or fringe of matter. The ebb and flow of the tide exemplifies the fluctuation of the outer consciousness breaking on the beach of the material world and receding back into the full flood of collective or absolute inner consciousness.

To turn to Russell's comments, he asks what is identity in relation to the human species? Definition of the essential identity of a person is much more difficult to achieve than the mere description of outer appearance by which we recognise those whom we know. The outer appearance, as we know, can be changed either by the passage of time or the onslaught of disease, or by artificial means such as the use of cosmetics and plastic surgery. We see, therefore, that the identity of a person is not the outer covering, but the inner self. Thus, when the body perishes, it is not the real identity which perishes; the real identity, the self that is intangible as far as the material world is concerned, survives and continues to evolve.

Now, the intriguing question, Russell stipulates, is where and how does identity commence? The materialist will presume that identity commences at conception or perhaps with actual birth. He cannot demonstrate that this is not so, but can only argue that what is now in manifestation must always have been incipient, for you cannot have something developing from nothing. Granted that identity becomes aware and palpable during the course of evolution or incarnation or unfoldment, but we cannot say categorically that there was a time when it did not exist at all in some form. In a sense, therefore, we date back to the beginning of time: we were in the beginning, and have advanced with the stream of life to the present. One begins to get the feeling of timelessness and continuity which are so difficult for the human mind to imagine.

This chronological development of identity gives us more clearly a picture of our continuing evolution. It is useless to try to trace specific developments, but we can perceive the general unfoldment that has taken place and continues. The text, "*As it was in the beginning is now and ever shall be* begins to take on a new, deeper meaning. *Before Abraham was, I am*. We can perceive life as a whole and gain a sense of unity. We can attach a purpose to life without which we feel lost, insecure, and futile.

Continuing Russell's line of thought, it might almost seem that one of the purposes of evolution is the cultivation of a sense of identity. It is this sense that distinguishes Mankind from the Animal Kingdom. But at the present time, identity is threatened by mass-orientation to material values which can easily overwhelm it through distracting it from its own stabilisation.

To grasp all the implications of our own identity (Russell says), and to become fully acquainted with our own identity, we need to know a great deal more about human nature in general. It is by comparison that we come by most of our knowledge in many fields, not least in the field of self-knowledge. We are taught so little about

168

ourselves in the majority of cases, and so little is explained to us about human nature, that we often know ourselves no better in old age than we did in youth. It is hardly surprising that there are so many misunderstandings between people, that so many find it difficult to live with others, and that so little tolerance is sometimes displayed between groups or between individuals.

Humanity's greatest problem is itself. Much of the suffering of human beings is inflicted on them not by "acts of God", but by other human beings. Many illnesses, both of the body and the mind, are caused by the thoughtless acts of others, by their cruelties and neglectfulness and disregard. Humanity's fight for survival and welfare is not a simple matter of dealing with the elements, of overcoming famine and drought, of controlling the pests which are Mankind's enemies, of finding and administering cures for its sicknessess, but of overcoming the inherent selfishness and greed of its nature, and learning to live at peace with one another.

There is a ruthlessness in human nature, Russell comments, which drives some members of the human race to stop at nothing to get their own way, and to have no scruples in employing violence to obtain their needs. It often seems futile to appeal to people's better natures which seem virtually non-existent in many cases. In their blind determination to achieve their goals, they are totally deaf to reason, apparently without any qualms of conscience, and devoid of compassion. It is as if the spark of divinity which we like to believe is contained in every human being has been extinguished and will not respond to any effort to rekindle it. In a word, it is as if a disease is eating into their very souls.

As long as the human race exists, it is bound to contain some disruptive elements, and there will always be the bigots, the aspiring dictators, the wanton destroyers. Peace-lovers must have prayed to heaven for peace so much that those very heavens must be endlessly reverberating with the clamour of their petitions. God does not wave a magic-wand and turn the violent-natured into peacable creatures, said Russell, and it is evidently heaven's edict that we ourselves must work out our own peace. Let us recognise that human nature changes little if at all, and having admitted that, we may find ourselves in a better position to negotiate with one another. We will be dealing realistically with the situation instead of escaping into idealistic daydreams. This may sound depressing. but the only effective way to cope with human nature is to face up to its weaknesses as well as its strengths.

We know there is much that is fine in human nature; we know it holds within itself a fundamental and prevailing urge to improve itself and its surroundings; and this urge must triumph ultimately. But the triumph will be reached only by consistent and united endeavours on the part of the human race itself, and by its response to the Creative Good or God.

The next section is a direct quote from Russell.

"I am far less of a cynic than I was, although I remain to be convinced of many things. I am, however, still very cynical as regards human nature, the more so, perhaps, because I can now see its pettiness in sharper detail. I am not sorry that I have left your world, for although it gave me a generous measure of success and wordly goods, it is hardly the place for the idealist which is what I was at heart. It does, however, provide much material for the philosopher; it is a rueful thought that a perfect world would be prone to make philosophy superflous. Bernard Shaw pointed out to me one day that a perfect world might also make God superflous. 'In fact', quoth he, 'If God did not already exist, Man's wickedness would make Him a virtual necessity.' "

"Shaw has a habit of expressing succinctly in a few words ideas that I myself would describe more ponderously and probably more ambiguously. That particular pithy remark of his did more to convince me of the existence of God than did many a church-man. How ironic that the wickedness of Man should strike a blow for the truth which the goodness of Man had failed to do as far as I personally am concerned.

"Do I believe in God now? Many people will want to know my answer. Yes, I now believe without equivocation, and with a positive intellectual comprehension which was and is the sole acceptable proposition as far as I am concerned. Have I seen God? That poses the next inevitable question. Not in that sense have I seen God. The eye cannot behold the glory of the countenance of God! Have I seen Jesus? This time I can answer in the affirmative. I have seen this Man who was God's representative on earth. In his presence I am awed, for his purity and compassion so flood his being that I feel I am in the presence of God. It is a disconcerting feeling to one who measures things by the intellect.

"You may not believe that it is I, Bertrand Arthur William Russell, who am saying these things, and perhaps there is no conclusive proof that I can offer through this somewhat restricted medium. Those with an ear to hear may catch the echo of my voice in my phrases, the tenor of my tongue in my tautology; those who do not wish to hear will no doubt conjure up a whole table of tricks to disprove my retrospective rhetoric.

"There will come a time, already inaugurated, in human affairs, when mind will be able to reach mind independent of material means. This mind-to-mind process will be the key to extended communication with discarnate minds. I am able to contact many minds in your world, but this is done without their knowledge because their minds do not recognise the interpolation of thought which they misinterpret as their own. As a rule, it is possible only to touch in thought those whose minds have a similar attunement. You need not fear that you are all being subjected to a continual bombardment of thought from discarnate (and incarnate) beings of all kinds; you have your own wave-length and can only receive upon that frequency.

"Experiments supervised by your present scientists will demonstrate that an interchange of thought is a far more common occurrence than envisaged. There is a network of thought-waves the same as there is a network of radio waves, and the two in your world are closely interwoven. You are on the verge of startling discoveries in this field, and it will take some time for the world to adjust to the disclosures. The need for a sensible and balanced approach will rapidly become apparent, and the charlatans on the scene will be able to take advantage of the discovery until a system of detection is sufficiently organised to discriminate between valid operations and simulated ones.

"Working with Mrs. Brown has been an interesting experiment in communication for me. I have been able to observe that the "line" of communication sometimes carries whole phrases in their entirety without so much as the loss of a single syllable. At other times, words have been mutilated or obliterated altogether, through no fault of mine or the receiver. Both she and I have sometimes been aware of these deficiencies, and endeavoured to correct them. She has been very doubtful whether she registered certain words accurately, and has queried several with me. Trying to check back with me has proved helpful, I believe, but we cannot guarantee a foolproof manuscript or what she said Tovey has dubbed a 'foolproof proof'.

"I have aimed at plain speech because I wish to be intelligible to as many as possible and not address myself specifically to the highbrows. The highbrows often consider it their exclusive prerogative to assess everything and interpret everything. I hope the populace will not allow themselves to be over-ridden by this small and often circum

171

scribed section of their community. The populace may not have acquired the same expertise in logic and argument as their highbrow counterparts, but they have a natural intelligence which is often quite as capable of grasping an understanding of the obstruse. Intelligence is not the monopoly of the rich nor the aristocratic,which is a fortunate thing for them because if it were, the structure of society, which is based on a framework of labour, would speedily collapse.

"I have taken a great deal of Mrs. Brown's time and energy, and hope that readers will feel it has been worth while. The world in which I now live is a world of ideas, but is, nevertheless, a very real world. There is, in fact, a permanence in this world where I now dwell which contrasts strongly with the material world, and the latter appears quite unsubstantial from my present dimensions. You can certainly understand that your world is a transient world where everything is subject to change and decay. It is so transient, in fact, that you would expect more people to seek for permanent values and for the stream of everlasting life.

"The material world is a world of ideas also – ideas being expressed in terms of matter or material substance. But matter has a relatively very slow frequency which responds only in a crude fashion. It has a clogging effect on mind and spirit which dulls the intelligence and weights the soul. Through struggling towards freedom from this clogging effect, Mankind's intelligence will become more powerful, and his soul will rise.

"I wish to mention another matter which could be of some assistance to many with their work or problems. Mrs. Brown could scarcely believe me when I drew her attention to the fact that a mental technique which she frequently employs was one that I, too, employed. She told me that as far as she can recall, she stumbled on this technique as a child. Having become aware of the fact that life consists of more than the material aspect, (through her inborn psychic nature), she realised that she could draw knowledge from other planes, from other levels of consciousness. As she grew up, she developed the habit of referring to the "Supreme Wisdom" for guidance and enlightenment. If she wished or needed to know what course to pursue with regard to some particular concern, she would (to use her own words) "tell God about it and wait for his answer". She was using the same technique as I used, although expressing it in different terminology. I had a practice of implanting my problems, especially in connection with my work, in my subconscious mind by

172

holding them firmly for a time in my conscious mind; I would then leave the problem to gestation, and in due course, the subconscious would give birth to the solution. It is such a simple process that any one could adopt it, although it requires a great deal of concentration and practice to perfect it.

"Mrs. Brown discovered that she could apply this process to many fields, including the psychic ones. By focussing her attention intensely she managed to achieve effectual communication with a number of musicians in my world, subject, inevitably, to variations in the degree of success. She would sit in deep meditation, seeking enlightenment, or in contemplation of God awaiting divine inspiration, and this prepared the channel for her to draw forth the hidden wisdom and achieve rapport with inspired beings or with the source of inpsiration itself.

"I knew, even in my lifetime on earth, that I was somehow tapping the roots of a universal intelligence, but this implied the existence of a Supreme Intelligence which people would classify as God. As this conception was somewhat untenable to me, I dismissed it and gave my subconscious mind the entire credit for the solutions I received, which certainly took the form of revelations.

"One does need the application of a certain amount of intelligence, of course, in this practice of sowing problems into the subconscious and reaping the solutions. There are some schools of psychology now giving instruction in the practice; some people will find that they possess a natural talent for the process, but others may find the required effort demands too much exertion if they are unaccustomed to mental concentration.

"In the world, people turn their attention to the conscious mind almost exclusively , and ignore the sub-strata of the deep intelligence latent within the subconscious. The conscious mind is like the top of an iceberg; submerged below the surface the greater bulk of the mind floats unseen. Most people remain on the surface all their lives; few have the time or inclination to plumb the depths and raise the treasures that await there.

"As a parting remark, I should like to tell people that they are far more fearfully and wonderfully made than they suspect. They are gods in the making, but the making has to be of their own. The tragedy is that so few make it.

173

CHAPTER 18

The piano that played itself, and other phenomena

Apart from the clairvoyance, clairaudience and other aspects of "mental mediumship", as such gifts are sometimes known, there have been occasional manifestations of a more physical nature in the psychic field. Perhaps it is a pity that such manifestations are not more common, so that a greater number of people could experience psychic activities that they themselves might see or hear. On the other hand, such occurrences might prove rather spine-chilling to the uninitiated!

We have all heard of hauntings of various places, and there are histories of famous and ancient buildings being positively spook-ridden. The research carried out by bodies such as the Ghost Club has accumulated so many records of such hauntings that unless we are utterly illogical or too afraid to believe in these things, we must recognise that they do take place, although we may not understand them.

I myself believe that many of these hauntings are psychic echoes of things which took place long ago, things that were so fraught with tragedy or terror that they made a vivid impression on the surroundings. I do not think they are always due to the presence of an active spirit, but to a "replay", to use a modern term, of acts that happened in the past. It may not be easy to determine which are echoes of the past and which are the activities of a ghostly presence. Research may eventually reveal how we can distinguish between the two.

Occasionally, I myself have witnessed the movements of earthly objects or heard with my own ears sounds that were clearly not accountable by what we call "natural causes". I am not particularly interested in such manifestations – which is perhaps the reason why

174

they do not occur very often in my presence – and I usually dismiss them as mildly interesting but purposeless.

One of these manifestations took place when I was in my teens and was having a discussion with a school-friend about religion. This friend of mine had been brought up in a Roman Catholic Convent, a place where the fear of God and the Devil and Hell-fire had been driven deeply into the poor girl's mind. She was a nervous wreck because she was only too aware – as any honest person – of her shortcomings, and lived in constant dread of the Hell-fire she was convinced must await her after death. She was also the victim of a sadistic father who got drunk regularly and caned her mercilessly on the slightest pretext. I often wonder what became of her. We lost touch during the war, in the same way as many people lost touch with friends or relatives through the breakdown of communications and the general destruction and upheaval.

I tried to give her some peace of mind, and to mitigate some of the harm done to her by the teaching to which she had been subjected. She asked me whether I believed in another life, and I replied that I not only believed but was sure of it because I had seen my own brother and conversed with him after he had died. I told her that he had assured me, since his passing, that God is a Being of Infinite Love, and not the vengeful, punishing deity as sometimes misrepresented to us.

My friend sat beside me on the settee in front of the fire-place. She stared into the fire, and said how awful it was to think that one day she would be cast into fire, the everlasting fire.

"Nonsense!" I cried, "You must put that idea right out of your mind. It is not true. God would not do a thing like that; if He did, He would not be a God of Love, Mercy and Compassion. God loves you. He loves us all, although we are not perfect."

"Oh! I wish I could believe that God loves me," my friend cried, wringing her hands in desperation," I wish your brother could give me some sign to show me that I won't go to hell when I die."

I was appalled to see such damage to a young, sensitive mind by misguided preaching. It seemed that my friend would go through life tormented by the fear that had been rammed into her. Silently I prayed for her to be helped, and for her to understand the great depth of God's tender, all-enfolding love.

Suddenly, we were both startled by a loud tapping sound coming from the mantel-shelf. We looked up, and watched spell-bound as a large, weighty vase which stood in the centre of the shelf, moved

175

backwards and forwards, striking the mirror which was behind it. It struck the mirror three times altogether, then returned to its central position and was still. For a moment, my friend and I were silent, speechless at this strange happening. Then my friend suddenly burst out, "It was a sign! It was the sign I had prayed for, the sign of the Holy Trinity. Don't you see, the vase struck three times, the number of the Trinity. I was praying to the Father, the Son, and the Holy Ghost for help, and that was the answer to my prayer."

She fell on her knees, weeping quietly, and stammering, "God be praised. He heard me . . . He answered me."

Was it my brother in spirit, knocking the vase against the mirror? Was he aware of her distress, of her dire need for reassurance, and had he caused the manifestation to give her comfort? Was it a divine intervention in response to her desperate prayers? Whatever or whoever produced the phenomenon, it was certainly miraculous in the effect on my friend. From being a trembling, fearful person, she changed into a radiantly self-confident young woman, assured of God's loving care for her.

I wonder sometimes where she is now. If she ever reads this, I would like to tell her that I have that vase to this day, and whenever I look at it, I am reminded of the "Sign from Heaven" which freed her from her burden of fear. Her name was Mary McGowan, and she lived in Streatham, and went to my school. I expect she married young – she was a pretty girl, and I hope she has had a happy life.

I must say that vase has never behaved like that since! But we possessed one object which often behaved in a strange manner. This was the old reconditioned piano that I managed to acquire several years after the War. It began to do its tricks in my Mother's time. She and I would be sitting quietly, sipping our afternoon tea in broad daylight, talking of little everyday matters, when the piano would suddenly decide to play! The lid over the keyboard was often left open, as my Mother had a theory that it was better for the piano, keeping it "aired" in some way. We would sit and watch the notes of the keyboard going up and down as if being pressed by unseen fingers. Liszt told me in later years that he was responsible, since he was trying to attract my attention.

Some years after my Mother had passed away, and also my husband, my daughter, then aged about seventeen years, was unable to sleep one night, She told me the next morning that she decided to get up and make herself some tea. Her brother and I were fast asleep in our respective bedrooms. She brewed some tea, and sat

176

drinking it in the kitchen at the back of the house, with our dog and cat beside her, when she heard several chords being played quite loudly on the piano which was in a room towards the front of the house. Thinking I had come down from my bedroom and begun to play, she went to the room to ask me if I would like a cup of tea – and the room was empty! She found I was still asleep in bed, two flights of stairs above, in the front part of the house. We reasoned it out that had a mouse been responsible, it might have made possibly some slight sound . . . although I doubt whether the weight of a mouse could produce so much as one pianissimo note! But a mouse certainly could not play chords loudly . . . unless it was a very musical and powerful one!! We presumed Liszt was the performer.

This story had a remarkable sequel. When I moved out of the large old house which was the family heritage, I had to go into a very much smaller residence. By this time, a kind and generous benefactor had presented me with a new, small upright piano, and there was scarcely room for this in my new home, let alone the old reconditioned piano. I was obliged to dispose of the old piano, and it became the property of a friend of mine with a spacious house three stories high. The piano had been installed in her house for about six months, when it gave cause for alarm. My friend had a lodger in her house, a young man who is a Roman Catholic, and he was the witness in this case to the activity of the "haunted piano".

One night when he was unable to sleep, he heard the "ghostly pianist" at work. A chord, not just a single note, was played clearly and distinctly, but everyone else in the house was in bed asleep. He said he was so scared that he almost rushed out of the house, but as it was the middle of the night, he thought better of it, especially as he was afraid he might rouse the rest of the household from its slumbers. My friend related the incident to me a few days later when we met, and said they had teased the lodger by saying he must have had too much spirit of the alcoholic type. He denied flatly that he had had anything to drink, and said he knew he had not imagined it because he is not given to flights of imagination. He did not know at the time, neither did my friend, that the piano had acquired the habit of playing itself – or being played by ghostly fingers. I had made no mention of the phenomenon when the piano changed hands, as I was under the impression that the ghostly playing only took place in my old home. I did not expect the ghostly pianist to be transferred with the pianoforte!

Since such occurrences do not convey any message, or any intel-

177

ligible message, as a rule, my own interest in them is not very deep. I prefer communication which is of such a nature that it provides definite indication of the communicator, and a message that is worth while. All the same, the experience with the vase had certainly accomplished a valuable purpose without my friend or myself knowing exactly who or what was responsible for the manifestation.

There was once a psychic manifestation at a Television Centre which was seen by several people. This took place in Birmingham at the Associated Television Studios while I was there to take part in a programme produced by Wendy Cooper in May 1971. Wendy wrote an article about this event in the Birmingham Post, and it was published under the Saturday Magazine section. She told the whole story of the interview, and mentioned the visible phenomenon under the sub-title, *The jacket moved.*

The jacket in question was the cover of my book, *Unfinished Symphonies.* Wendy had obtained a copy of the book to look through before meeting me. It was the first time I myself had seen the illustrated jacket of the book, and after I had looked at it, Wendy placed it on the piano stool and we moved away from the stool to sit and converse on two chairs while waiting for the set to be prepared for the broadcast. In Wendy's own published account she wrote, "In the past I have certainly been somewhat sceptical where the supernatural is concerned, and none of the mediums or clairvoyants I have met and interviewed has done anything to change my mind.

"Rosemary Brown has – or at the very least she has forced my mind open to the fact that there is something about her story and her music that defies rational explanation.

"The whole business is extraordinary, and made the more so because it is happening to seemingly such a very ordinary woman. There she sat, middle-aged, middle-class, from Balham, explaining to me simply that Liszt was there with us, and that he always went with her to concerts or television shows concerned with her music.

"Occasionally she asked him questions and gave us his answers. At one point, *Liszt actually picked up and moved the illustrated jacket of her book,*" The emphasis is mine. It seemed extraordinary that Liszt should be able to demonstrate such a phenomenon in a bustling television studio, full of technicians and apparatus.

My mother and I often witnessed an unusual phenomenon in our old house at Balham. On the landing, there was a row of hooks, about half a dozen, on which we used to hang our coats. When we first became aware of this phenomenon, there were only three of us

178

living in the house. My middle brother had passed on, and my elder brother had married and moved away. There were just my parents and myself left.

We would hang our coats up by the loops provided for that purpose, simply slipping each loop over a hook. When we next went to fetch our coats, we would find the loops wound over and over so tightly that we had a job to get the coats off the hooks! This happened repeatedly, and my mother took it as a sort of joke on the part of some spirit. Or else she would say, "Ah! the fairies have been at their tricks again."

We even tried to wind our coats on to the hooks in the same way, but found it completely impossible. There was obviously no means by which human agency could get those loops twisted into so many tightly-wound coils.

This particular phenomenon was all the more fascinating because it used to follow us wherever we went. We would find our coats with the loops twisted into umpteen coils in the houses of other people whom we visited, much to the mystification of our hosts or hostesses. Once, after my Father had passed away, my Mother and I managed to scrape up enough money to afford a week's holiday at Christchurch, where we stayed in a small guest house. To economise, we shared a double-room. We hung our coats on the hooks on the door. Sure enough, the same thing happened there, and my Mother said, "The fairies have come with us."

I always used to sleep poorly on the first night in a strange bed, and so I spent the hours sleepless after we had first arrived at Christchurch. There was no-one in that room but my Mother and myself, yet overnight the coat loops were twisted so much that we had to break one of the loops of one coat in order to remove it from the hook. My Mother had slept soundly through the night, unaware of what was happening, and although I had felt a presence in the room, I had seen nothing unusual- though in the darkness I can see clairvoyantly just as clearly or sometimes more so.

Since my Mother passed away, this phenomenon has ceased. In some way, it was apparently connected with her because it followed her from place to place. I came to the conclusion that it could have been caused by someone in spirit who was linked with her, trying to attract her attention. After her transition to the Spirit World, I suppose it was no longer necessary for the person responsible for the phenomenon to indulge in the looping of the loops! Perhaps the person concerned was able to contact my Mother in the Spirit World,

179

and reveal his or her identity to her.

It is a wonder that there are not more cases of phenomena that can be seen or heard by people in general. Certainly a great deal of scepticism would be sorely tried if such happenings were common! But Liszt said that most spirits avoid such activities because they do not want to scare us "mortals", and they do realise that many of us would be frightened to death by psychic manifestations. We have been brainwashed heavily down the centuries into a fear of such phenomena. Attempts have been made and are still being made by some people or organisations to cut us off from the World of Spirit. We cannot be cut off, of course, since spirit is all-pervading and transcends matter; but we in this world have obstructed endeavours to make a break-through because of our fears, superstitions, and prejudices. It is very difficult for spirit to manifest where an atmosphere of antagonism confronts them. In fact, it is very likely that many a self-respecting spirit will not trouble to exert himself or herself to put in an appearance under such circumstances. Even in this world, we are hardly inclined to stir ourselves to visit those who will treat us as unwanted guests! If we feel ourselves to be unwelcome, we usually keep away, and no doubt this applies with equal force to the dwellers on other planes.

It is love which overcomes the barriers of time, space, and death. It is the most powerful force of all, and as people grow more loving (not in the sentimental or sexy sense, but in the true meaning of the word "love") perhaps the gap between matter and spirit will be bridged more and more fully. Love is a dynamic force, a source of energy which can be used to build lines of communication; it is love that can bind the world together in peace and harmony, and the dearth of love that is threatening to destroy the world and those who live in it.

Love in this sense simply means caring about other people. It is the love which Jesus tried to teach us in order to save us from ourselves and from one another. Only through caring about other people and other nations can we hope to build any kind of worldwide alliance which can deliver us from wars and the destruction of life and property. Only through caring can we foster world trade and mutual assistance. And it becomes more and more plain that nations and peoples need each other in order to survive and prosper.

When we have established world peace, and have learned to work for others as well as ourselves, when we have evolved into peaceable beings radiating goodwill, perhaps conditions will be more favourable
180

for the great Worlds of Spirit to blend with us in harmony and help-fulness. Our very harshness must repel the great souls in the "higher" realms; our discordant vibrations must surely have a shattering effect upon their peaceful natures. Small wonder, after all, if we hear little from those other planes of life. The world is like a battleground, constantly torn by conflict, disagreement, intolerance, and all the ills caused by human beings opposing one another, attacking one another, demolishing one another. Would angels wish to tread amongst such people? Amongst people who reject God and deny others the right to live in peace? It must be well -nigh impossible for those who belong to the Celestial Realms to penetrate our dense vibrations, and to make any impression on our unheeding natures. There are many in the world who are good-living, God-fearing people; but there are also many who are cruel and Godless. Nations are still divided against nations, and people divided against them-selves. There is so much antagonism, even between different religious groups who all profess to believe in God, that the psychic atmosphere surrounding our planet must fairly bristle with hostility and discord, which must continually rebound on to us.

If we want to commune with the saints and the sages, we must become peaceloving; if we want to walk with angels, we must fall in step with them; if we want to hear the still small voice from on high, we must be still and listen. Many at present do not want to commune with the peaceable, do not want to walk in the ways of peace, do not want to be guided by the Cosmic Wisdom: the loss is theirs, for by being warlike they deny themselves peace, and through turning a deaf ear to the voice of Wisdom, they go headlong down paths of destruction.

We are passing through times of crisis, and the whole world has become caught up in a maelstrom of economic upheaval. At the same time, a great many people have become disillusioned with orthodox religions, and need a new vision to give them hope and inspiration to work to improve our world. Perhaps this is the time when advanced souls and enlightened beings in other spheres feel the urgency to try to reach us, and to try to touch our consciousness. If they feel this way, we can be sure they will make every effort to contact us either directly or indirectly.

I hope this book will help their work, help to rekindle the light of inspiration in our minds and compassion in our hearts. We need the God-intelligence to be quickened within us to guide us through the dark and troublous times.

181

CHAPTER 19

Liszt's message to the world

I am certain that the composers appreciate the genuine love and affection which many people – of both sexes – feel for them. They have indicated that they are sometimes very moved by the world's remembrance of them, and that they feel honoured when their music is performed and applauded.

We are very obsessed with sex in our world today, and it must be difficult for people to grasp the idea that sex is only an aspect of a soul. I myself have come to regard people, not so much as men and women, as souls incarnating in a male form or a female form. When one thinks how little difference there is between female and male babies in their behaviour and reactions, and how little difference similarly between elderly women and men, one can more easily see the fundamental resemblance. During the years between babyhood and old age, when the physical characteristics take over the soul, the outer manifestation is so predominant that we are inevitably confronted by a sharp division.

Liszt, to me, is a soul, a devout soul of noble qualities. I think of him, not as a man – that was only his earthly manifestation – but as a spirit. And the same applies to the other composers and other spirits. Mundane matters, it is evident, no longer concern the souls of those who are of a spiritual nature. The earth-bound might still try to attach themselves to earthly objects or surroundings, but they would discover eventually that this is useless, and turn their attention to more elevated subjects.

I asked Liszt once whether it worried him because he is labelled a womaniser. He replied that it no longer troubles him, and that, as it is true he was like that, he has no right to complain.

"I earned myself a bad name in some respects," said he, "And I

182

fear that I deserved it. But how many people in the world are any better than I was? People are so ready to point the finger of scorn, and to forget their own sins."

He said that it does not really matter what people think of him, as long as his music enriches the world, and gives pleasure, or, better still, has an elevating effect, "The sum total of one's life is the real test. I hope that the world is the richer for my having lived in it in spite of my many peccadilloes."

He always speaks with a quiet sincerity that would surely disarm the scandal-mongers of this world. Chopin made many romantic conquests, but whereas Liszt confesses that he used to boast of his personal conquests, Chopin was more discreet about his. They said once, "Men are men, and women love to be loved: if we had been immune to their charms, we would surely have become great bores, preoccupied with ourselves and unchivalrously failing to pay tribute to their beauty and worth."

Perhaps there is something in what they said, or perhaps they were just making excuses for themselves!

Now to come to the serious side of Liszt's nature – the real Liszt. I asked him whether he would like me to pass on a message from him to the world. He looked very thoughtful, then said, "The message I would give the world is a very simple one, yet I deem it to be a message of the greatest importance. I would adjure people to do two things which any religious teacher of discernment and sincerity would teach. One, seek the truth, and never cease to seek it even when you think you have found it. Two, promote the welfare and happiness of others with all your power. In this way, people will be preparing their souls for the Life Hereafter, and making the world a better place. Everyone longs in his or her heart for happiness, yet too few are prepared to do anything to create happiness. How can you expect to receive that which you are not willing to give to others? The simple rule of life is that you reap what you sow; this may not be very obvious in your world since misguided people defeat the Cosmic Law by breaking it, and throwing it into chaos, but sooner or later the Law, which is inexorable, adjusts the scale and metes out justice. So it pays people to keep the Cosmic Law for their own sakes."

A simple message, perhaps, but none-the-less, very solemn words to a world full of self-seeking people with only a minority prepared to work for the good of the whole. It is the struggle for survival which no doubt makes people callous and greedy, in other words, they are motivated by a lack of security. But Liszt may be right: the only way to security is through the promotion of the common welfare and universal happiness. If people could see that this promotion would benefit themselves as well as others, and help to anchor their own security, they would probably be more ready to further it.

As regards the "truth", Liszt said it has no bounds, and that it is humanity which tries to set limits for it. We may catch sight, so he says, of one ray of truth, and think we have seen it all. And we each think that our ray of truth is the only one or the right one – that is, unless we are really enlightened people!

Liszt has not said anything new, we might conclude. Perhaps there is nothing new to say. But it is positive that we need to be reminded or remind ourselves of certain spiritual home-truths which it is so easy to forget in the scramble of contemporary existence. As he says, we can flout the Cosmic Law – don't we all at times! – but inevitably it will catch up with us. And I think he means this to be applied on a national and international scale. It is not so easy to find ways and means of being good neighbours to other nations, but there are growing efforts on the part of many groups, both official and unofficial. World survival may depend on these efforts.

As Shaw adds, "It is easy for a man to be a good neighbour when his belly is full, and his granary overflowing; but the hungry will clamour at his gates if they are not also fed."

Liszt said he knows how anxious many people are about the sequel to their actual passing. Naturally, they wonder where they will find themselves, in what sort of state, and how they will adapt to their new life. We have already been told that we are building our own future every moment of our lives, and that we will inherit in the Next World what we have built while here. As that world is a world of ideas, although a very real world, we will find that our hopes, desires, and above all, our expectations, supply most of the conditions for our new life. Hopes, desires, and expectations are, after all, ideas, and if we have ourselves created conditions favourable to their realisation, we shall experience fulfilment of these ideas.

For instance, those who earnestly wish or expect to see Jesus will be drawn to him by the propelling power of their own innermost impulse. One gravitates in the Next Life naturally and without effort towards those whom one loves and we go where our inclinations guide us. In this our present world, we are often unable to be with or see those whom we love because of certain circumstances; in the Next World, we are free from the interference of material obstacles and so we are reunited with our dear ones. In this world, we often have to live in an environment which we find disagreeable; in the next one, we are no longer limited by material considerations, and we are able to choose an environment which is congenial to us.

The Next World or Plane is, in fact, for most people a kind of paradise, according to Liszt and other spirits. But over and over again, they emphasise that it is a paradise into which we enter only if we have the right spirit, that is, a spirit that is imbued with right motives. We may have many shortcomings, but if we try to do our best, we will find the door to that paradise is open. It is the first lodging-place for the majority of people, but there are many planes and places, suitable for every kind of spirit – many mansions. As we evolve, we can progress from one plane to another until we reach the highermost, and dwell in the Presence of the Creator.

There are some who by their own actions have shut themselves out of paradise. But a change of heart, and a sincere attempt to improve, will lead in time to that paradise. As Liszt expresses it, "God never turns away anyone who truly repents." How do people travel or move about in the Hereafter? A question that is often posed. We all know what it is to be with someone in thought, or to be in one place, but be far away in our thoughts. In the Next Life, when we wish to be with someone, our very thought places us beside them; when we wish to be in a certain place, we hold it in our thoughts and find ourselves transferred to that place. Movement needs energy, and the energy is supplied by the force of thought or desire. Movement is therefore a thought-transportation. Thoughts are wings.

Do we need sustenance in the world hereafter, is yet another frequent question. There is, of course, no need for physical sustenance, for the physical world has been left together with the physical body. However, there is a great need for spiritual sustenance, a need which is felt by many still in the material world, but by many more in the World of Spirit because it is a world where Spirit predominates.

One can rest in the Next World if one feels the need, and newly-arrived souls often do need to rest and recuperate from their earth-lives especially when ended through ill-health that has been prolonged or caused much suffering; in such cases, the spirit has been taxed to its endurance by the suffering, and a period of restoration is necessary. But there is no enforced rest, and most souls wish to engage in some kind of activity, because continued rest usually proves boring.

What kinds of activity are available? That is the next question. There is an infinite variety of activities available in the fields of the arts, the sciences that appertain to the Hereafter – or the sciences that

185

are related to the material world, if one wishes to study them; there is opportunity to study or create in all branches of literature, music, dance, painting, sculpture, and so on. Life in the Next World is not an unrelieved state of solemnity, but a place of joy and laughter, where many kinds of worthy recreations can be followed. There is also ample opportunity for service to others, both amongst the dwellers in the Hereafter and amongst those still on earth.

People wonder – if they believe in another life – what kind of surroundings they will find there. Those who dwell in spirit tell us that there are beautiful landscapes and gardens there, cascading waterfalls and still lakes, great trees and many lovely flowers; the difference from earth lies in the richer colours which glow with life, and the much larger range of plant and tree life. There are also buildings of many kinds for various purposes, and people have their own home or place which is created for them according to that which their life on earth has made possible, or which their own thoughts have built in a manner of speaking. It is strange how many people seem to think there will not be room for all earth's millions and millions of souls – but in the Hereafter there are not earthly boundaries, nor geographical limitations, nor lack of space! People tend to think in terms of our dimensions which is understandable since those are the only dimensions they know.

In the Hereafter, we are drawn towards those with whom we have affinities, and these need not be members of our own family nor even people whom we have known on earth. Since the Hereafter is a sphere where spirit is all-powerful, souls are no longer governed by the laws of matter but by the laws of spirit. There are no material barriers to keep people apart, only barriers of understanding or, rather, the lack of it. People do retain their biases, their prejudices, and their self-opinionated attitudes for a time until they begin to see more light. Those who are the most baffled in the Next Life are the ones who believed that only the people who subscribed to their particular belief are granted Eternal Life; they find people who did not hold the same beliefs, and yet have manifestly reached the Spirit World. They have to go through an adjustment of outlook which can be hard if their false ideas were strongly entrenched.

Moving into the next stage of Life, Liszt wishes to state, is not the same as moving straight into the Highest Sphere or the plane most people would call Heaven. Not many of us are ready for that High Place when we first pass over, and it may be quite a long time before we are fully qualified. Even when we are fit for Heaven in that highest sense, a number renounce their right to enter, choosing instead to sacrifice their passport to Everlasting Bliss so that they may instead help those who have not yet made the grade. Possibly Liszt himself is amongst that number, though I doubt whether he would admit it. He is, so I have found, in many ways a very modest soul, a soul of great humility, in spite of the popular image of him as a bombastic personality.

None of us can really tell, apart from one or two exceptions, so he informs us, just how far we will find ourselves along the Path of Enlightment or the Way of Unfoldment or Spiritual Progress. Some, he says, will find themselves very much farther along the Path than they dreamed; others, who considered themselves far ahead of their fellow-beings, may find themselves lagging behind.

In his own words, "It behoves a man to walk in humility, not knowing when his hour will come, or how he will stand in the Light of Judgement."

Often it turns out to be the least that is greatest, and the greatest least. Our standards are so much of this world, with wordly success or popular esteem as the measure of a person's value or importance; but in that Other World, a person's stature is measured by his or her integral worth, states Liszt. Thus the roadsweeper may turn out to be a saint, and the peer of the realm an unrepentant scoundrel; the half-wit can prove to be an angel, and the intellectual nothing but a fiend; the illiterate peasant may transpire to be a soul of true refinement, and the over-bearing pedant to be merely a vulgar upstart. Beneath the veneer, or lack of veneer, lies the true soul, the secret self of each person. It is this real self that places each soul automatically in its true setting.

Liszt does not mean to imply that we are all hypocrites, or whitewashed sepulchres, but says that we judge too often on face-value, seeing only that outer mask which life and we ourselves have given us. There are hidden riches, he says, in every person, which for the greater part are left buried. Millions of souls never have a chance to develop their personalities or cultivate their talents; this very fact alone, he says, should make us realise the necessity for another Life in which to develop.

The seed, the embryo, is placed in this world, and pushes its way through matter, metaphorically speaking, emerging finally into the World of Spirit. Whilst the seed is buried in the earth, it cannot know what the world above is like or suspect that it exists. If it were told about it, just as likely it would not believe that such a place could

187

exist. Completely clogged about with earth, and cut off from the air, it would seem that that was all there was. How similar the situation, in the case of human life, encased in the physical vehicle in a physical world, and unable, perhaps, to imagine any other kind of environment or a spiritual world. It is very difficult for some people to picture a non-material place of habitation. To many people, the only reality is made up from things that can be detected by the five senses of the body; yet a little thought might extend their idea of reality, for when Man's imagination conceives a notion that leads to the creation of a work of art or a symphony, or to a magnificent building or a fine bridge, or to a great machine or a powerful satellite, it demonstrates the reality of that notion. The outer accomplishment is the visible or audible expression of the inner reality. In any case, the Next Plane of existence is not a transparent place, but one consisting of substance equally real and solid in a different degree to our own earth world.

There is, of course, one great difference between this world and the next: in our world, we have to exert ourselves to survive, but in the next our survival does not depend upon our exertions. Here we often have to struggle to obtain food and shelter, but since our life needs neither of these for its continuance in the Hereafter, we inherit a freedom from reliance on material things which in itself is like a taste of heaven. Greed, which often arises from fear of deprivation, is rampant on earth, which we do not need Liszt to remind us! This greed gives rise to contention and frequently to strife, and we can see that many of our troubles in the world spring from material problems. We cannot escape material problems while we are here, but they are part and parcel of the challenge to Man's spirit; and as we draw near to the end of the Twentieth Century, these material problems are clamouring for attention, and cannot be shelved by any nation. We are being brought face to face with our present realities, and can no longer ignore the cries of the hungry and oppressed. The plight of those in want is brought home to us now not only in newsprint, but also by radio and television. Many people have been living in ivory towers, but we are beginning to discover that one nation cannot survive whilst others go down: we will sink or swim together. We have to learn a great lesson, Liszt advises: that Man cannot survive, let alone prosper, unless he co-operates and shares with his fellow-beings. It is a spiritual lesson which we will be obliged to learn, if we have not already done so, through the sheer force of material circumstances.

There was a Man born nearly two thousand years ago who tried to teach us the necessity of co-operating one with another, who tried to make us see the wisdom of sharing, and to realise that we turn a deaf ear to the needs of others at our own risk. He was, Liszt construes, no unpractical dreamer, no unrealistic idealist, but a Man centuries ahead of his time, able to foresee the economic and social disasters that will overtake those who fail to practise policies of exchange, or in simple terms, give-and-take. The world's resources have to be shared if we are to avoid world-wide chain reactions of the imbalance that results from non-circulation. It is, as Liszt says, a matter of common-sense and not a question of being pious. Those who have no compassion and will not share out of kindness will slowly realise that it is good policy for their own sakes to share, exchange, and co-operate. They may well learn to be unselfish for selfish reasons!

Liszt is not urging us to practise principles which he himself did not practise. Accounts of his life describe his great generosity and his willingness to help his fellow-musicians. He was generous with his great talents, often performing to raise money for worthy and charitable causes; he gave freely of his time and energy to teach many pupils without charge; he assisted many an aspiring composer or performer to climb the ladder to success. With that total lack of jealousy so characteristic of him, he promoted the works of contemporary as well as past composers, and even supplied musical themes and ideas to others who were seeking inspiration in their work. No doubt he was self-indulgent in some ways, but as long as this indulgence caused no unhappiness to others, it was, perhaps, not such a grave sin.

I know him as a soul who not only believes in the Christian principles, but endeavours to practise them faithfully, with sufficient enlightenment to refrain from bigotry and condemnation of the beliefs of others, and sufficient compassion to care about those who suffer.

I, for one would like to express my gratitude to him for all his good work.

CHAPTER 20

Ghosts make news for journalists

Criticism is sometimes levelled against reporters in general, alleging that they are a hard-headed, hard-hearted lot who will spare no-one to get a story. In my experience, this is not the case at all, at least, not with the majority of journalists. I have, naturally, had a mixed reception from the Press, but on the whole I feel it has given me a fair hearing and a fair deal in its reports.

There have been occasional misquotes about me which may have arisen because some point has not been made clear, or through hurried editing or type-setting. The Press in this country has a high standard generally speaking, and coverage of my work has mostly been unbiased even if sceptical. There have been the inevitable snide remarks and nasty insinuations here and there – I dare say as a result of some journalists not knowing what to make of my work, and deciding to play it safe by making a show of sarcastic disbelief! They may even have been afraid of laying themselves open to ridicule if they ventured to hint that my work appears to be authentic.

When being interviewed by the Press, I have sometimes been given staunch support from the Spirit World. It is good to know that there are kindly souls on my side there, and this knowledge helps me to bear with the over-sceptical here. I was very fortunate in having an "unsolicited testimonial" from Tom Blau, the brilliant photographer of Camera Press Fame, when his "departed" mother was brought by Liszt to communicate with him. I am most grateful to Tom – and so is Liszt – for allowing me to publish an account of that event in my first book. Two other people connected with Fleet Street have been good enough to give me permission to relate further instances of spirit communication which took place quite spontaneously and unexpectedly. One is an account of messages for Unity Hall, who

190

writes for the *News of the World*; the other concerns messages for Vicki Mackenzie who writes for the *Daily Mail*. I wish to express my deep appreciation to them both for allowing me to quote from their own reports.

Vicki was sent by the *Daily Mail* to interview me about my work. The interview was quite long as Vicki questioned me conscientiously, and she wrote an excellent account which sadly was jostled out of the London Edition by more topical news. However, it was published in the Northern Editions. When the interview was almost finished I saw the spirit of a woman standing near to Vicki. Much that this lady had to say cannot be published as it concerns private family matters (so often the best "evidence" turns out to be too personal to be made public!). I described the lady's appearance, and mentioned a ring with a large stone which she said had belonged to her, but that she never wore because she felt it was too large. She said that this ring and some miniatures were still in the family's possession, and that if Vicki checked, she would find that it was so. But let me quote Vicki's own account:

"Towards the end of my interview with Rosemary Brown for a *Daily Mail* feature story, Rosemary told me she could see a woman standing near me. As Rosemary began to describe this woman, small, dainty, with a round face and an un-English accent, I thought it sounded rather like my Czech aunt who had died a couple of months beforehand. Apparently this woman was dressed in a rose-coloured, crêpe-de-chine, waisted, dress with a camelia on the collar. However, since I had only met this aunt about ten times during my whole life, I would not really be sure whether it was her or not, although I did know she was always very fond of me, just as Rosemary told me she said.

"Rosemary then told me that this woman was saying something about a large ring with a big stone she had had, although never wore. She was giving details, too, of some miniatures that she had of some of her family. Rosemary drew with pencil and paper what she had gathered was the size of them. And there were other messages of love and of a personal nature which tallied exactly with my experience at that time.

"That evening I rang my uncle, my deceased aunt's husband, and asked him about the ring and the miniatures (which, of course, I had never seen or known about). He was amazed and said that there were in fact two rings, each with a large stone which my aunt had never worn because she felt they were too large for her small hands.

191

And there were three miniatures standing in a glass case containing pictures of my aunt's cousins, miniatures two inches high, exactly the same size as Rosemary had drawn them. When I mentioned the dress, my uncle thought for a moment, then said she had worn a waisted dress with a white camelia on the collar, *long before I was born.*

"Both my uncle and I were astonished and thrilled with the accuracy of Rosemary's description of my aunt and her belongings because it seemed to make my aunt come alive again – even though neither of us had seen or heard her since her passing. And for me, who had no knowledge of the objects described, it was ultimate proof that my aunt had been seen by Rosemary Brown."

I think many people will be grateful to Vicki for having the goodness and courage to let me make this known to the world.

Before I go on to Unity Hall's account, I would like to mention an occasion when communication from the Beyond occurred during an interview with Georgina Nazer who writes for the Wimbledon News. Like Vicki, she had been sent to interview me for a "Profile" which was published in June 1973. I saw the spirit of a man standing beside Georgina, and wondered whether to take the plunge and tell her. Never knowing how such information will be received, perhaps with apprehension or disbelief, I do hesitate sometimes before passing on the details! However, Georgina seemed a very sympathetic person, and not the type to get nervous, so I took the plunge. I will quote her own account.

"By the way," said Rosemary, "Your grandfather has been standing beside you for the past few minutes. I wondered who he was, and he just informed me in a gruff voice that he was your grandfather."

"At first I thought 'Ah ha, she says this to everyone.' But she described him so well, and knew so many things about the family that this, coupled with the fact my grandmother was to go into hospital the very next day, made me think. She could, of course, have read my mind" . . . could I? What makes people so often try to explain such happenings as mind reading? What a remarkable gift I must have if I can read such a wealth of details (of which the person is obviously not thinking at the moment) from the mind! Such a feat, if one does not accept the true explanation that the information is furnished by spirits, would throw a startling light on astonishing mental abilities.

Georgina continued:

"But somehow it didn't have the flavour of a party trick. But why

192

my grandfather?"

Why not?

"How did she know such utterly typical details about him? My grandfather came because apparently he was worrying about my mother, to whom he was very close, and trying to support and comfort my grandmother, who was very lonely and sad after nearly 60 years of marriage, and after having known him from birth."

I always think how sad it must be, after spirits have managed to establish contact, to find themselves met with disbelief. But we can be comforted by the thought that disbelief does seem to be melting away in the world, and that evidence of Life after Death is steadily accumulating through the good work of many dedicated mediums, and the occasional spontaneous experience of the non-psychic or slightly psychic person.

Peter Dorling once told me a remarkable story of spirit manifestation which was witnessed by two friends of his, husband and wife. This couple were visiting the wife's old college at Cambridge for one of those "Old Girls" functions. They were crossing a wide lawn in the grounds, when the lady spotted an old college friend coming towards them.

"Oh dear!" she exclaimed to her husband. "There is so-and-so coming towards us. We can't avoid her, and she *is* such a chatterbox."

Her husband looked at the "Old girl" approaching them, and replied that they would just have to be polite.

"Strange," his wife observed, "She is wearing exactly the same clothes as she wore when we were at college together twenty years ago."

They drew abreast with the girl, who just smiled at them, and walked past.

"Phew!" sighed the lady in relief, "What a mercy that she didn't stop to talk."

Husband and wife went into the college, and were later engaged in conversation with one of the dons, when they mentioned having seen the girl in question as they walked across the lawn.

"Are you sure?" asked the don with a startled look.

"Why, yes," replied the wife, "And I noticed how strange it was that she was wearing the very same clothes that she wore when we were at college together."

The don was quiet for a moment. Then he said slowly, "That girl committed suicide soon after you left the college."

The most extraordinary feature of this case is that the husband was

193

a witness to this phenomenon. The wife's vision could be explained away by the sceptics as a trick of the memory; not so the husband's because he had never known nor met the girl whose apparition appeared.

A great many people have experienced single instances of psychic occurrences or know someone who has experienced one isolated happening. There can be various explanations for them, such as psychic echoes of past events. In cases where the apparitions, ghosts, spirits, call them what you will, volunteer information which they themselves would not have known prior to their death, we have to look for something more than a mere echo. When the couple Peter Dorling told me about saw the spirit of a former college student, it was probably an actual vision of a real spirit because it recognised and smiled at the wife. A psychic echo could hardly do that.

Now that we know that sounds and images can be conveyed by television and radio respectively, possibly we are one step nearer understanding how sounds and images can be conveyed from the World of Spirit to our world of matter. When sounds or images happen spontaneously or without warning, however, we can only study them in retrospect instead of during actual occurrence.

The best results in spirit communication often come spontaneously. I think this could be explained by the probablility that results are obtained more readily when there is complete relaxation, and no attempt to force communication. For a period of six months, I worked for one day weekly at the Spiritualist Association of Great Britain as a clairvoyant, partly as an experiment to discover whether it is possible to function psychically to order, and partly in the hope of helping a few people.

The Association is unable to pay anything above a moderate fee to mediums or clairvoyants who work there – almost a nominal fee if the mediums have heavy expenses such as fares, which most incur in travelling to and from the place. So no-one can suggest that mediums who work there are making exhorbitant profits for their efforts. Those who operate privately may make a great deal out of their work. I am not critisizing them, however, because mediumistic work can be extremely exhausting, coupled with which mediums run the gauntlet of sceptics and hostile critics, and often deserve any reward they receive for giving their time and energy to their sitters or clients.

The results that I obtained during my work at the Association, as far as I can judge from sitters' comments, almost without fail achieved some good evidence and clear contacts. Sometimes, I was

194

told, the results were brilliant, at other times good but not sensational. This satisfied me that it is possible to sit continuously for a variety of people from all walks of life with differing view-points and histories, and still get results. But it demonstrated plainly that the sitters themselves can either assist or hinder results according to their own attitude and emotional state. It is extremely difficult to obtain good results for a very antagonistic person; the hostile vibrations set up evidently deter those in spirit, and certainly make it hard for the medium to get in touch with the World of Spirit.

Although I was sitting, of course, at routine times and by appointment, I tried to remain relaxed and not allow any tension to arise. The moment tension develops, communication is hampered. Yet mediums must sometimes be worried by the responsibility they undertake, and perhaps become over-anxious to produce satisfactory demonstrations. Truly their lot is an unenviable one, especially when they have sitters who expect them to solve all their worldly problems for them!

While I was working at the S.A.G.B. I came to know some of the mediums who worked there regularly. Without exception, they seemed to be sincere and activated by good motives to try to give comfort to the bereaved and evidence of Life Hereafter to inquirers. Yet some of them appeared to fail lamentably when put to the test by anonymous reporters from a national newspaper. I remember one day I had a gentleman enter the room for a sitting with me, and I did not know him from Adam. Liszt, however, seemed to be on the *qui vivre*, because he told me quickly that the man had only come because he was doing research. I passed this information on to the man, who admitted that was the case. Next Liszt said that the man wrote reports on his research, and I passed this on as well, and the sitter acknowledged it to be true. By that time, my mind had become wary and not conducive to communication. In spite of this, there were some contacts made, and some information furnished, which the man grudgingly, it seems, agreed was correct. There appeared to be a bitterness in his attitude which did not help to secure harmonious rapport with spirit. I felt he was one of those who would not believe though one rose from the dead before his very eyes!

It seems common-sense that a friendly attitude towards spirit will encourage contact. Would we walk into a hostile atmosphere if we could avoid it? Of course not, and neither, apparently, will spirits. Also, communication seems to take place more easily when there is no demanding nor exacting attitude on the part of medium and

195

sitters. In the same way as we try to avoid people who are demanding and exacting in this world, so spirits, too, seem to shy away from this kind of thing. It is best to let *them* say what they want to say, rather than ply endless questions to them and try to extract what information we want. Sometimes they do offer to try to answer questions, although, of course, they cannot guarantee to know the answers. On the whole, if they come to see us, it is usually because *they* want to say something, and they may not like being subjected to any attempt to quiz them. When it comes to the kind of person who is a clever-stick bent on trying to trip them up and discredit mediumship, it is not at all surprising if results are confused, misleading or inaccurate. Sitters or investigators who practise deception are guilty of wreaking havoc by setting up the equivalent of atmospheric disturbances which interfere with reception in radio and television.

Journalists are usually open-minded, which they need to be if they are to make unbiased reports. Their duty, we would take it, is to cover the news as comprehensively and accurately as possible. In this country, since we have a certain range of freedom of speech and writing, we are fortunate enough to be given generally reliable accounts of events supplied by a press that, for the greater part, takes a pride in its integrity. Political currents may sometimes have some sway, but in religious matters discrimination is rarely to be detected.

Perhaps it is this very attitude of impartiality in journalists that has created favourable conditions for contact with spirit during interviews with some of them. Journalists have to be good listeners, too, and this must be helpful. The next account of successful communication from the Hereafter is provided by Unity Hall, who can be judged to be a shrewd observer and has no religious axe to grind.

I first met Unity nearly four years ago through my work. I took to her immediately, finding her a sympathetic listener with keen insight into the frailties of human nature. Before long, I found myself confiding in her about the way I had been "pushed around" by bossy people and been the victim of many acrimonious attacks in print and speech (even by some whom I had regarded as my friends)! "Well", she said, "your work is naturally very controversial, and some people will be unscrupulous enough not only to be derogatory about it, but also to try to defame you." It has been alleged more than once that I was doing it all for money (that's a laugh – I could have earned far more as a typist or teleprinter operator over the years than I have accrued from royalties and the occasional fee for playing the piano!), but, as Unity pointed out, most people think first and foremost of money and would suspect others of doing what they themselves would do and of being "on the make". I suppose it is true that we judge others mostly by our own standards!

What was most amazing of all with regard to adverse criticism were the allegations that the music is "no good". That, perhaps, is really the least cause for concern, since in the past there were critics who said that Schubert's music was no good, that Chopin's music was no good, and so on ad infinitum! At one recital, critics were overheard in the bar during the interval to be actually conspiring together to decide how they could "scotch" the whole thing. One was heard to say that he did not want a woman muscling in on his territory! Together, the conspirators admitted that they could not deny that the music was in the style of the composers concerned. So they decided to say it was rotten music in so many words!

Mercifully – for the sake of the composers striving to establish the authenticity of their break-through – a large and growing number of musicians pay tribute to some of the music, singing its praises. Novello's have now published a first album of a few of the piano pieces, and this has wrung a measure of respect from some of the detractors of the music. As someone remarked sagely, publishers cannot risk publishing anything of doubtful quality. The publishers introduced me to the Director of Music for Jersey and the Seychelles, and I was absolutely thrilled when he told me that, had I composed the music myself, he would have made me a doctor of music on the strength of it.

Unity received communications on two separate occasions. The first one took place when she and I and another guest were relaxing after dinner, and I became aware that the spirit of a young man was standing behind her with one hand on her shoulder which she could not feel and just as well because it might have been a little un-nerving for her! I described his appearance, and she was able to identify him. Then he proceeded to give a message about something so secret that it fairly took the wind out of her sails. It was a secret known only to her – but our secrets are often known by spirit, as in this case.

The second occasion was at my home, just as we were finishing a meal, and taking coffee. Beside Unity stood the spirit of another man, and he so much resembled Stan Laurel (of comedy fame through his dual act with Hardy) that I very nearly began to chuckle. The spirit even had the same little quiff of hair standing up on his head!

He was plumper in the face, and of stockier build, so that I could tell that it was not Laurel the comedian. Having described his appearance to Unity, I then told her what he had to say. It was Unity's father who had very recently passed into the Spirit World. He spoke of a number of family matters, of which I could not have known, and sent a comforting message to his wife. He came across so clearly that Unity was quite moved – Fleet Street has a heart, though it may not wear it on its sleeve!

The sequel to this manifestation gave cause for rejoicing. Unity passed the messages faithfully on to her mother who naturally had been grieving and unable to sleep. Unity said that after receiving the messages, her mother had her first good night's sleep since her father had died. It might have been only a coincidence that she had a good night's sleep, but I like to think that Unity's father had managed to reach his wife (or widow) with the messages and to give her some comfort and reassurance.

This brings up the point sometimes argued about Spiritualists and others who believe in another life: that we should not grieve for someone who has passed away. This, in my opinion, is sheer non-sense. Even if we know there is Life after Death, even if we know our dear ones who have gone beyond the veil are near to us and watching over us, if we are human and love them, of course we miss their earthly presence, the little endearments of sharing daily life, the affectionate conversations. Unless we are without feelings, we are sure to feel some sorrow, the same as we feel when close friends or loved relatives emigrate to a distant country and we are unlikely to see them for a long time.

To indulge in unrestrained grief, however, is possibly rather selfish, for we are probably just pitying ourselves for our loss. Also, we should not like to think that our loved ones who have passed on can see how deeply we are immersed in sorrow. They would want us to be as happy as possible, and our sadness might well cloud their new-found release. To go to the other extreme, and suppress all feeling, is not a wise course, as I myself discovered.

My beloved mother died in January 1961. Only seven months later, my dear husband also passed away. Because I did not want my two small children to be surrounded by a miserable atmosphere, I kept my sadness buried deep inside, and fought hard not to give way to tears, even when they were asleep. It was, so my doctor told me some months later, a great mistake on my part. In February of the following year, I fell seriously ill with gastro-enteritis or something of the

198

sort. When I had recovered, the doctor told me I had had a close call.

"You've been suppressing your grief," he stated perceptively, "And it has taken its toll by undermining your health."

I may owe my life to the neighbour who lived opposite me at that time. I had struggled on for several days, becoming steadily worse, but thinking that I might be better the next day. Then one morning I found myself too ill to be able to sit up in bed. My daughter, poor child, was suffering from an attack of asthma and in no fit condition to go out for help. We had no telephone, and the only person left to fetch help was my son who was only just five years old.

I asked him to bring me a pencil and paper, and I wrote a short note to say that I was very ill and needed the doctor, and could someone please telephone one. Then I sent the little chap off to a nearby neighbour whom I knew had a telephone. To my astonishment, he returned to say that the lady in question was too busy doing her weekly wash to telephone. I sent him off again to another neighbour on the opposite side of the road, instructing him to cross carefully. Back he came again, to report that this lady was too tired to do anything!

By then, I was getting desperate. I felt that if I did not get medical attention, I might well slip into the Next World myself.

"Try Mrs. Jenkins opposite. Perhaps she will help," I said.

My children both knew the plump, kindly lady opposite who was the mother herself of two grown sons. She came straight over with my son, took one look at me and exclaimed, "My God! I'll get the doctor."

This dear lady – a Roman Catholic incidentally – was goodness itself. She took charge of the children, and told me not to worry about them.

"I'll take care of them until you are better," she volunteered.

But for her, I could have died in the bedroom at the top of the house without anyone knowing. She was a real Christian, God bless her.

CHAPTER 21

Whence and whither

Two imponderable mysteries are expressed in the words heading this chapter: two mysteries which many seek to solve because as beings in a transient world we feel the need for some explanation of Man's origin and his destiny. Since we live in a world of causes and effects, that is, a world where the past has shaped the present, and the present is shaping the future, some of us look inquiringly into the past for clues to the continuing pattern of our existence. But the distant past is not very accessible, and we do not know how far back the past stretches behind us. We cannot even be sure that our past began on this planet. So the past remains shrouded in mystery.

The future, too, must remain a mystery since it has not yet happened – at least, not as far as we are concerned. It seems to be still in the melting-pot, still being moulded from the present. The past is over and cannot be altered; can we direct the future as much as we wish? That is really the important question for humanity.

To some extent, we can detect the Law of Cause and Effect at work. We know that certain actions will produce certain results. There appears, however, to be an element of chance in operation, and it is probably this element which supplies us with a gleam of hope regarding the shaping of our future. If there were no element of chance, we could plan and carry out everything with mathematical precision, and create a robot-style existence. Without an element of chance, there could be no free-will; without free-will, we would be mere puppets without any self-engendered volition of mind or body. We could not then be held personally responsible.

However, we recognise that the laws which govern the universe appear to be immutable; hence we have immutable law encountering something which is quite incongruous to its nature – the element of

200

chance. Is there really no such thing as chance, after all, or is there what we might regard as a flaw in the working of the universe? Does this give some indication of a plan gone wrong? Would not a perfect plan have made provision for all events and chains of events? The more we think about it, the deeper the waters in which we find ourselves.

If we examine the matter more closely, we will find that the apparent element of chance is, in fact, subject to the same immutable laws. An accident happens as a result of certain consequences, therefore, it is still directed by the law of cause and effect. If I step rashly into the pathway of an oncoming vehicle, it is sure to collide with me; but if I am cautious, and try to ensure that no vehicle is within striking distance of myself, I can cross the road in safety. This points to the possibility of some control of the chance element. We have a degree of free-will, as far as we can judge, but we know that we do not always operate our free-will wisely and with foresight.

We can now deduce that matter is subject to immutable laws, but that mind seems to have some choice. How far can we extend our choice in everyday matters and in matters of eternal values? Every day choice is largely conditioned by our phsycial needs and by the governing influences exerted over us by state, country, climate, social standards, and so forth. In matters of eternal value, we have a much wider choice, so the dwellers in spirit would have us believe. In the material world, we are subject to the laws of matter; in the spiritual world, we are not subject to these laws, but we are subject to the laws of spirit. These laws are also immutable, so we are told by spirit; we could hardly expect them to be anything other than immutable if there is a constant principle governing everything. Wherever we look, in the physical world or in the spiritual world, there are evidences of this constant principle in operation. I should, perhaps, use capital letters when speaking of it, since this Principle must be the Creative Source or Creator. It is reassuring to know that there is a constant factor functioning: how much more vulnerable we would be, were the whole universe devoid of this stabilising influence.

There are laws, Cosmic Laws we might call them. How, did these laws come into existence? Did they form as Creation came into being, automatically relating themselves to each phase of evolution? Did the laws come first or did Creation come first, or did they happen together? We seem back to the old question of the chicken and the egg, and which came first. Whichever did come first, there must have been a triggering off of the whole process. What or who triggered off the Cosmos? "God", the religious will answer; and the scientist will promptly ask "What is God, or what do you mean by God?" We can only reason that God was the beginning and was *before* the beginning. Whatever or whoever began it all *was* before it all began! Infinity presents itself, incomprehensible to the limits of our understanding.

Once, when I was in contact with Einstein, I asked tentatively whether he could say anything to help me to understand these great cosmic processes. He said in reply that each universe is a vortex of energy, and that there are countless universes. What are these vortexes of energy, and how do they arise, I wanted to know. Where do they come from, in other words, and what sets them in motion?

"You must realise, my child," said he, "That energy existed in toto."

In toto? I made a mental note to look that up to get the exact meaning.

"Also," he continued without a break, "That energy is indestructible. You can only change energy into another kind of energy, which is one of the basic principles of science. You cannot annihilate energy: you can only push it into another dimension. This is what is happening in the multitude of universes all the time; energy is being transformed into other types of energy, and is thus responsible for all the manifestations of life."

Energy, then, is the essence of Creation, I thought. As if he had read my thought, Einstein spoke again.

"Energy is the impulse of the Instigator of all manifestations. The thought-waves of the Almighty, if you like to put it that way. Energy proceeds from the Almighty, from the heart of Creation, from the Central Mind, the very nucleus of all energy. Don't ask me about that nucleus of energy. It defies definition. It defies analysis. It cannot be approached by mere man, even in his spirit body. It possesses a concentration of power so intense that it is indescribable even in scientific terms. It is self-charging, inexhaustible, perpetual. An ancient soul with whom I have conversed in one of the thought-spheres over here informed me that to approach that nucleus, you must first discharge all your incipient energy, become empty of energy so to speak; then and only then can you move into its sphere. It is like speaking in riddles because the matter is so complex. Only an empty vessel can be filled from the source of energy. It is a paradox because energy can only be shifted to another level, and cannot be destroyed. Energy levels, energy levels. . . ."

202

He seemed to go off on a trail of thought, as if still pondering on the meaning. I felt that I had set off on another unending path of inquiry. Somewhat whimsically, I reflected that if we could tap that energy, we could overcome the energy crisis that has hit the world.

When I have had the opportunity to ask several of the wiser souls in other spheres to throw some light on Man's ultimate destiny, their replies have all concurred with one another, yielding the same information although worded in varying phraseology. Humankind, according to them, is destined to attain reunion with the God-head after evolving through eras towards complete enlightenment. But, they all insist, reunion will not spell cessation of individuality or activity, instead, there will be an amalgamation of individuality with the Whole, and renewed activity as a result of that merging – or Spiritual Marriage, as some of the sages prefer to express it.

Meanwhile, as they all point out, we can take but one step at a time, and should relate ourselves to the present which is, for us, the immediate reality. They do not recommend that we should brood over the past or dream of the future, but pay attention to the moment, to each moment, learning all we can as we pass through each one; and by constructive thoughts, by positive speech and action for good, build an auspicious future through judicious application to the present.

Many people do not bother about the future, either their own or anyone else's. But the march of time moves forward, carrying us all into the future. We are advised not to waste time dreaming of the future, but this does not imply that we should ignore it or dismiss it as if it is non-existent. Whenever we have a margin of choice between positive and negative, between constructive and destructive, between beneficial and detrimental, that is our chance – the element of chance or freewill – to shape the future one way or the other. This marginal choice is our opportunity to introduce influences that can set off chain-reactions of either a good or an evil nature, that can head us towards either heaven or hell.

We are given a picture of the human race as an evolving species with opportunities to exercise a certain amount of freewill during its earthly incarnations. It is emphasised that as we exercise the faculty of freewill, we will increase its efficiency and scope, learning to choose more and more wisely, and expanding our capacity to exert it more fully. Throughout life in this world, our will or choice will be constantly challenged by the will or choice of others, obstructed by

203

material circumstances, and sometimes defeated by opposing forces. No matter how much we try, we will not always be able to have our own way. This, some of the discarnate communicators state, is to enable us to learn the great lesson of selflessness, and to realise that others have their rights and needs. If we were never denied what we want, we would almost certainly become completely selfish; if we always had our own way, we would never learn to give way to others. Thus limitations are often opportunities.

The earth world is portrayed by spirit as a stimulant to thought and growth of mind; but it will only stimulate us to think and grow when we respond to its challenge. By thought, they do not mean the idle drifting of the mind, or the aimless and casual passing thoughts of the non-thinking person: they mean applied thought, concentration of thought, analytical thought, all thought where an effort is made to direct it. It is thought that has accumulated knowledge and accomplished great feats of architecture, engineering, and technology; it is thought that has created great works of art and music. Thought is indeed a resourceful and powerful force, and we do not know how far it can carry us or how much it can achieve. We know little or nothing about thought-waves, but it is now becoming evident that they do exist. Since thought results in so many accomplishments and is obviously so important to us in our progress and evolution, the more we can discover about it, about its nature and functions, about its power and qualities, the more we shall come to know the secrets of the Cosmos.

It is Man's ability to think which distinguishes him from the animals, as we all realise. It is Man's ability to think that can raise him to the stature of a genius, a saint, a superman, How important it is that we learn how to think with the greatest possible efficiency, clarity and understanding. For it is apparent that the power of thought, rightly used, can lead us into an age of peace and plenty, of widening horizons and greater vision. Thought can help to free Man's mind from the bigotry which sometimes threatens to cramp his spiritual unfoldment. Thought can help him to understand himself and others – and God. Thought can even help him to understand the bigot who is locked in his self-made mental cell and afraid to step outside into the great unknown. Thought is the initiator of speech and action, the mother of invention, the father of ideas. Thought is the beginning, the making, and the end product. Thought is latent energy. It is up to us to develop its potentialities.

Tracing the history of the human race, it would seem that it has moved from an unthinking state, or an animal state, towards a thinking state. The development of mind through thought has brought about enormous changes in Mankind's life down the ages. The life of animals, however, has not changed significantly except where human influences or climatic changes have affected it. Humans have the power to change and improve their lives in a way denied to the animal kingdom. Yet they often waste life on an incredible and terrible scale in wars. We obtain more power to destroy, and use it very often in a totally indiscriminate manner. To the animal kingdom, if they could but judge, we would probably appear to be both gods and devils. Whether we behave like gods or like devils depends on our thought. If we really think things out to their uttermost, we will surely realise that wars are not beneficial to the human race, and may culminate in a massive conflagration which consumes all. But it seems we do not yet think things out fully. We see one issue at a time, and do not seem capable of seeing all the other issues. We do not see or choose to see all the possible repercussions. We cannot be bothered to think!

Exchanges of thoughts and ideas can help to usher in an age of world-wide and lasting peace. A refusal to exchange ideas and consider the ideas of others is calculated to ferment further trouble. The diligent use of thought and its well-judged application may lead to the solution of many current problems, and provide the foundation for negotiations on a mutually beneficial footing. Astute thought can enable us to become aware of all the implications of an individual or national or international situation, which in turn makes it possible for us to react in the most advisable manner. Most of us act and react impulsively without due consideration of all the facts.

It does not seem possible that thought can hand us the key to all mysteries; if it could, we would long ago have solved all the questions regarding life, death, God, and so forth. For centuries, probably for thousands of years, Mankind has devoted thought to determine whether God exists, whether there is an underlying purpose to life, and given consideration to many other obscure and involved problems. Answers have never been reached that satisfy everybody. There are people who maintain that there is no evidence of God's existence, and people who maintain that it is unthinkable to deny His existence. Those who are sufficiently clever at manipulating words are able to argue so plausibly at times that they can either prove or disprove practically anything. To rely upon words alone can be a precarious practice. We need to go deeper than words which

205

are, after all, only the representatives of ideas, and often very ineffective ones. At its best, language is full of limitations and lends itself to misinterpretation, particularly during the process of translation. When people speak we need to look beyond the face-value of the words they are using to ascertain what they are trying to express.

Thought is capable of conceiving things which cannot be adquately expressed in words. This may account for Mankind's need for music and art; in such realms we can find outlets for themes which cannot be clothed in mere words. Both music and art can soar above thought, and transport us into the celestial spheres. They are as necessary to Man's evolution as language and mundane communication. Whenever Man has aspired to become something more than animal, he has reached out for finer meanings and outpourings, and enriched himself and others by making music and creating art. It is as if he knows instinctively that Humankind is intended to be beautiful and noble, and he responds by trying to produce echoes of this vision in earthly terms.

This brings us to the probable destiny of the human race, though some, as usual, will enter into dispute. In his highest moments, Mankind, both in everyday life and in his vision of eternity, seeks and endeavours to create around himself that which is good to survey and to hear. He has a constant urge to improve, embellish, and uplift. This is the voice of his true self, of the spirit of God within him. It inspires him to seek perfection, and to create it within himself and all about him. It is the voice of God telling him that he is made in the image of God. It rests with each and every soul to reflect that image in its true likeness.

CHAPTER 22

Voices of eternity

One of the most moving and momentous meetings I have had as a result of my work took place in the residence of the Bishop of Southwark. He had very kindly invited me to lunch with him one day, and I arrived at his house feeling a little awed at the thought of taking a meal with a bishop. He and his chaplain soon put me more at ease with their kindliness and warm hospitality. They made me feel that I was in the presence of true Christians who did not look down upon the humble.

As we lunched, the Bishop asked me various questions about my work and my psychic experiences. In response to his prompting I admitted that my visions had included some of several saints and of Jesus himself. I rarely speak of these special visions, since they are so sacred to me that I guard them from the ungodly.

All I will say in this book is that I have been the awed witness of manifestations that have left me in no doubt that Jesus was the instrument of Christ, and died upon the Cross because his teaching was an unprecedented challenge to the self-righteous and the self-seeking. Some of these manifestations took place during my husband's life, and we shared together some truly remarkable and overwhelming spiritual occurrences. I must emphasise, however, that I do not accept the Bible as being literally true, and that I am convinced that honest and thorough investigation into its validity would reveal that it has been mutilated through mistranslations, through copyists's errors, and occasionally through deliberate falsification. Of course, I am not alone in this conviction and am acquainted with the fact that theological scholars and researchers are amongst those who share my conviction. However, the great message of Christ shines through the obscurities of wording and faulty reportage: that is, seek God,

207

and care for others. The same message runs through all true religions.

After we had finished lunch, the Bishop tested me by prevailing upon me to try my hand at psychometry. This is a branch of psychic science which I am not in the habit of practising, but I have found it will work successfully. With practice, it would very likely improve, as all activities do with constant application.

The most dramatic moment came when the Bishop handed me a large book which was entirely covered with plain brown paper, so that there was no clue whatsover to be gleaned as to its title, nor author, nor contents.

"Take this, and see what impressions you get," he said.

I held the book – quite a heavy tome – and became aware immediately that a spirit was building up or becoming visible to me. I began to describe him, and to tell the Bishop how he was robed. I could not think of the correct name for the tall headgear the spirit was wearing, but I described it in my own words. The Bishop told me that I was giving a description of Pope John the Twenty-third in his papal regalia.

The next event to take place was one which I experienced with misgiving: I felt myself being taken into a trance – a thing which I usually resist strongly as I prefer to remain fully conscious and know what is happening! I informed the Bishop that I could feel myself being drawn into a trance. He told me that he was quite accustomed to witnessing such occurrences, and that I would therefore be in safe hands if I allowed it to take place. I drifted off into unconsciousness, still feeling apprehensive.

When I came to, I found my cheeks were wet with tears.

"Why have I been crying? What happened?" I asked, somewhat embarrassed to find myself in such a state.

"Peter spoke," replied the Bishop.

"Peter who?" I asked.

"Apparently it was Simon Peter," answered the Bishop to my astonishment.

I felt very shaken that I had allowed myself to go into trance and have so exalted a soul communicate – that is, if it were really Saint Peter. The fact that I have often seen a spirit claiming to be Saint Peter made me feel no less taken aback.

"But why should Saint Peter come and speak?" I asked the Bishop, wondering what Peter had said, and whether it could really have been the saint himself.

"It was perfectly logical," replied the Bishop, "The Pope would be

208

regarded as Saint Peter's successor, and you saw Pope John before you went into trance."

I felt a little reassured.

"Now open the book, and look at it," instructed the Bishop.

Carefully I opened the book he had given me to hold, and discovered it was a biography of the life of Pope John the Twenty-third. So I had seen the spirit of Pope John appear when I took the book about him in my hands! Suddenly, I felt very humble, and very moved to have had the privilege of seeing him. And to this day, I have been overwhelmed by the thought that Saint Peter himself apparently spoke through me, a humble housewife and lowly aspirant.

Since that day, I have seen Pope John many times, and received wise counsel from him. I was wondering one day whether he would have wanted me to become a Roman Catholic, but he said to me, "All that matters is that you are a Christian."

And that, perhaps, puts Christianity in its true perspective. I do not know much about Pope John, of course, but from what I have learned of him, it seems that he had an exalted breadth of view, and saw beyond all the petty, man-made divisions of the Christian faith.

How can we hope for Christian principles to triumph when Christian opposes Christian, and differs on so many issues? The fundamental principles of Christian behaviour are to be found in all the great religions, although each religion makes its own interpretations and regulations. But orthodox Christianity often wears blinkers which permit only a narrow vision, and makes it blind to the great universal truth that the enlightened can discern in the true significance and meaning of Christianity.

Slowly the whole world may realise that the same sacred water fills countless kinds of vessels; that the same holy breath is breathed into an innumerable diversity of souls; that the same divine fire is kindled in numerous dispositions of hearts; that the same hallowed earth is to be trodden on the way to God by an endless variety of pilgrims. Gradually it may dawn on us that no-one holds the monopoly of the truth, that no-one possesses God exclusively, that God is truly everywhere and available to all.

We destroy the wholeness of truth by cutting it into tiny pieces. We envisage the Almighty as a limited being who is biased in favour of people who hold specific beliefs. There is a steady growth of disapproval in the world towards discrimination against anybody on account of their colour or nationality, on account of their class or creed, even on account of their sex – perhaps the most lingering and ingrained prejudice of all. Can we picture God practising discrimination towards humanity, and refusing to grant eternal life to anyone other than a mere handful of souls, whose set beliefs conform exactly with a certain bigotted, hide-bound pattern? Especially when we remember that those bigotted patterns have been woven, not by the hand of God, but by human beings themselves! We try to cut God down to size – our size – He, who is limitless, all-embracing, and all-comprehending, and beyond our puny understanding.

That outburst is my own personal outcry against the bitter vendettas that rage between religions, and even within religions. I think of all who have been martyred for their beliefs, whose very martyrdom should shame us into exercising tolerance. Our beliefs change down the ages, new religions spring up and fade away, and in recent times the public has fallen away from orthodox religion. We tend now to conduct our lives on what is definitely known and can be scientifically borne out rather than upon beliefs which some deem to be unreasonable or irrational. Perhaps we are moving into an age of much-needed tolerance, for the intermingling of various nationalities all over the world calls for such tolerance. We have to learn to respect the beliefs of immigrants if we are to live and work side by side with them in peace. We have to realise that their religions are just as true to them as ours is to us, that their sacred books are equally authentic to them as is the Bible to a Bible-orientated Christian.

I have been asked whether my psychic and mystical experiences have led to any conclusions on my part or made any conspicuous difference to my outlook. As human beings, we are always drawing conclusions about all manner of things, and many of our conclusions are faulty because we do not allow for the fact that we are not acquainted with all the relative data. Even when we believe we have collected all the available data concerning a subject, we may be missing out a single factor which is so vital that it could alter our entire train of thought. Therefore the conclusions to which I have come should be regarded as preliminary attempts to summarise my experiences. The parapsychological field still lies largely unexplored, and new aspects are continually being revealed.

As regards the psychic vistas, these are only just beginning to open to the world, and many hesitate to explore them, and some try to prevent or discourage others from exploring them. But Mankind is imbued with a sense of adventure and curiosity, and will go on exploring and experimenting as long as the human race exists. There is an unquenchable thirst for knowledge in the human mind, and an insatiable hunger for spiritual enlightenment in the human soul. The inextinguishable spark kindled from the divine fire which the Creator has breathed into us can light great beacons to illuminate our way. The human spirit is destined to triumph over all obstacles placed in its path by the ignorant and bigotted. All the indications I have had point steadfastly towards an expansion of human consciousness unparalleled by anything that has taken place in the past. Mankind is travelling towards consciousness of its true self, and through the achievement of enlightened self-consciousness will follow on to God-consciousness.

In its highermost expression, psychic experience blends with spiritual experience almost inextricably. That is possibly why we find so many descriptions of psychic manifestations throughout the Bible. But psychic power, like all other powers, can be used either for good or for evil, either for constructive or destructive purposes. We must harness the psychic faculties to be used in the service of the Almighty and for the good of Mankind. We must use the psychic energies to create stepping stones towards peace. We must direct these energies to heal not only sick bodies, but sick minds and sick souls.

We are all using psychic energy throughout our lifetimes, whether we believe in it or not. But it may take many decades before we begin to understand the nature and functions of psychic energy. We live in a world charged with many energies or latent energies; we do not understand them all and are not even aware of the existence of some of them.

There is boundless scope for investigation in the psychic fields for those who are intelligent and brave enough to set foot into them. We need qualified people to carry out investigations, scientists, parapsychologists, and experienced researchers. We need investigations by people who are completely impartial: those who are either pro or con belief in psychic powers may tend either to force the pace or to try to halt it according to their personal leaning.

My own experiences have led me to realise that there are many pitfalls in the psychic field, especially for the over-imaginative, the over-ambitious, and the wishful thinkers. I believe we have to endeavour to exclude emotion from serious investigations, and to avoid any personality cults, as these are bound to lead to dead-ends Unfortunately, mediums – and guides, let it be said – occasionally begin to regard themselves as oracles, and this is sure to end in disillusionment. Spirits in the Hereafter do *not* know everything, and if they claim to do so, you can be sure they are not very enlightened ... or very honest!

It is clear that psychic research and paranormal investigations, if conducted expertly and with total impartiality, will reveal extensive and important aspects of human nature, of the mind and psyche, hitherto undreamt of in our philosophy, We shall be able to penetrate more deeply into the mechanisms of the brain, of which most of us use about one-third. That other two thirds, when put in to use, could produce an influx of genius such as the world has never known. And, goodness knows, we need every atom of intelligence that we can muster to help to solve the problems that face us and to overcome the barriers between us and ignorance. Since Einstein has stated quite categorically to me that intelligence does not depend merely on the number of healthy brain-cells possessed, we might profit through our endeavours to learn how to tap our entire available psycho-mental resources, including those of the extra-sensory fields. Intelligence is a quality or entity which operates through the brain and through other senses, and a knowledgeable use of the extra-sensory-faculties provides an additional and valuable outlet for the inherent intelligence.

Through our fears, superstitions, and prejudices, we dam the flood of Cosmic Intelligence which, rightly employed, could produce a race of super-beings. We are, so Einstein and others in the Beyond assure us, far more wonderful than we dream, with tremendous un-tapped powers which could transform us into veritable gods in a kingdom of shining achievements. Too easily we accept ourselves to be insignificant as others would persuade us; too readily we adopt an attitude of inferiority which is so often imposed on us by others; too quickly we believe it when we are told that we are of no consequence in the great scheme of things. Each and every single soul has its part to play in the Grand Plan; and all are part of the great whole which we call God. We may not always behave in a manner worthy of the whole; some of us may even try to separate ourselves from it; but intrinsically and irrevocably, we are inseparable fragments of the mighty Cosmic Spirit.

The light thrown on the hidden side of our nature through new facts uncovered by investigation of E.S.P., could be of assistance in the treatment of disordered and criminal minds. It could also be a lamp to guide us on the path to the Omniscient, Omnipotent,

Omnipresence. For if we are part of the whole, as we are so frequently reminded, in discovering truths about ourselves, we would be discovering truths about the Almighty.

My mystical experiences have certainly deepened my belief in an Almighty Spirit; indeed, they have heightened my growing consciousness of the Presence of God. But mystical experiences are so personal that they can mean little or nothing excepting to the person who passes through them. To say that I have felt myself enfolded in a holiness so intense that it has created a sense of ecstatic upliftment, are just so many words, empty to all except those who have had a similar experience. Some psychiatrists will explain such experiences as hallucinations – but how do they know? Unless they can DISPROVE the existence of God, they cannot argue conclusively that such experiences are mere delusions.

My visions of Jesus and some of his disciples have not transformed me into a Bible-punching fanatic. That Jesus lived a life teaching about God and healing, I can believe; that he died on the cross seems to be an historical fact borne out during my own contact with his spirit, and by Liszt's intimation that the Holy Shroud is evidently the authentic shroud from the body of Jesus. But it is so apparent that some words attributed to Jesus were either never uttered by him, or else have been misreported, that I find the only reliable course to follow is that of the spirit of Christianity rather than the letter. Many generations had come and gone before written reports of his life and teaching were made, and during that lapse of time, and the passing by word of mouth of details, it is inevitable that discrepancies and misquotes arose. Since I find myself sometimes mis-quoted almost the next moment, I can well imagine what happened to the sayings of Jesus! I have read in print statements attributed to me which I have most certainly never made at any time. The human mind is constantly liable to embroider, to exaggerate, even to twist, accounts of people and events, as demonstrated by conflicting accounts made by witnesses in the Courts of Justice. The New Testament story of the life of Jesus conveys an immortal spiritual message, tells us clearly that life continues after death, and that we should care about other people as well as ourselves. It exhorts us to turn to God, which all religions do. Jesus is reported to have said that no man cometh unto the Father but by "me". Were these his exact words? If so, did he intend that to be taken literally, or was he trying to make people realise that no one can come to God through another person, or second-hand, but that each must come himself

213

or herself through the ' me": in each one of us which is part of the whole "Me"? Each, in other words, must seek God for himself or herself, and cannot pass the responsibility to another person. We must come individually to God in a spirit of humility and repentance, and no-one else can do that for us. Each one of us, that is, can approach God only through Christ within, having allowed Christ to enter into us or be born within us. Our interpretation is perhaps at times too literal and at times too shallow. Real Christianity is, we can assume in all reverence, far richer than many of us have realised, and bears not a narrow, parochial message, but offers a world-wide, universal message that incorporates all religions.

If I had had only the Bible on which to found my faith, I think I would have found it inadequate and illogical and minus sufficient proof of its authenticity. The New Testament, for all one might know, could have been concocted by a group of people – years after the death of Jesus – to found their own branch of religion. And from the time it was put on paper, it could have been doctored by a succession of hands causing it to veer farther away from the original facts. What, it might be asked, was it that led me to accept the Christian way, if I feel so much doubt and uncertainty about the Bible? Simply this: my own personal experience of the Presence of Christ, my own visions of Jesus and of certain disciples, and the indelible impression left on me by the sheer wonder of the Infinite Love enfolding me, a mere speck in creation. There are things which one can feel but cannot find words to express; there are visions, such as that of the Christ Spirit, which are too glorious to be described in words. The most that can be given is an assurance that my mystical experiences have been real, intensely real, and alive to me, and that they have imbued life with an inner meaning which has enabled me to see beyond the changing scene of everyday existence into the ever-present Reality of the Eternal Now. I am not saintlier nor wiser than anybody else, but somehow – perhaps because I have no pretensions – I have been blessed with a glimpse of light, and touched with a breath of awareness of the Supreme Life.

That is as much as I can say, as I am prepared to say. In common with many others, I have felt myself sustained throughout life by a spiritual strength from beyond our mortal ken. I have not had an easy life. It has been fraught with tragedies and disappointments. It had been dogged by poverty and ill-health. Together with a multitude of other people, I passed through times of great danger and hardship during the 1939–1945 War. I was born in London, and lived there

214

right through the war. I witnessed many of the horrors of the bombing, and saw at first hand some of the terrible suffering it caused. Yet all the time, it seemed to me that God walked beside us, seeking to restore peace and reach out to the wounded of body, mind and heart. I have also experienced heart-breaking loneliness which has been made bearable only by the sense of the nearness of God.

This sense of God has been constant all my life, and has always been keenest during my times of need and trouble. At times, through inattention, through foolishness, through carelessness, the sense has been dulled; but I have found it always there, waiting to reawaken in my consciousness. I cannot believe that anything so durable, so steadfast and unwavering in the face of all the contingencies of life can be without reality, without sound spiritual foundations, without an authentic source. Its sheer persistence, even when I questioned it and everything under the sun, moon and stars, is in itself sufficient to constrain me to believe in a God-head, in a God-behind-it-all, in Providence. Perhaps many more people share this sense than is realised. Can we all be mistaken? Are we all indulging in a kind of glorified daydream just to reassure ourselves? Perhaps there is a still small voice in us that whispers the truth, though many of us do not heed it, and the over-intellectualised brain may deny it disdainfully. Each one of us has to decide whether it rings true or not, knowing that there is no material corroboration to settle the matter one way or the other. God seems to have left us out on a limb, but perhaps it is not really like that. We have become accustomed to trying to weigh everything up with our physical senses and by material means; this may be the whole point of it: that we have to learn to exercise our spiritual senses and our spiritual awareness in order to transcend earthly limitations.

This does not imply that we should live in the clouds or lead impractical lives ignoring the harsh realities of the contemporary world. On the contrary, what it should bring about is an increased awareness of the true values of human life, and a greater ability to cope with all the exigencies that face us. It should give us a true sense of perspective, placing each moment of time in the context of Eternal Life. We should hear the Voices of Eternity urging us to triumph over the present, over time itself, knowing ourselves to be an immortal breed.

CHAPTER 23

Poetic inspiration

Little attention is paid these days to poetry, except in schools and colleges. This seems a great pity because poetry often says to us things which are rare yet would seem commonplace in ordinary prose. Poetry is a crystallisation of thought which in a few words can speak volumes. Poetry has the gift of endowing with beauty the everyday, apparently dull, details of life. It can help us to appreciate the wonders of the universe, and the miracle of living; to rediscover the eyes of childhood that gazed in awe and admiration at the multitude of marvellous things about them which we adults, with our dulled senses, fail to perceive. Poetry can develop the aesthetic senses without which we are mere animals. It is the language of lovers, mystics, and idealists, and has certain qualities, when at its best, to inspire us with valour, fire us with noble enthusiasms, and also to soothe us in torment or sorrow. Poetry is the music of words, and springs from the same fount of inspiration as music itself. Poetry can speak in god-like tones and awaken our higher selves.

This chapter is included for the benefit of those who love poetry, and the possible interest of the unpoetically inclined. I am not naming the poets from whom I believe some of the inspiration is drawn because their concern is not so much to prove their identities as to present a few poems for reading and enjoyment. In any case, the tedious process of trying to provide proof to satisfy public and individual scrutiny has become very wearisome. After some years of dissection (often of a ruthless nature) by critics of all waters, I feel driven to adopt a take-it-or-leave-it attitude which itself may invite some criticism! After all, it makes no difference to me personally what people believe or do not believe, and their attitudes do not alter the facts regarding life after death.

The quality of communication on the poetic level may be affected by the seemingly inevitable fluctuations during contact with spirit. It can be as clear as a bell or muffled and disjointed. I believe, however, that the following poems were noted down by me with few, if any, errors in transmission.

THE SCEPTIC

When darkness throws her mantle o'er the earth,
And owls begin to hoot their nightly dirge;
When trees their darkened shapes with shadows knit
Because the gloom makes tree and shadow merge;

When cats steal silently amidst the grass
Until they meet a foe upon the prowl
Which makes them spit in startled enmity,
And rend the air with shrill, blood-curdling howl;

When moonlight sheds elusive, pallid light
That makes the landscape look half real below;
When all the atmosphere is strangely hushed,
And lakeland waters gleam with eerie glow;

I fancy then that I believe in ghosts,
For everything appears to shift and change;
Familiar landscapes loom unrecognised,
Their well-known features blurred and lost and strange.

Vague spectres seem to rise in misty forms
To sway uncertainly about the place;
With writhing, wraith-like shapelessness they drift
Dissolving, melting into empty space!

What tricks the moonlight plays, I tell myself!
They are but shadows of the trees, I vow,
Which wave about as breezes stir their leaves,
And make the creaking branches shake and bow.

As soon as dawn arrives, the spell is gone.
How sceptical I wax in daylight broad!
I know that there are no such things as ghosts –
At least, till darkness falls, I feel assured.

RETROSPECTION

If I could love as once I loved
With carefree heart, unclouded mind,
And know again those years of joy
Which now, alas! are far behind;

If I could tread the hillside paths,
And tirelessly the steep ways climb
To stand aloft on mountain peaks
Oblivious of age and time;

If I, without the fear of chill,
Could brave the wind, the storm, the rain,
And not grow breathless when I run:
If I could do these things again –

I'd sacrifice my hard-earned rest,
And gladly, too, would I forego
The idle ease old age endows,
The chair beside the hearth's warm glow.

Elysium could wait a while,
And let me linger here below.
Mid Nature's beauty with my love
A fairer world I scarce could know.

CONTENTMENT

What does the townsman know of life?
I pity him.
He cannot hear the songbirds sing
Their morning hymn.

The sun arising o'er the hills
To gild the skies
A glory sheds that is not seen
By townsman's eyes.

The miracle of each new Spring
That life unfolds,
And country lanes fresh-clad in green
He ne'er beholds.

As swelling buds unfurl their leaves,
And blossoms flower,
With thankful mind I live and drink
Each peaceful hour.

Oh! not for me the city rush,
The crowded train,
The jostling, noisy, tinsel world,
The fevered brain.

Content am I my days to spend
In quiet retreat,
Unknown, unpraised, but praising God
As think I meet.

HUMILITY

A canopy of stars is overhead.
The moon comes gliding from a veil of cloud
Where lately she withdrew to hide unseen,
Escaping for a time the star-strewn crowd.

Across the fields of heaven now she moves
With slow and stately gait she makes her way,
Until with humble grace she yields her light
Before the rising sun at break of day.

The sun, ablaze, its daily debut makes,
And steals the heavenly scene with splendour bright
Oh gentle moon, fear not the posturing sun:
He, too, will dim before the Greatest Light.

The Preservationist

Unsullied brooks flow still
Past narrow gorge and hill
Where human feet no footing find
To tread beside them as they wind
Through deeply-wooded dells
Where drink the shy gazelles.

The waters calmly slip
Below the cliff's high lip
Where Nature holds unchallenged rule,
Unspoilt by human hand or tool
In places too remote
For human eye to note.

I watch the stream grow wide,
Its open course espied
By trippers far too rushed to prize
With leisurely observing eyes
The beauty of the scene,
The water's satin sheen.

Oh Nature, hear me speak!
Your hidden haunts I seek
To keep for ever wild and free
That here your heart may always be
Enshrined in pure delight,
Untouched by human blight.

Justice

If dreams of immortality are vain,
And human life is but a transient strain
Or should the final trump card dealt by death
Annihilate our souls at our last breath –

Then we into oblivion would sink,
No more to fear, no more to feel or think,
Escaping life and death and all their powers;
It seems the final triumph would be ours!

220

The freedom which devoted Buddhists court
Would thus be gained by everyone unsought.
Our souls would melt to nothingness and cease
To shuttle back and forth in search of peace.

How easy all our sins to shrug away
If after death there is no other day;
No just deserts, reward or punishment;
No need to beg forgiveness and repent.

But Nemesis is not to be outdone:
Another life awaits for everyone
Where all will reap the good that they have sown,
And each for every misdeed must atone.

To Sorrow

What might thou be, oh Sorrow, that thy touch
Can harden many hearts like granite gray,
But other hearts can soften like the light
That dawns so tenderly at break of day?

Storms of Life

West End shoppers, window gazing,
Tourists mingling, drop-outs lazing –
Storm-clouds gather, must take shelter.
Down the rain begins to pelter.
All the crowds, disordered, scatter.
Harder falls the pitter-patter.
Deep in doorways people huddle.
Lovers take the chance to cuddle.

Pavements now are all deserted.
Faces looking disconcerted,
Peering out from all directions;
Window panes with blurred reflections
Busy streets have been disrupted,
Life and movement interrupted;
People anxiously awaiting
While the storm is unabating.

221

All activity is halted.
Hopes and plans are rudely jolted.
We must face the unexpected,
Brave the storm though unprotected.
Life can be so disconcerting,
Indiscriminately hurting.
We must weather every season
Though we may not know their reason.

FICKLE LIFE

Oh hapless life, you took within your grasp
My helpless, trusting soul from time of birth.
You carried me, unknowing as I was,
Through childhood's fleeting years of carefree mirth.

You offered wine to me while I was young,
And let me savour first love's blissful taste;
But when my lips would fain more deeply drink
You dashed the cup away in cruel haste.

At length, I met a soft-eyed, gentle girl,
And shared with her a happiness that's flown,
For death grew jealous, seeing me so glad,
And snatched away my bride to be his own.

And now I sit considering my lot,
The way of life with all its good and ill.
What's given us is taken soon away.
We end our life, as we began, with nil.

But when the time to move on comes at last,
And elsewhere we awake from that last sleep,
Perchance we'll find a harvest waits us there,
And all that we have cherished we shall reap.

HOPE!

Oh, be not sad when Summer
Spreads her wings and flies,
And lets the Earth grow colder
'Neath the wintry skies.
For there's a time for resting;
There's a time for sleep,
When the World lies cradled
In its Maker's keep.

The Earth will re-awaken,
Heralding the Spring,
And Summer soon will follow
As the seasons swing.
For there's a time for waking;
There's a time to smile,
When we find Death's slumber
Lasted but a while.

THE EXPLORER

Discovery! I stand here at your brink,
And steel myself the final plunge to take.
Shall I uncover buried deep below
A precious pearl? Or find my life at stake?

I gather all my quiv'ring faculties
To hold their throbbing energy in rein,
While deep within my heart I breathe a prayer
That all my efforts may not be in vain.

The enemies of progress throng me round,
And mock me as I wait the last commands.
"What sheer foolhardiness inspires you thus?
"Why cast yourself to death?" are their demands.

They heed not tales of noble fights men fought,
Of all the heights they scaled and depths they trod
As they sought wider knowledge, greater power;
Of epic trails they blazed in search of God.

223

Were they to read what I read, time-engraved
Upon Creation's universal face,
Then they might understand what sends me forth
Aflame with hope, uncharted paths to trace.

Then they might know what joy unbounded comes
To those who bear the torch of quest along.
When breaks on us the glorious light of truth,
All earth with music rings, all heav'n with song.

TRUTH

Truth was a string of beads around God's neck,
Held with a thread of pure, unbroken thought;
Each bead a precious stone, a jewel rare
That God Himself from great ideas had wrought.

God made the World, then He created Man,
Endowing him with brains that he might think
And share the pure, unbroken line of thought;
The waters of eternal truth to drink.

Mankind was feckless like a little child,
Clutching at all it saw with eager hand.
The string of beads transfixed its greedy eyes;
It grabbed them clumsily and broke the band.

And so the precious thread was snapped apart;
The sundered beads were fallen far and wide.
Now Truth in fragments lies about the World,
Its unity destroyed, its power denied.

BITTER-SWEET

As the past recedes,
Should we extract what's sweet,
Leaving the bitterness to die?
Frail in human needs,
Should we aim to unseat
Echoes of woe from days gone by?

Sweetness on its own
Might in an excess cloy.
Catholic be our appetite!
Scorn to taste alone
Banquets of endless joy:
Bravely partake what's hard to bite.

How our soul may waste,
If like a child that sups
Sweetmeats until "Enough!" it cries,
We indulge our taste,
Sipping the syrup cups,
Shunning the food which fortifies.

Can we but be brave,
Bidding our courage meet
Feasts thst are spread with grief or pain,
Self shall not enslave:
We shall not know defeat,
A noble soul-hood thus attain.

CLAY

When you have spent your life and nothing's left
Except the dying embers from the past
Which lend no heat to warm your cooling blood;
When every day on earth might be your last:

Will you look back as most incline to do
To seek some comfort from the days gone by;
Or try to find some meaning in it all,
And some good reason why you should not die?

We vainly dream our time will never come,
But come it must each one of us to claim.
Death lies in wait to take us unawares,
Or slowly may invade our mortal frame.

225

Yet many live committing cruel deeds
As if they are exempt from heaven's law,
And will not have to give account one day
When they themselves their final breath shall draw.

With death upon our heels all through our life,
The path of good we wisely should pursue,
But foolishly we follow harmful ways
And habits that our souls will surely rue.

A rude awakening awaits the soul
Who disregards the laws which govern life.
To make another suffer by our deeds
Will bring upon us misery and strife.

Though cynics shrug in hardened unbelief,
They cannot be too sure it is not so:
That every time with wanton-ness we wound
We lay up for ourselves a future woe.

You plant a rose-tree and in season due
The roses breathe their fragrance on the air.
Neglect the garden-plot that is your soul,
And useless weeds will quickly flourish there.

The Potter placed some clay within our hands
For each of us to mould upon life's wheel,
And when the wheel for us no more will turn,
Our handiwork at last we must reveal.

Then crooked vases, ugly to behold,
Mis-shapen souls, the Potter's eyes will see:
Rejected for their self-inflicted flaws,
Unworthy shall they prove for Him to be.

So, cast upon the Potter's wheel again,
The clay must be re-formed with greater care,
Until the wheel of life, revolving still,
We learn to use to mould a finer ware.

Then summon all your skill and use it well,
And from your clay a noble vessel build;
So shall your work be well-performed at last,
Your vessel with eternal joy be filled.

CHAPTER 24

John Lill

John Lill contributes the fine article incorporated in this chapter. In fact, I feel that it is so complete within itself, and speaks with such eloquence and clarity of thought that it needs no introduction or additional explanation.

As I read it, I experienced a directness of impact that springs from an unequivocal character – that same unequivocal quality which distinguishes the very soul of Beethoven. While emphasising the wisdom of developing our innate spirituality, the article carries a no-nonsense tone which bears witness to the unwavering strength of mind and courageous ideals of a young man who is not only a great pianist but without doubt a great soul.

It is for all the world as if Beethoven himself had seized the pen and joined forces with John Lill to speak out boldly at a time when many people take refuge in pseudo-scientific rejection of Mankind's spiritual potentialities, and many more display fearfulness of losing face by their practice of disowning all belief in psychic faculties.

Thousands of people have allowed themselves to become totally obsessed with an all-devouring materialism; thousands have become dehumanised by consuming passions for power, position and prestige. Here, in John Lill's article, some of us may hear the purposeful voice of a prophet with a Churchillian capacity to rouse us from our spiritual lethargy and our intellectual teetering, to rouse us into stripping away the sophisticated pretentiousness which too often is mistaken for superiority.

227

My View of Spirituality by John Lill

When something is so much part of your soul and you have lived with it all your life, it having helped you more than you can say, you feel a little awkward at the prospect of writing about it to others. Awkward, because you have taken it for granted as the major and logical essence and helper of your work and life, seemingly, on earth, and it feels peculiar to think that there are still many people without it. What I mean, of course, is deep inner conviction in spiritual existence, assistance, and development.

In my work as a concert pianist I give about a hundred concerts every year in many countries. I was born in London in 1944, and have never known life without being able to play, however roughly. On fairly good authority from my mother, I seemed to have shown enormous enthusiasm for music at an early age, and was picking out melodies at the age of 3 or 4. I had written a sonata (it must have been terrible) at 6, and I gave my first concert at 9, which I do remember! For me it seemed so natural to play the piano that I was unable to understand why my school-friends preferred kicking a ball about, and seemed unable to share my enthusiasm for music, and especially for my great god of music, Beethoven. My obsession for him was overwhelming, and I seemed to learn nothing else apart from his compositions.

I have little memory of the first few years, apart from the odd occasion, but it comes as a great surprise to be told by friends and relatives who heard me then, of the extent of my passion for music. I remember being unable to realise how it was that my hands were moving as they were, and my musical memory was as cast iron as my non-musical memory was comparatively poor. I learnt the sonatas, symphonies, and concertos of Beethoven from memory by the time I had reached my middle teens, and had by then, incidentally, learnt that other composers had existed, too! No wonder people must have thought me more than a little touched, coming from a very poor family (but emotionally very secure) in the East End just after the War, with no ancestry of musicians, as far as I can make out.

But difficult as life was then, I never felt alone. Solitary, yes, but even in those days I was aware of a rock-like force injecting me with my indescribable passions for music making and for Beethoven. Why

228

he was such a father figure to me was never questioned, but I am sure that thousands of performers and listeners must derive colossal strength and optimism from his music.

I was, by now, continuing my studies at the Royal College of Music in London, and it wasn't long before I was more or less forced to leave on account of the amount of concert work I was getting. It was simply too much to do both. Since then, although there have been lean times, my career has developed slowly and solidly. Perhaps the most remarkable example of spiritual guidance, so far as I am concerned, came in 1970. My mother had suffered a serious stroke at the end of 1969, and I felt that it was essential to move her from the pokey terraced house with very difficult and noisy surroundings where we lived, to a quieter home. It was impossible for me to afford to buy a house, unless I won a major competition. There was nothing to be done except try one, so I decided to go to Moscow to have a shot at the International Tchaikowsky Competition. My friends thought it was very unsafe, as to do badly might prejudice my career, which was gradually establishing itself well. However, I felt compelled to go to Moscow, and all the time I was there, I felt conscious of a great spiritual force helping me through the weeks of tension and bringing me to the ultimate victory of winning the first prize. This meant that I was able to buy a house for my parents and move them four months later to quieter surroundings where my mother could live a more peaceful life.

I do not believe that the spiritual force which I felt guiding me through those nerve-racking weeks was purely the product of my own imagination. Words cannot explain the colossal confidence and power which I felt before I played in the final round, nor explain the uncanny message which I received, telling me that I would win, before my final performance. In competition with 67 other young professional pianists from all over the world, this was indeed an extraordinary experience. I know that there was an entity outside my own conscious mind which was able to inspire and control me, and from which I could draw power when I most needed it.

I have given this brief resumé of my background, to try to explain to you the extent of spiritual help of which I was aware, and from which I benefitted, and still do, in the face of difficult, envious, and sometimes hostile people and situations. Whilst practically never going to church, and having no so-called religion in the fashionable sense in those days, I was nevertheless given indefinable security and confidence by what is virtually one and the same thing. Spiritual

229

enrichment really does begin where everything else (especially material things) leaves off, and for those who feel that I may be speaking in a pompous or conceited way, may I remind them that everyone receives help, but not all avail themselves of it.

It was not until April 1973 that I first had direct contact with those in spirit – and being hard-boiled and a bit thick-skinned about such matters as direct contact, I never thought it possible. I will not explain how or why it occurred because mindless experimentation, and irresponsible dabbling into something so important is pointless and sometimes dangerous psychologically, especially to those who do it for fun. Those who do not regard it as fun need have no fear, for they surely feel as secure as possible in the knowledge that they are right. Since those in spirit made contact with me first, I did not feel too bad at trying to communicate, in order to get the completion of a message I had received earlier, and, amazingly, I was able to make vivid contact straight away.

I was still very doubtful as I felt spirits always signified dubious or evil influences (and indeed there is much truth in the fact that the least developed persons stay closest to earth, and often try to communicate, hence my previous warning). Imagine my astonishment when I communicated at once with Beethoven. By now you will all regard this as predictable fantasy, hallucinatory or subconscious, and with good reason – I did, too! But when you converse with somebody, and many others, for what averages an hour or two a day (often much more), and receive such facts as are only known to the spirit which prove, on checking to be correct 100 per cent of the time, even the biggest cynic has to think again. I have been told countless facts and names which, I stress again, were completely unknown to me but with the aid of reference books and encyclopaedias, were and are proven completely correct every single time.

I was asked one day by Beethoven himself whether I would be interested to go to a lecture given by Rosemary Brown. I had heard of her, and believed her to be genuine, but had never heard her speak or heard her compositions. He gave the whereabouts and time – we enquired, and all was correct. We went along to the lecture, and the music I heard seemed to be genuinely in the manner and style of the composers of the past who were named, and who, not unnaturally, continue in another wavelength or vibration.

Some of the music was simplified in a way, it seemed, because not being a professional musician she is not always able to take down very complicated music as yet. Besides, it seems to me that their aim

230

is not necessarily to try to transmit great music, but simply to prove their existence. Listening to her speaking and playing, I was at once moved by her sincerity, for all was obvious to me (and, in any case, was predicted by Beethoven himself).

During the lecture, I interrupted rather brusquely, announced myself, and stated that I believed her to be entirely genuine. That is how we met. She later told me that Beethoven had warned her of a possible interruption that evening by me! We do not meet often, for we are both very busy, but when we do it is a wonderful pleasure to realise that we both make regular contact with the great composers and others who are much more concerned than one thinks about their representatives on earth. What is more gratifying is when we are both given the same message independently which we discover to be identical through later comparison (as often happens).

I am still hard-boiled, at least when it comes to matters of proof, but it would be simply impossible and idiotic for me, with all my experiences so vivid in my memory, and communicating every day as I do, not to realise the obvious and forceful reality that has now been proved to me a thousandfold. Quite apart from this, I have recently met clairvoyants, people who can do automatic writing, and many others who still further one's already comprehensive grasp of the potential powers one may achieve. Instead of hiding one's head and pretending that there is no continuity of life, often from ignorance or fear, one should face the logical and obvious conclusion that even if there were no "proof" by any of those, including myself, who have been fortunate enough to communicate directly, it would still be an insult to one's logical commonsense to think that after such a short life on this earth, with the beauty, art, purpose, and obvious plan of the whole vista and cosmos so perfectly conceived by God, and already partly apparent to us, that death be final.

I have really nothing to add, having possibly spoken too much, realising how quick some people are to try to do one harm by assuming one is in touch with what they call the supernatural etc. However, that is their loss. Actually, when you consider how many people make contact, it must be admitted that people do very well to see spirits at all. Fancy being able to "see" an unmodulated radio or television wave, for example. How some people can be so pompous as to feel that science now knows all the answers, when so much is still unanswered, is a mystery to me. After all, was it not true, that there was a time when you would have been spat upon for even whispering to a friend that the world were anything but flat?

231

What continues to give great pleasure is the fact that one can ask literally any sensible question, and those in spirit will always give helpful, often profound replies, In fact, I have asked so much about the enigmas of life, and the answers I have received could fill numerous text books. I did start writing them down, but there is too much. Their kindness, generosity and sense of humour are also not generally realised by those who feel that serious spookiness, or trances in darkness are necessary. It is simply not true.

I have not spoken about the important and personal reasons behind my life and communication. Some things are better not publicised, at least, not yet. If and when I do publicise the main reason for my existence, it might create a great many waggling tongues. I have been told it is now my job and vocation in life to make sure that I do with my greatest powers what I have always felt and have been given the gift to do. Surely nothing can give greater ecstasy or agony than such a vocation.

Finally, may I just say (it sounds like politicians' pre-dinner verbiage) that since the last year of true awareness, my life has become greatly enriched, is happier, healthier, and I do not believe I have every played better than now. Don't you think it is worth coming to terms with your true powers in order to develop them, and to tear away from the attitudes, conventions, and superficial escapisms of our decadent money-obsessed age, and to have them replaced by long-term values of indescribable strength and richness of mind. It is surely worth the switch.

Perhaps I may be permitted to comment upon John Lill's fine testament to the spiritual help and guidance we receive if we attune ourselves sufficiently to the spiritual planes. When I give a lecture-recital, I have to limit my choice of pieces to the not-too-difficult since I am not a trained concert pianist. Therefore the music John Lill heard me play did not include any of the really complicated pieces which I receive and which demand a first-class performer to play them competently. It is worth noting that Peter Katin, for one, remarked (both when recording some of the music for Philips and when broadcasting on television) that some of the pieces are extremely difficult. What the composers have given me so far may not have excelled what they gave in their life-times, but they have certainly transmitted a generous quantity of music which many musicians have acclaimed to be of excellent quality and construction.

232

After all, it is no easy task to take down music note by note while it is being dictated from someone in another dimension – people probably have not the slightest idea how laborious a task it is, how delicate the balance of such contact, and how tenuous the line of auditory reception.

I should like to add one other thing. There is a vast difference, of course, between communicating with the planes of consciousness where the average (possibly spiritually unawakened soul) dwells, and communicating with the higher planes of consciousness. I must be excused for using the expression "higher planes" which is rather a misnomer, for these planes are not higher in the sense of distance. I am referring to the planes to which spiritual consciousness is the sole means of entry, planes into which the materially-minded, the spiritually dense, and the degenerate person cannot penetrate. Saints, highly-developed souls, and the spiritually quickened can descend from these planes to lower planes to assist those who are still struggling there. These high souls can reach us here on earth at times, but usually this can only happen when we raise our own consciousness to meet theirs. This is why I believe it is important to embark on communication in a prayerful frame of mind, otherwise one may get contact only with those who are still very limited in their spiritual development and knowledge. This is not displaying spiritual snobbery: all souls are potentially equal in quality, but some have advanced farther in their search for the highermost.

If we are content with messages from dear Aunt Maud, who was quite a nice soul but is hardly able to think or talk of anything but the fish and chips that she loved to get from the corner shop and her husband's shortcomings, then we will not care if communication of a more enlightening or uplifting nature is not forthcoming. But if we really want to learn, to unfold our higher nature, and grow nearer to God, we will surely endeavour to reach up to the higher planes from which issues divine inspiration, wisdom, and an expansion of consciousness.

Ordinary messages from souls who have passed on may be of great comfort to those whom they have left in this world, therefore mediums who render the service of establishing contact for this purpose are providing a valuable link. We were, after all, instructed to comfort those who mourn. Often this first experience of the bereaved in communication is a stepping-stone on the way to further enquiry, study and application. It can be the first step towards increased spiritual growth. Those who use mediums solely to extract

233

endless messages for their own satisfaction are unlikely to be making any worth-while progress, or becoming wiser or better persons.

To communicate simply for the sake of communication is likely to be a useless occupation. It would be like talking for the sake of talking when little that is of note may be said. Motive in communication is the all-important issue. To decide to while away an hour or two chatting with the "dead" can be as much a waste of time and energy as gossiping with a neighbour can be. Results that are rewarding in the spiritual sense will probably ensue only when there is an unselfish purpose in the attempt to communicate. I feel there is a need to stress this because some people do stop short in their development through contenting themselves with the trivial and the commonplace.

Have I a final message for readers of this book? Only to repeat the words at the end of chapter 21. In his highest moments, Mankind, both in everyday life and in his vision of eternity, seeks and endeavours to create around himself that which is good. He has a constant urge to improve, beautify and uplift. This is the voice of his true self, of the spirit of God within him. It inspires him to seek perfection, and to create it within himself and all about him. It is the voice of God telling him that he is made in the image of God. It rests with each and every soul to reflect that image in its true likeness.

THE END

APPENDIX I

A message received by Rosemary Brown from Bertrand Russell in which he comments on current tendencies

The future of any country, it is manifest, depends largely upon its economic and social development. It does not rest, as some may believe, entirely in the hands of a minority. Yet there is always the need, if not the desirability, of governing controls and distributive maintenance if a balanced production and subsistence level is to be retained.

Surplus profits on the one hand can lead to a deficiency on the other hand with a concomitant collapse in national economy unless the profits are devoted at least in part to the furtherance of a general increase in prosperity instead of remaining an individual source of advantage.

Capitalism as we have known it during the past few decades may well be dying a natural death through the recognition by those whom we may label "capitalists" of the expediency of permitting employees to equate their labours with the value of their products or services instead of being apportioned an arbitrary wage for the work performed. This is no idle sentimentality, but a practical approach to the encouragement of goodwill between employers and employees without which co-operation is likely to become stultified. Co-operation, besides being keyed to be the password to a sustained and evenly distributed prosperity, available to all, could prove to be the indispensible element in the survival of the human species.

All nations have a history of fluctuating fortunes which may have seemed frequently unavoidable, and which were certainly unplanned. It is only in recent times, that is, since the turn of the century, that a worthy proportion of thought and effort has been given to the welfare of the masses upon whom the entire economy of the country depends.

Religion was exploited to exhort people to accept their lot and

235

their so-called place in society as the Divine Will: an empiric mandate since no-one can define the Divine Will with conclusive argument. As a result, the oppressed, hypnotised into acceptance of this situation, were generally unprotesting and obsequious, defeated by their poverty and social impotence from negotiating for fairer treatment.

The spread of education has enabled the masses to become more articulate and capable of calling into question much that was formerly accepted as inevitable in working conditions and pay. The challenge to current Capitalism stems to a large extent from the workers' increased awareness of the structure and function of business concerns, and their growing recognition of their own essential role as the very basis on which the tycoons build their financial empires. At the same time, those situated (however haphazardly or hazardously) at the summit of the class and wealth pyramid may affect less indifference to the lot of their less fortunate brethren, partly through a growing realisation that a nation, to keep the wheels of industry running smoothly, must look after its workers on all levels, and partly to appease the demands of public opinion which is now a force to be reckoned with due to its power to make itself heard via the news media.

World-wide changes in the structure and conduct of economic priorities are inevitable and advisable. Workers must participate more fully in the life of the nation both for their own sakes and for the sake of the nation as a whole. Privilege must always walk hand-in-hand with responsibility or run the risk of becoming licence. And it should always be remembered that the smallest cog in a machine can bring it to a standstill if it is not given due attention and care.

Since the ideal of government by the people for the people has emerged in opposition to government by a despotic individual or a group of tyrants, endeavours to create a perfect system of government still continue and should continue for improvements can always be made. Retaining a system that is sufficiently fluid to allow desirable adjustments to be made is the nearest to a truly democratic norm that it is perhaps possible to attain. A system that is totally inelastic is doomed to snap because of its political inability to expand its scope to measure up with world expansion.

Government by the people can be conducted only by an indirect process, since it is palpably impossible for all the people to govern by direct means. It may not always be easy for the average person to decide who will best represent his interests or his will because each political candidate will do his utmost to persuade the electorate that he stands for the most desirable party. It is a great pity that an outline of planned policies of each party cannot be drawn up and presented to the electorate by a totally disinterested committee: but where could one find a totally disinterested committee? (Since everyone is involved in – and affected by the results of any election.)

If each candidate could and would adequately promote the interests of each and every member of the electorate, the need for opposing parties would in all probability become superflous, for the aims then of every party would be identical. Conflicting interests constitute an almost unavoidable feature of any nation, especially when that nation is absorbing a quantity of mixed immigrants with different cultures and needs. The ideal candidate would be one who could reconcile these conflicting interests to the satisfaction of all concerned which is a task in which he is unlikely to succeed.

The politician must become a master of compromise if he is to balance the needs of all sections of the community, but compromise will not be easy to achieve if he has well-defined aims to pursue. He walks upon a tight-rope which will throw him if it is either too taut or too slack. His motives may be admirable but his performance poor which may lead to the electorate substituting him with a candidate who has less worthy motives. Benevolence of spirit is not enough in a politician; the public look for results, expecting a member of Parliament to be something of a magician at times.

Politics nowadays cannot be confined to national issues; they are speedily becoming a matter of international bearing. This makes the politician's task more onerous, but he may be able to turn this to advantage if he can grasp the general situation and gain acceptance on an international as well as a national scale. There is no longer any room for insular policies, but he may find some of the electorate slow to realise this fact.

The world needs men of vision and courage, men who will not court popularity at the expense of wise and long-sighted policies that may not meet with the approval of the impatient who clamour for immediate results. Yet if they do not draw some measure of popularity, they will not be elected in the first place; or, if already elected, they will not remain in power longer than the populace will tolerate.

A cool head, a steady hand, and a warm heart: these are the attributes which are perhaps the most essential to the present-day successful politician. Men of such stature are rare, and if we find any amongst us, we should be wise to heed them.

APPENDIX II

The Music – an opinion from Professor Ian Parrott, MA, DMus (Oxon), FTCL, ARCO

In her Autobiography, "Unfinished Symphonies" (Souvenir Press, 1971), Rosemary Brown has described in fair detail how many of the large number of "received" compositions came to her. For the psychical researcher it is remarkable that the phenomenon should occur at all. In some ways it is similar to mediumistic "automatic writing", but musical notation is harder to write down than the language of words. Rosemary has had only a limited knowledge of the rudiments of music, but this has helped to keep her a clean vessel and indeed it has helped her to be receptive. She is humble about her extraordinary gift. In "Performing Right", May 1970, she wrote: "I would be proud indeed to claim these compositions as being "all my own work"; such a claim on my part would not only be dishonest and presumptuous, but would also oppose the composers' efforts to display their individual surviving consciousness."

For the musician, naturally, it is not sufficient that there should be a communication with the "beyond". Some quality should emerge. This, I believe, the discerning reader will find. Also some style. We must realise here that sceptics, although often claiming to be scientific, can go to ridiculous lengths to laugh things off if they do not wish to believe them. That is why I find *Grübelei*, for example, so satisfying – for the sceptics. It is not, on the one hand, a pale imitation of Liszt's early manner; nor, on the other, is it utterly unlike anything he wrote. It is something in between: rather like the sort of experimental composition that he might have written next, had he lived longer in this world. Let us not forget that any stylistic imperfections or impurities in some of the other pieces might be due to the difficulties of communication. Rosemary, after all, is not a consciously constructing music student deliberately imitating well established

238

models. And, if it comes to that, I know no brilliant music students or after-dinner entertainers who could produce anything at all like her results.

Rosemary's work may remain controversial for some time, but I, for one, am prepared to back it.